PSYCHOANALYSIS AND PAEDIATRICS

Françoise Dolto

PSYCHOANALYSIS AND PAEDIATRICS

Key Psychoanalytic Concepts
with Sixteen Clinical
Observations of Children

Translated from the French by
Françoise Hivernel and Fiona Sinclair

KARNAC

First published in English in 2013 by
Karnac Books Ltd
118 Finchley Road
London NW3 5HT

First published in France under the title *Psychanalyse et pédiatrie: les grandes notions* by Françoise Dolto © Éditions du Seuil, 1971 and 1976

Liberté • Égalité • Fraternité

RÉPUBLIQUE FRANÇAISE

This book is supported by the French Ministry of Foreign Affairs, as part of the Burgess programme run by the Cultural Department of the French Embassy in London.
www.frenchbooknews.com

ISBN-13: 978-1-85575-812-4

Typeset by V Publishing Solutions Pvt Ltd., Chennai, India

Printed in Great Britain

www.karnacbooks.com

CONTENTS

ACKNOWLEDGEMENTS

Our warmest thanks go to Sian Morgan, our special advisor and friend, for her selfless devotion and attunement to Francoise Dolto's work and her thorough editing of this text.

We would also like to thank the following:

Dr Penny De Lacey for overseeing the translation of the medical vocabulary.

Bridget Matthews for all her work on the manuscript.

Laura Minogue for her occasional assistance with the complexities of translation.

Oliver Rathbone (Karnac) for his patience during the lengthy fine tuning of the translation and Kate Pearce our Project Manager.

The French Institute in London, especially the Cultural Attaché Paul Fournel, for awarding us the Burgess Grant.

ABOUT THE AUTHOR

Françoise Dolto was a paediatrician and psychoanalyst. Her life witnessed an extraordinary evolution from a relatively conservative family background, at a time of very restricted opportunities for women, through the Second World War, to the turbulence of Paris in the 1950s and 1960s. Having been analysed by Laforgue, she began her analytic career as a child analyst, much influenced by Sophie Morgernstern; she became a member of the Société Psychanalytique de Paris, and was a close colleague of Lacan. Dolto made a number of original contributions to the understanding of neurosis, psychosis, psychosomatic medicine, neonatology, female sexuality, education, and religion.

'Psychanalyse et Pédiatrie 'was her medical thesis, written in 1938 and was to be the first of many books. She was unusual in her capacity to write not only for her professional colleagues but she also wrote and broadcasted about children for the general public, for ordinary families. In 1979, Dolto opened the first Maison Verte, where she would put the findings of psychoanalysis at the service of very young children. Dolto continued to write and teach until her death in 1988.

ABOUT THE TRANSLATORS

Fiona Sinclair has been in clinical practice for many years, teaching and supervising trainee psychotherapists. She previously held an honorary psychotherapist post in the Young People's Service and in the Psychotherapy Department, Fulbourn and Addenbrooke's Hospitals, Cambridge. She is a founder member of the Site for Contemporary Psychoanalysis. Her paper "In the teeth of death: synecdoche" was published in *The Death Drive* edited by Rob Weatherill (Rebus Press, 1999).

Françoise Hivernel, PhD, after a career in archaeology, she graduated from the Contemporary Freudian Training of the West Midlands Institute as a psychoanalytic psychotherapist. During her training, she worked at the Psychiatric Hospital in Fulbourn and subsequently held an honorary psychotherapist post at the Psychotherapy Department, Addenbrooke's Hospital, Cambridge. She now works in private practice with adults. She is joint editor with G. Hall and S. Morgan of *Theory and Practice in Child Psychoanalysis: An Introduction to the Work of Françoise Dolto* (Karnac, 2009).

INTRODUCTION BY THE TRANSLATORS

It is our great pleasure to have been able to translate into English the first book ever written by Françoise Dolto, her work has been translated into many other languages.

Françoise Dolto's thesis was first published in 1939, and this translation is of the 1971 edition published by Le Seuil, Paris. Most of the original footnotes have been incorporated into the text and bracketed, in accordance with the rules of the publisher of this edition, Karnac, except for a few bibliographic references.

As is usual in translation, we have had to grapple with a writing style that does not always translate easily, and we hope that readers will understand that our translation is also an interpretation, while we have kept faith with the original as much as possible. The colloquial is always a thorny issue: French babies are born in cabbages, English babies in gooseberry bushes!

Françoise Dolto also presents a challenge of her own, which is that she quite simply invents words, or slightly deforms them, in order to give an impression of how the child expresses himself or how he might experience the speech of adults. Again, we had to use our judgement to interpret Dolto's intentions as accurately as possible.

We also decided to unify the grammatical style of the text, as the narrative often jumps from present, to future, to past. Similarly, the personal pronouns jump from "I" to "we", and in some instances it was difficult to decide whether the "we" indicated the presence of colleagues or was the "royal We". The same applies to gender; sometimes it is not entirely clear whether Dolto is referring to a boy or a girl, and again, for the sake of clarity, where it seemed important, we made a choice.

Because this is psychoanalysis, Dolto is constantly alert to, and showing the reader, the unconscious communications of her little patients. It has not always been possible to translate these as the play on words is untranslatable, such as that between *mère* (mother) and *mer* (sea). We hope these are self-evident in the text.

Equally, for the contemporary reader, the traditional male/female roles and Dolto's use of them in her work sometimes make for difficult reading. We can only say it is worth the effort for the reward of experiencing almost at first hand Dolto's extraordinary, radical way of talking to children.

FH & FS

PREFACE TO THE 1971 EDITION

Despite many lacunae, I believe that this book will enable doctors, parents, and educators to gain an understanding of the relevance of psychoanalysis to intellectual and character development; and that it will facilitate an understanding of general health matters in human beings, who must confront their sexuality as it evolves. For the last thirty years, psychoanalytic enquiry has enabled a deeper understanding of many of the questions raised here. The interaction between the organic, functional, and internal disorders, and the development of sexuality, have become obvious to doctors, some of whom now specialise in psychosomatic medicine. Since 1939, society has been in the midst of huge change. Pedagogy is faced with an increasing number of children presenting learning and behavioural problems, as well as not being able to adjust in all sorts of other ways. Pedagogy has therefore had to fine tune its teaching methods and ways of helping children who have fallen behind. Medico-pedagogical consultations, almost everywhere, are responding to parental worries over the problems faced by their children: difficulties with speech, writing, reading, motor control, school attendance, or just obeying rules. In the meantime, living conditions in towns mean that the time and space within which to live have been compressed. Awareness that one is responsible for one's

xvii

self awakens in young people, often in a milieu where parents do not know how to listen or can no longer be trusted. The family, which in the past was a safe, holding place, a refuge, has become a transient place in which to grow up, but into which, through the eyes and ears, enter all the reverberations of the world. More than ever, each human being, whose body is sheltered from the recurrence of ill health, notices that its affective and psychic shortcomings put him in danger of losing his mental equilibrium. He has to acknowledge in reality a sexuality that he knows very well in his imagination to be the root cause of his anguish, and to own a fecundity, his capacity to reproduce, in order to reconcile himself to his own death. The twentieth century, which discovered the power of the atom and found ways of harnessing it, is also opening up to the unconscious power of the libido. The sense of personal responsibility could not be greater.

I dedicate this book to paediatricians.

Françoise Dolto, Paris, 1971

INTRODUCTION

It is not widely known that Freud, far from being a philosopher with original and revolutionary ideas, was, before becoming a psychiatrist, a laboratory scientist. He trained himself in the rigorous discipline of scientific experiment and investigation with a microscope. With the objectivity that this first training helped to develop, Freud applied himself to the study of psychological phenomena. In his eyes, his theories were no more than working hypotheses until his clinical studies could confirm them. Consequently, we stand as witnesses to the evolution of his various theoretical conceptions. Faced with problems for which he could not find an explanation within the scope of his first postulation, he would return to the clinical, always back to the therapeutic work, to confirm or invalidate his views.

In this way, Freud progressively elaborated and brought an essentially original doctrine to the public; a public which was either entranced or indifferent.

He was, above all, a doctor. He wanted to care for his patients, his aim was to heal. In chemistry, his first researches had a practical aim—and the subsequent discovery of the effect of cocaine crowned them all—in the same way, his painstaking researches in the psychological domain were conducted by a doctor's desire to heal mental illnesses which did not respond to the usual therapeutic interventions.

We have often heard colleagues repudiating in all good faith any real foundation to psychoanalytic theories, treating infantile sexuality as a pure invention, its manifestations, if not inconvenient, at least not interesting enough to be researched. Even the Oedipus Complex is accused by some of being either just a theoretical construct or a monstrous conflict reserved for some abnormal individuals.

But those who live or work in continuous contact with children, if they are honest enough to note what they see, will bring many observations to support the discoveries of psychoanalysis.

Or, if it is only a question of speculative pleasure at seeing one's hypothesis confirmed, one could admit that this question may not interest those who are kept away from such theorising by their social roles, that is to say, educators and doctors.

Sometimes, it is forgotten in these polemics that if psychoanalysis opens new avenues of research to the historian, sociologist, psychologist, its main interest, to which no doctor can remain indifferent, is that the psychoanalytic method born from the clinical has a therapeutic aim.

Armed with our scientific systems of observation and with an extraordinarily developed and nuanced therapeutic arsenal encompassing pharmacology as it does today, we still see many cases which do not yield to our treatment. The embarrassed doctor will try his array of medication for cases such as insomnia, physical weakness, lack of energy, panic attacks, anxieties somatised into digestive or cardiac problems, most often without any long-term success.

Physiological reactions of fear, of stage fright, of angst, of disquiet, and all other organic problems which have a psychological root related to a known objective cause, and disappear with it, are acceptable; but for troubles of a similar type, whose cause is no longer objective, the sick—because these are people who suffer, and ask to be treated—hear the GP say that "It's nothing, it's just stress".

That emotional conflicts can trigger serious disorders in general health, we will give but one example:

Josette, a little girl of three and a half, was brought to see Dr Darré at the clinic of Les Enfants Malades because of a worrying overall condition: weight loss, paleness, anorexia, lack of interest in playing, nervousness, insomnia, or nightmares from which the little girl woke up in the grip of a panic attack.

The mother traced the onset of these problems to a fortnight earlier: at first, she did not pay much attention, but the symptoms continued, becoming worse, and the child's misery, even when not in the grip of an attack, made her decide to go to the doctor.

The physical check-up revealed nothing, and the doctor prescribed a barbiturate and something to stimulate her appetite.

Eight days after this, Josette was brought back again; she had lost a pound in eight days. She is permanently miserable, does not have a temperature; the child who had been dry for over a year has started to wet her bed again.

Because people know I am interested in the psychological dimensions of the symptom of enuresis, my colleague called me, saying: "perhaps what she suffers from is more in your domain". I started very carefully to question the mother about dates.

We learned that the nightmares started three weeks ago. The behaviour of the girl changed at the same time; from being a lively and happy girl she became taciturn and indifferent. The parents were scolding her for waking up at night, panic attacks followed, and, her condition worsening, Josette was taken to hospital.

Apparently nothing had changed in the immediate surroundings of the child which could have disturbed her. I ask where Josette sleeps: in her parents' room.

— But, adds the mother, my husband and I feel that she is too old now and we decided some time ago to buy a sofa-bed so that she can sleep in the dining room.
  I check dates with them.
— We took that decision about three weeks ago, and we even bought the sofa, but of course we have not yet changed anything, we are waiting until she is better.
  I point out the coincidence between the dates.
— She is far too young to understand, replies the mother. She did not even know. Her father and I haven't spoken to her about it, and, to convince you, Doctor, I can assure you she has not noticed the new sofa, which is in the dining room. She is still a little baby.

I could see the child on her mother's knees looking at her with a somewhat bewildered expression. She looked at me as soon as I spoke about the coincidence of the beginning of her problems with the appearance of the sofa-bed.

Through these symptoms, the root cause of which was unconscious, the child expressed a refusal to leave her parents' bedroom, to abandon her mother to her father.

We did not go into the genesis of each of the symptoms: nightmares, night terrors, anorexia, enuresis, and loss of interest in the sort of things you would expect for a child of her age. Everything pointed towards an anxiety that was bringing on regressive neurotic symptoms.

Understanding the conflict at play in the child, we explained to the mother in front of Josette that her child was suffering psychologically, that she needed help in tolerating the idea that she had to separate from her parents, and in becoming a big girl, of which she was afraid.

I explained to Josette that she wanted to remain like a baby so as not to leave her mother. Maybe she believed that she was loved less and that Daddy wanted to get rid of her? The little girl was very attentive, listening and crying silently. The parents stopped the medication and followed our advice.

That same evening, Daddy and Mummy spoke to Josette of the forth-coming change. Daddy cuddled her more than usual and talked to her about her future; he described the big girl she was going to become, and of whom he would be so proud; and the school where she would soon be going with other children.

Four days later, the mother came back and told me that the child had calmed down. She had slept without a sedative, a light sleep, but one without nightmares. The enuresis had persisted for the first two nights, but the child was not told off about it. There had been no bedwetting for the last two days, the child had recovered her appetite, and she was happy during the day. She asked numerous questions. (The anxiety had disappeared and the child had regained a normal way of being.)

I suggested that she should now sleep in the other room, and I explained this to Josette, who agreed. I advised the father to go and kiss the child goodnight. And I added that under no pretext should the parents have her back in their bedroom.

Eight days later, the mother comes back with a laughing and proud Josette. Everything is fine. Appetite, sleep, and happiness are back. The child is putting on airs of becoming a little girl, and it is she who has asked her mother to go and see the doctor to tell her that she is cured—see p. 116.

This is only one of many cases where the usual medical intervention is inadequate. These are cases which never make it to the psychiatrist, remaining with the general practitioner. Only the physical symptoms seemed to worry the parents. But a thorough questioning guided by the knowledge of neurotic mechanisms lead to their origin: a psychological trauma.

Similarly, in taking a history of a somatic case, we have to predict what we are looking for whilst listening to what the patient is telling us. In the same way, in order to study behavioural difficulties, we have to know how the psyche works.

All doctors should have knowledge of the pitfalls encountered by an individual during the course of his psychological development; this particularly holds true for paediatricians, on whom, in collaboration with teachers, the onus of the prophylaxis of the neurosis falls; but also for all the other doctors who, confronted with a specific inexplicable organic manifestation, find themselves floundering but dare not say so to the patient, leaving him to despair and go from one doctor to another who, in turn, repeat their previous colleagues' behaviour by sending the patient away. And this despite the fact that these patients are people who are suffering and that psychoanalytic treatment could help, if not cure.

A doctor who lacks knowledge of the structure of the mind reminds us of a surgeon who, faced with an abscess about to burst, tries to hide the swelling and smear it with analgesics instead of draining the abscess. Sedatives and "a change of scenery" fall into that category.

Nature, it is said, can do the work itself, hence patients are being told such things as "with time", "be patient". Yes, but the pus will ooze for a long time and the scar will be ugly. The abscess could also become encysted and, although apparently eliminated, the seat of the infection can reawaken during a phase of lower general resistance or of an injury at this sensitive point: anxieties, obsessions, depression, insomnia, cardiac or digestive troubles, appear suddenly in an adult because of an unhappy emotion or event which he could have surmounted were it not for the neurotic infantile trauma ready to reawaken.

It therefore appeared to us interesting to draw attention to the cases of illnesses seen daily by doctors—and not by psychiatrists—and whose diagnosis as well as treatment should be psychoanalytic.

The importance of infantile traumas in all the works devoted to psychoanalysis is sometimes surprising. However, everyone knows that in all individuals the most dangerous illnesses and the shocks which traumatise the most are those which attack an embryonic organ; an organ with the least resistance or an organ which has already suffered a previous lesion, for which healing is not yet assured. What is true in the physical domain is also true in the domain of the psyche.

The cases of which we are about to talk are amongst the simplest ones, without having been simplified artificially.

The cases which go directly to the psychiatrist will only be alluded to, because we have purposely eliminated them from this work.

The symptomatology of adults is richer, and the different reactions more complex, but at root level the same mechanisms are always at play. Also, and apart from some general clinical points, the limits of this work[1] do not allow us to write about adult observation. In all adults, even in those who are psychologically healthy, it is possible to find, when certain difficulties are encountered during life, traces of the castration complex, at least in the evidence of the unconscious activity that is the dream.

It is, of course, through psychoanalysis, as we must not forget, that the universality of the conflicts encountered during human development have been recognised, especially the Oedipal conflict, which definitively marks a subject according to the manner in which he responded to it at the time.

Françoise Dolto

Chapters One, Two, and Three are theoretical statements; the reader could go directly to the second part of this book (p. 111) which is definitely more concrete and clinical, and could come back to the preceding chapters at a later stage, if something seems obscure in the discussion of the clinical observation.

---

[1] D. Lagache (1966). *La Psychanalyse* (Paris: PUF); A. Berge (1951). *L'Education sexuelle et affective* (Paris: Scarabée); J. Favez (no date). *La Psychothérapie Cahiers de pédagogie moderne* (Paris: Bourrelier).

THEORETICAL PART

CHAPTER ONE

Terminology

We will try to show as briefly and as clearly as possible the meaning of some terms.

What is the meaning of the term "castration complex", around which the discussion in this book will be articulated?

A *complex* is an indissoluble link between:

> On the one hand, *drives* which have different aims, sometimes contradictory, each of which seeks dominance.
> And on the other, *prohibitions* of a cultural order, which militate against the realisation of some of the goals of the drives.

The *drives* are primary, aim-oriented impulses of a physiological nature which demand satisfaction. Some of these drives are in conflict with the *prohibitions*. These drives and prohibitions being unconscious, the link between them—the complex—is also unconscious.

But the reactions engendered by this unconscious conflictual situation manifest themselves through behaviour. The subject then thinks and acts despite himself according to motives stemming from unconscious determinants, whilst his need to make sense of them always manages to enable him to justify his actions in his own eyes. He can also experience, powerless as he is to modify them, psychosomatic symptoms coming from unconscious determinants—the instinctive nervous system being the medium through which unconscious affective states are displayed. In the same way, he externalises many conscious states, through tears, blushing or goose pimples, for example. *Castration* means, in day-to-day language, a "destruction" of the genital organs, which does away with sexual needs and concomitant sexual behaviour; but for Freud and psychoanalysts, the term "sexual" does not only designate the physical aspects linked with the genital act of procreation; it also encompasses all that is to do with hedonistic activity, which is to say everything which has to do with pleasure-seeking.

Castration, in psychoanalysis, then means "the frustration of hedonistic possibilities", a frustration of possibilities based on seeking pleasure.

We will see that hedonism does not remain centred on the same areas of the body during the different stages of development, and an account of this evolution will be given in Chapter Two.

The present chapter is devoted to the account of "the nuts and bolts" of the adult psyche, if we can be forgiven for using such an expression.

Despite our desire to use as little scientific terminology as possible, some of it is unavoidable, unless we wish to burden our text with lengthy and repetitive paraphrase, which will render it incomprehensible. I would like to add that, personally, I very often use non-classical terminology, which seems to me useful to complement the usual terms, clarifying them without losing the meaning.

Components of the personality according to Freudian psychoanalysis

We will give a brief description of the personality, but we must not forget that we are talking about artificial, useful schemata constructed for psychological study, and be wary of taking these as real entities and watertight compartments.

The id, the ego, and the superego

The *id*: Source of the drives and a blind libidinal force, which, like a river, needs to flow. The libido is to sexuality what hunger is to nutrition.

The *ego*: Locus of satisfactions and of conscious discomforts. It is the circumscribed kernel of the personality. It is organised, lucid, and coherent. Through its mediation, the id gets in touch with the external world. Initially, it acts as a buffer between the id and the external world, then, at around six to seven years old, between the id and the superego.

The *superego*: A kind of authority figure constituted through the integration of allowed and forbidden experience during the first years of life. Locus of an inhibitory force that also operates blind, the superego is incapable of developing appreciably on its own after the age of eight, even if life circumstances totally modify the conditions of the external world.

When we are saying that the id and the superego are the seat of blind forces, we are referring to their unconscious functioning. Moreover, the ego is also only partly conscious We need to repeat here that this is just a schemata; what is important to understand is that the unconscious, from which affective strength stems, is from very early on "divided against itself" (id against superego).

Conscious, unconscious, and preconscious

The set of thoughts that we can have in mind at a given moment constitute the *conscious*. All those which are outside our conscious field at any given moment are said to be *unconscious*. But, amongst all these, it is necessary to distinguish those which can be recalled at will—(*preconscious*)—and, on the other hand, the *unconscious* properly speaking, which will always remain practically speaking unknown.

But the unconscious is not an obscure receptacle of useless and mute psychic representations.

Through studying the phenomena of post-hypnotic behaviour observed by Hippolyte Bernheim, a French specialist in hypnotherapy whom he visited,[1] Freud noticed that an action which had been ordered by the doctor under hypnosis was emphatically inscribed on the conscious mind, whilst neither the memory of the order to perform the action nor the memory of hypnosis could be accessed.

Furthermore, if the subject performing an absurd order was asked about the reason for it, he always invoked a justification that seemed good enough in his eyes, although it very often went against all logic: *the thought of performing* has passed from the unconscious into the conscious, loaded with the incitement to act; but *the thought in the form of*

---

[1] Freud also translated two of Bernheim's papers into German.

an order received under hypnosis does not become conscious, despite the fact that it is the trigger to action. For example, a subject opening his umbrella in the middle of a meeting, according to the order received under hypnosis, might reply to the questions of the group that "I want to see if my umbrella is working". A psychic phenomenon can therefore be unconscious and effective.

Freud's observation of hysterics caused him to conclude that external hypnotic suggestion and the internal suggestions of hysteria are almost identical phenomena.

In other types of neurosis, and even in the psychology of a healthy person, psychoanalysis points to the predominant role of unconsciously active ideas; the driving forces that an individual alleges to justify his actions while the real motivation escapes him are called *rationalisations*.

However, one must notice the following difference: the action ordered under hypnosis, once performed, ceases to play a role in the unconscious of the subject; however, the unconscious force emanating from the subject himself tends to repeat itself indefinitely, according to a rhythm which varies with each individual. This is the reason why neurosis cannot be cured spontaneously.

Freud proposes the hypothesis that all psychic phenomena tend towards becoming conscious. They are only stopped in their path if they face resistances, and this is no conjuring trick, it is a game of *opposing forces*.

Once the process is triggered, the affective charge which supports it has to find an outlet; it is part of the expression of a libido which, no more than "life", can be conjured away. We can modify the manifestations of life; but once triggered, life can only be stopped by death, meaning the complete destruction of the living being. Similarly, the libido cannot be cancelled or lessened in its dynamic quantity.

Should it happen that, right from its beginning, the libidinal thrust finds prohibitions in the external world, the representation is repressed; but the underlying affective charge remaining, it is transformed into *extreme anxiety*.

Anxiety, an unutterable malaise, sees its intensity depend on two factors: on the one hand, the importance of the affective charge detached from its original hold; and on the other, the degree, more or less total, more or less explicit, of the inhibition imposed on the drive.

If the affective charge finds a way to graft itself onto another idea, better tolerated by the outside world, a *symptom* is formed: an unrecognisable use of the repressed drive. This appearance of the symptom *frees the subject of his anxiety* and gives him an immediate feeling of well-being.

It is only during the first years of life that drives come up against the external world; the prohibitions, which they come up against after their first experiences, will soon invade the very personality of the subject (the superego).

A classical experiment will allow us to understand the formation of the superego. If some fish are put into a bowl and the bowl is divided into two by a transparent pane of glass, the fish on either side desperately try to swim through the transparent wall and crash against it ceaselessly; until the moment when they act as if they "had lost the will" to exit the compartment which is reserved for them. From then onwards, they will never crash against the glass wall again, and if, after a few weeks, the partition is removed, one notices that the fish carry on behaving "as if it was still there"; the prohibition has been internalised and is by now part of the "personality" of the fish.

This is how the superego acts. It processes prohibitions from the external world so as to avoid disappointment; but once formed, the superego is rigid. Because of it, the drives are spontaneously constrained, even before becoming conscious, as soon as they arouse an associative resonance to those which initiated the repression from the external world and were followed by anxiety during the child's early experiences. This is the inhibitory mechanism to which the name of *repression* is given. This process is *internal*.

Repression only affects ideas. The affective charges which sustained the ideas (and which, as we have said before, cannot be destroyed) provoke in the conscious of the subject, through the accumulation of nervous unsatisfied tension, an anxiety from which he suffers and whose cause he does not know. The term "primary anxiety" is kept for the suffering resulting from a conflict between libidinal drives and the prohibitions external to the subject. The anxiety produced by an internal conflict between the superego and the id is called "secondary anxiety".

Anxiety tries to liberate itself by producing a symptom, which will then allow an emotional discharge (the affective charge attaches itself to another idea). This transmutation may be tolerated or not by the external world or by the conscious part of the subject. In the case of repression, the instinctual relaxation cannot occur, and a new anxiety will lead to another symptom, still propelled by the same libidinal charge, which has been disconnected from the first repressed idea. It can, therefore, lead to such an intricate situation, and the symptom be so far removed from its point of departure, that only very slow "analytical" work will find its cause.

This allows us to understand why psychoanalytic psychotherapy can be beneficial for children, whose superego—if it began forming around seven to eight years old—doesn't reach its final rigidity until the end of puberty. On the other hand, it will be necessary to use a long therapeutic process, which a "true psychoanalysis" represents, for an adult, with his double difficulty of an even more rigid superego and a long personal history.

We can compare the libido to the water from a spring. It has to flow; if it is prevented from welling up where it emerges, it will appear somewhere else. When the water first appears, it is called a spring; it does not have to go further than a few metres before it becomes a brook.

If one wants to stop the flow of the brook, one has to dam it; but that dam needs to be reinforced again and again as the water pressure rises, and however large the dam, however powerful its walls, it will only be an obstacle to water for a certain length of time, beyond which it will be breached, unless some small gaps allow for an overflow, or, there again, if there is an outlet through which the reservoir can discharge, powering a hydroelectric plant, for example.

It is the role of the superego to favour "sublimation", which is the deployment of the libido into social activity which is tolerated or even stimulated by the external world.

But if the outflow is not in proportion with that of the spring, the water must find additional openings: this is the role of the symptoms; and these breaches occur at the points of least resistance.

This is what happens when drives cannot reach the conscious and awaken or reinforce symptoms corresponding to an early developmental period which were tolerated at the time. The libido is tempted to retrace an old known path, and to proceed to this or that re-investment around "fixation points", depending upon an array of conditions which in the past had led it to emphasise this or that symptom when it appeared.

So, back to the metaphor; under the thrust of a flood, the water from the reservoir will first break through the flood gates which close the access to beaches where the water was allowed to stay temporarily when the dam and the hydroelectric plant were not yet functional.

The big difference between what happens to water on the surface of the earth and what happens with the libido inside an individual, is that the inhibiting force, which opposes the expression of the drives, stems from the individual himself.

The dynamic element of the id is the libido, and the dynamic element of the superego is the same libido.

Thanks to the superego, an extraordinary amount of work is saved for the ego, thus avoiding the constant tedious work of choice and renunciation. The goldfish are at ease in the bowl, which at the beginning was constricting them.

If sublimations make full use of the dynamism of the repressed drives, and if the superego gives enough rein to the id to gain direct satisfactions, all is well, repression is quietly operating, and there is no anxiety.

But if the possibilities of sublimation are insufficient, or if the id is very violent and powerful, a tension ensues; the superego then has to become extremely strict and one witnesses the appearance of reaction-formations either with the agreement of the ego—perversions; or without its agreement—specific neuroses.

But if the vital thrust of the id is forever monopolising the imperious vigilance of the superego, the libido may become more or less totally blocked, and is then used against itself. This force, trapped in unconscious mechanisms, is not available to the ego, and therefore for the subject's conscious activities.

One could believe, then, that the subject would be relieved if some of his blocked energy were returned to him. But this is not the case. A sort of metabolic deviation would lead the newly liberated energy in the opposite direction to the one sought.

In other words, rather like the clever and apparently paradoxical processes of some endocrinal or biochemical reactions, as Jury and Fraenkel (French translators of Freud[2]) noticed, if the analyst triggers a repression in order to bring about a letting-go, he may just be reinforcing the repression. Effectively, it would go back in equal measure to the two antagonistic parts of the unconscious (the id and superego), and this only worsens the conflicted state.

---

[2] P. Jury and E. Fraenkel translated Freud's 1926 paper into French: *Inhibitions, symptome et angoisse* (Paris: PUF).

And this was the error of the first years of the psychoanalytic method, when naively it was thought that it was good for patients to be told the meaning of their symptoms. Even nowadays, those who, armed with notions of psychoanalysis, aim to interpret symptoms and dreams may find what has an anecdotal effect can also bring about painful and even dangerous side effects for neurotic subjects.

At the same time as the ego of the subject desires in good faith to submit to analytic treatment and help the doctor with the best will in the world, as soon as psychoanalysis attempts to separate the two antagonistic forces, the subject deploys an unconscious latent opposition, just as if he was organising a defence. The name given to this phenomenon is resistance.

The same mechanism that produced the repression kicks in as soon as the analytic interpretations give a glimpse of a possible relaxation of repressed ideas and memories; at this signal, the vigilance of the superego is reinforced tenfold.

This mechanism, however annoying during treatment and even for the dissemination of psychoanalytic ideas, nevertheless has its uses; it keeps the personality in equilibrium.

It suffices to think of the discharge of libidinal force which is expended, for example, during an acute manic crisis, to understand how the strict governance of the superego is helpful in making sure that the drives of the id are not too liberally removed from its control.

Consequences for psychoanalytic technique

This is why psychoanalytic method aims to circumvent *repressive* mechanisms and not what has been *repressed*.

Psychoanalytic treatment is based on the analysis of resistances. This was particularly true in 1939. Since then, the technique has evolved and, although analysis of the resistances is not neglected, interpretation bears mainly on the drives, the obvious expression of which, through desire being forbidden because of the resistances, is from then on disguised as demand.

This is not an intellectual interpretation, which the doctor gives to his patient as the key to a riddle. The treatment is achieved through "the transference", which means the unfolding of an emotional relation from the patient towards the doctor; it can be positive, negative, or more often mixed.

Transference is present in all human relationships. However, in ordinary life, the reciprocal attitude of two individuals depends on a number of factors. Understanding precisely and correctly what belongs to the subjective attitude of each, what to external circumstances, and what to the influences of other individuals blended into their relationship is an impossible task.

The originality of the psychoanalytic method is to permit the observation of an individual's behaviour to be as objective as possible. The patient's relationship to the therapist is outside social space and time; the patient does not know the therapist as a social being and knows nothing of his personal opinions and reactions; the patient will never hear from him the slightest value judgements.

Experience shows that, from the first sessions, a subject will "see" his psychoanalyst in such a way and react towards him as if he were truly as he imagines him. Another patient will see the same psychoanalyst in a very different way. The psychoanalyst will therefore be able to "analyse" why the subject reacts as he does, and "why" that patient bestows that personality upon him.

That is to say that the doctor needs to know himself well through his own completed analysis. Thus he will only use as material for analysis the reactions of his patient, which do not conform to reality, and he will not react through love or hate, that is to say emotionally, when his patient compliments or scolds him for one of his actuals characteristics.

good relationship with the mother whilst the refusal to comply will be likened to a punishment, or to a falling out with her.

Through mastery of the sphincters, the child discovers the notion of his power over what is his private property: his faeces, which he may give or not. The autoerotic power is over the bowel movement, the emotional power over his mother, whom he can reward or not. This gift to the mother can be compared with all the other "gifts" that one "presents", money, ordinary objects which become precious because they have been given, including a baby, a little brother or sister, whom, in childhood fantasy, the mother produces through her anus after having eaten miraculous food. (It is likely that anal libido is more than just linked to the orifice, it is a diffuse libido "spread over the inside" meeting up with oral libido. The pleasure is of a narcissistic autoeroticism of feeling oneself "master of one's nutrition and one's growth" from one end to the other, it could perhaps be said. This is the discovery of sadistic pleasure. In the same way, "sadistic" can be understood roughly as in the same vein as "I do something to you with my body", "I want to have the right of life or death over objects, over living matter, over you—as I wanted to have over my poo".)

But being obliged to empty his bowel at fixed times, often with difficulty, not being allowed to wait for the pressing and spontaneous need to do so, not being able to play at holding it back, constitutes a renunciation, from the point of view of the child. The ban on playing with faeces, in the name of a pretend disgust shown by the adult (even when she doesn't feel it), once again creates a renunciation.

Now, the child only renounces a pleasure in order to experience another, that of satisfying a beloved adult. Identification, a mechanism already known at the oral stage, is one of his pleasures.

But the *mode of relating* inaugurated with regard to his faeces does not disappear, because, seeking to imitate the adult in his gestures and in his words, yet he is still not participating in the adult's mode of thinking and feeling. Therefore, the child will need substitutes onto which he can displace his feelings: these will be miscellaneous objects, which at this age he drags around and which no one is allowed to touch without provoking his rage, his "wilfulness", his "naughtiness"; only he has the right of life or death over them, which means hugging them, destroying them or throwing them away; in other words, giving them life, or not, just as he does with his poo.

Then, instead of playing with his poo, he absorbs himself in making mud pies and paddling in mud and water; and *because of this* unconscious *displacement*, the severity or otherwise of the parental attitude towards cleanliness in general, including the sphincters, will foster or hamper the happy development of the child and his adaptation to the social world; this is reflected being at ease in his body and in his manual dexterity.

If, on the other hand, through play or occasional constipation, the child withholds his poo, the adult often responds with aggression, suppositories, or even an enema. For the child, it saves effort, providing the erotic satisfaction of *passive seduction*; but this can be painful, and may make the adult cross. Emotional ambivalence emerges again and is linked by association with a budding masochism.

There is more, as far as behaviour is concerned: the child now reaches a very satisfying stage in his neuromuscular development which creates in him a need to use opposing muscle groups at will, flexing and relaxing them. This now gives him the ability to imitate the adult, not only in his words but in all his gestures. He is active, noisy, brutal, aggressive not only towards objects which are within his reach, as during the oral stage, but which he grabs and tears, beats, throws down on the floor, just as if he were taking malicious pleasure, which is accentuated if he notices that it annoys the adult. The identification has been successful. It is because he loves the adult that he plays at being annoying and fighting with her. The ambivalence that appeared at the end of the oral stage is taking shape and growing.

But the child uses his muscular aggression with no other rule than his "caprice". Once again, it is the role of education to familiarise him with the rules of society.

When the child disobeys, he is scolded (in his eyes, deprived of love), he is smacked and, however aggressive a child is, however strong his resistance, he is always the weaker and has to submit.

But in so far as a sympathetic upbringing will have allowed the child to *substitute symbolic objects* for his poo, for his muscular development he needs to be given *time daily* without parental restriction, during which he is able *to play as roughly and as noisily* as he wishes. This is of utmost importance to safeguard his future life and libido; without this, the child will feel crushed under the sadistic domination of the adult (not that the adult is necessarily sadistic, but because the child projects his frustrated sadism onto the adult) and future activity in all domains will depend on a need for punishment which will lead to seeking occasions in which he is passively beaten and dominated.

The formation of *conscientious personalities* can be traced to *the anal stage*: people who are sober, work hard, are serious and scientifically minded—those who find pleasure in conforming to new demands made on them. We may also find the obstinate, the sulky, the stubborn, those who like to shock with their mess, their dirtiness, their lack of discipline, or again those whose meticulous ordering, close to obsession, renders them unbearable to those around them.

Interest in faecal matters is sublimated in painters, sculptors, those who love jewellery, collectors of all sorts, and all those who are interested in banking and the manipulation of money.

One has to attribute possessive characteristics in adults to the dominant components of the anal phase, qualities such as meanness and avarice (money representing excrement for the *unconscious* of the anal stage). Finally, the *sadistic and masochistic components* of this phase explain *perversions* in the adult. In perverts there endures an exclusive libidinal interest in the anal orifice in the sexual act, to the detriment of the vagina, the anatomical existence of which is unknown at the age of infantile fixation.

The love object sought by individuals of this character type is not a priori heterosexual. The subject seeks to rediscover in relation to the object the emotional experience he had with his mother based on the image the infant felt in his own body. There is thus an unconscious homosexuality which rules over his choice. The genital characteristics of the object of desire could be said to be parallel and secondary. The important thing is that the individual rediscovers the feelings that he experienced with the dominant and idealised adult in the pregenital stage. The magical value of the parent or carer overwhelmed his whole body; the same thing happens even when his spoken wish brings him into conflict with the dominant partner.

To subjugate or be subjugated is the acme of this all consuming love relationship. This is an ethic of possession, which finds its end and justification within itself. It is therefore a latent and unconscious homosexuality which underlies the choice of object, whether the person is of the other sex or not. The searched-for complementarity is not subordinated to the creative efficacy of the two partners, but to the reinforcement of a feeling of power socially (as much active in one as passive in the other).

They are frequently very enmeshed in reciprocal dependency and narcissistic equivalence.

It is important that the object is either very weak or very strong. The subject revels in a converse dependent role. In the case of a woman the object is often coupled with a husband or worrying child, or the object may be burdened by an illness or other calamity. For the child the (phallic) woman has "other things", "a third term", in her life. If the "third" disappears and the object is available at last, its value is lost as a sexual object. When this anal character is predominant in a woman, she can make a good and faithful employee to a demanding master, through whom she gains narcissistic advantage for having been chosen as his victim. She could also be manipulated by a man, as in a couple formed by her husband and his mother, or whomsoever exploits her, therefore justifying her withdrawal from genital activity which could gratify her as a woman.

Such characters dominate today's society at all levels of our culture—so-called Christian—in a capitalist system. The homosexual anal superego is dominated by fear of a rejection which annihilates, or by a success which reifies or stifles, taking no account of the human value of sensitivity, creative originality, or the vital and poetic radiance of the individual.

As far as sexual behaviour is concerned, extreme examples in women include the prostitute and the virago from a romantic, sentimental point of view: the child-woman is often inverted and masked as a vamp or virago, or she is a faultless wife and mother, a paragon of domestic virtue, smothered in self-sacrifice. Frigidity in women and impotence in men comes from over-investment in action, doing, or forcing the other to do, over feeling authentically expressed.

As far as sexual behaviour in men is concerned, extreme types include the pimp and the pederast. In social behaviour, such types are found in roles of leaders or self-selected victims, or else are sublimated, as in the case of doctors, surgeons and educators. Surely neurosis derives from anal fixation, much of the symptomatology common to hysteria and obsessional neurosis, organic pathology involving chronic ill- health and its corollaries, hypochondria and psychosomatisation, all in the service of a perverted anal type of narcissism. Medication obtainable without prescription is justified socially because it is of commercial value. The expected magical potency of miracle medication bought secretly is an indispensable aid to tolerating life in cases in which a particular type of libidinal object is missing or cannot be found, and the dependency with regard to these remedies is at least as large and as indispensable as that towards a person.

Thought process at the anal stage

This period, that of the initiation into ambivalence, is a time of increased perception of oppositional pairs precisely because of the discovery of ambivalence.

Based on a dualistic schema derived from anal investment ("passive—active"), the child establishes a series of understandings qualified by the actual relationships the child has with those around him. Any new piece of knowledge is identified with the object he already knows.

Every woman is a Mummy; good—bad. Every older woman is a Granny; good—bad, big—small. This is how his exploration proceeds, looking for similarities.

Objects that oppose his wishes are "naughty", and he attacks them; he is on bad terms with them and with whatever resembles them or is associated with them. But when his will comes up against that of the adult, he cannot win, for in a situation in which he is "naughty", he is punished (or imagines that he will be) and might lose the friendship of the adult. This is a story of dualities, good/bad, nice/naughty.

The child gives in because he *needs* the adult continually, the almighty, "divine", and magical big person, and it is in obeying her or not that he renders her favourably disposed towards him or on the other hand indifferent, or even dangerous. On other occasions similar to those of which he already has experience, to be "well behaved" will mean to choose to act according to what he knows the adult expects; this can corrupt the ethical code of the child for whom to be well behaved can come to mean being passive, immobile, and without curiosity.

We can, therefore, see that spontaneous aggressive drives and aggressive reactions against everything that opposes him have to be deferred and displaced. When the adult is involved, and in play these drives and reactions will be displaced onto objects reminiscent of the adult; by association, it is the source of *symbolism;* or through representation as in a doll or animal, it is the source of fetishism and totemism in children. (In Totem and Taboo, Freud raises the question of totemism, not in the clinical sense in which we understand it at present but in a historical and religious sense.)

The mere fact of directing his affects (which were aimed at the adult) onto these objects gives them a subjective reality, which the child will take as objective reality—of this he has no idea, not having yet the sense of "connection", of causality; he only apprehends objective reality through the pleasant or unpleasant repercussions which it has on his own existence.

So we see at the anal stage a thought process characterised by mechanisms of *identification and projection*: these projections always take place in the dualistic frame inherent to the sadomasochistic ambivalence of object relationships. This is the time of phobias and of animal totems, through which anxiety is expressed through the object invested by the child himself with magical power. This object, generally an animal, represents for the child's unconscious the adult from whom the child has withdrawn his aggressive libidinal investment so as to project it onto its replacement, the feared animal. (This is a key process, the abnormal persistence of or deviation from allows the later constitution (and the eventual therapeutic understanding) of hallucinatory neurotic constructions.)

Phallic stage

The phallic, erogenous zone, penis or clitoris, awakens as early as the oral phase. It may be triggered by repeated nappy changing, the urge to urinate and accompanying excitement. However it may be, all mothers are aware of how babies play with their hands, rub their thighs together when being changed and how they prattle away during the process. This may continue in spite of the occasional "tap" if whoever is taking care of the baby is strict. But most often, this *baby masturbation* is negligible and will stop of its own accord, reappearing only during the third year.

This indifference to faeces has been encouraged in the child in the name of what is "nice", and is accepted by him to "please" his parents and to "buy" their protective love; his success in this is all the greater because his interest is now centred on the phallic erogenous zone. Physiological tension in boys at this age is visible in erections which can happen when peeing or pooing; disassociated from the function of excretion, it becomes a pleasure in itself.

Until the child is potty-trained, peeing discharges the urethral/phallic tension arising from natural libidinal drives. Secondary masturbation appears when full potty training is achieved. Prohibiting masturbation may result in the return of urethral incontinence with or without thumb sucking.

The general existence of *this secondary infantile masturbation* has long been unrecognised by adults, because of the repression imposed by the civilising superego. However, many parents have noticed it and reprimand it strongly. Not daring to acknowledge, or remember that they did the same, they pretend that their child is exceptionally "depraved" or "anxious".

It has to be recognised that when this masturbation is very obvious, and persists in front of adults, in spite of their initial prohibitions, it demonstrates that there is a neurotic reaction added to the libidinal drive: there is anxiety, seeking punishment, or provoking a reaction, which, more than anything else, points to the absence of real emotional attachment to the adult who is present.

Sexual curiosity begins before the third year, during the anal sadistic phase. The aim is primarily towards *knowing where babies come from*. This interest is often awakened by a new birth in the family or by identification with a playmate who is unhappy, or pleased, by the arrival of a brother or sister. The question is generally dodged by adults, who speak of gooseberry bushes and of storks, but the child discovers very soon that the mother has a big tummy before the newborn arrives, and then that she breastfeeds.

The insistent "why" of the four-year-old, who does not even listen to the adult's response, only appears after the first reactions of the adults to directly sexual questions and the notion of the "forbidden" which the child picks up.

Various theories are hazily constructed, linked to the level of anatomical knowledge at this age: conception through the digestive tract, birth through mother's defecation with father's role in the shadows, obscure but probable, rarely confirmed, even less signified, by the parent (so therefore negated).

Then comes another question. *What is the difference between girls and boys?* There again, the adult usually avoids answering. The child then uses his own personal knowledge and, going back to his experience of giving or withholding his poo, where the dualism is characterised by the opposites active and passive, he says to himself that "the boy is stronger", which is generally true during early childhood. (I once heard a two-and-half-year-old girl saying in admiration: "Boys are *stroooong*", with her hands clasped, watching two little boys fighting.)

Very soon children notice when they need to pee outside, that boys pee standing up, which girls cannot do. This is considered superior and taken for granted by the boy, whilst the little girl fantasises that her clitoris will grow.

The boy, frightened by tales of genital mutilation, becomes fully aware of what until now he has refused to see: the girl really doesn't have one. This happens around five or six, an age when conversation with other children, and most of all sexual games between boys and girls, will leave him with no doubt on the question. Before the age of six, he still thinks that the girl "has a smaller version", unable as he is at that age to think other than in relation to himself. But usually, despite his acceptance of the lack of a penis in girls, the belief that his mother still has one, persists. The mother cannot lack what she has given. It is through her disfavour that the girl does not have one.

Thought process at the phallic stage

As the child develops, the mother looks after him less and less, materially speaking, and desires, of whom she is the object, result in fantasy and day-dreaming. These are part of all the active physical expressions of the child, including, amongst others, masturbation. For the girl, this is still clitoral.

Where the mother is generally well-balanced, the feel of these masturbatory fantasies is sadomasochistic with a predominance of sadism in the boy and of masochism in the girl.

It is not so long ago that these arms of hers, and these movements of hers, were associated with his own passive efforts. The erotic glance cast on the mother makes the child, an active participant in all she does, integrating his autonomous passive sensations; he is fascinated by the repetitive and wordless activities of the mother who is absorbed in herself.

When the mother is not there when he wants her, the child calls and looks for her. If he finds her, she may be busy and reject him by saying "Later on, now I am doing this or that", the child asks "why?". "So that you can have something to eat", answers the mother, "so that the house is cleaned, "so that Daddy is happy; go and play!'" The child obeys, taking with him whatever he can from his mother; her words, which he repeats to himself, often aloud. Or else he remains quiet, watching her.

Observation of mother's activity and thinking over her words, which have a sonorous resonance for him, and which he memorises in a rhythmical way, sometimes aloud, leads the child to acquire two notions of considerable importance, that of time and motivation.

Until then, the child acted according to his drives, for the sole pleasure of their immediate satisfaction. He did not know how to defer them and reacted immediately if the drive was not satisfied with a "tantrum". The uselessness of this furious protest and, on the other hand, the emotional reward for "being good", being able to wait for "later" promised by the loved adult, all teach the child the notion of "time". Previously, everything happened in the present. Now there is a "later", and a "tomorrow" when "later" arrives after the night. As a matter of fact, the child will not be able to differentiate "tomorrow" from "next week" or "next year", or again from "soon" for a fairly long time. It is only later that he will understand the notion of the past which is translated by the words "once" and "yesterday" applied to the immediate past as well as to the more distant past from the present, and which because of this fact get confused with his fantasies.

The second notion: through observing his mother's activity, with his attention focused on all that the loved object does, and in waiting for his mother to at long last look after him, a period of learning patience emerges. This is animated by intelligent observations depending on the individual rhythm of each child, but also on the emotional presence of the mother, her gaiety, her words, shared with him whilst she is doing the housework. The child can feel anguished by his mother's abandonment even when clinging to her, or be totally brought to life by her infectious joy whilst she is busy in the next room. The child learns to notice the many reasons for her movements and actions. He notices that the same object has several uses, and in this way develops the capacity to generalise based on his observations.

"What's it for?" becomes his leitmotiv confronted by anything that interests him. For the first time, he detaches himself from his exclusive interest in things related only to him. For example, the fire and all that was hot, "burnt", was "bad", and to be fled from. Now "the fire is for warmth" and is "pleasant when one is cold", heat is "used for cooking", and so on. And Mummy is there "to look after him, to cook, to clean", and so on. By extension, he wonders about everything that interests him "what is it for?". The day will come when he also wonders about his penis, and he answers "for peeing", but noticing that girls do without one, he tries in vain to find another purpose for it and, not finding one, he values even more the magical superiority it confers on him.

This is where *primary castration anxiety* may come into play (see next chapter).

Learning through trial and error, the child now holds the key to solve many problems. For example: he was too small to reach what he wanted and used to say "can't" whilst calling the adult to his rescue; now he gets a stool to make himself taller. This is when he longs to "act like a grown-up", like those who have more than him.

This longing engenders *ambition*, the wish to make up for his inferiority through the practical exploitation of his knowledge. This is, without any doubt, the emotional basis and the starting point of a greater and greater interest that the individual brings to learning, knowing, and it is the beginning of being able to value "Knowledge".

We have not as yet spoken about another discovery, that of death. It happens naturally around the same time, because for the child to take an interest in death, he has to have been made aware of it. He will not be aware of it if he has not sought equality of strength, movement, and knowledge with adults. His ambitions have got to come up against reality.

In observing animals, he discovers death. Finding a butterfly, a bird, a lizard or a fly, *immobile*, he asks "Why isn't it moving?" and back comes the reply "Because it is dead". Does every living thing die? Why do animals die? Because they are very old, but also because they have been attacked by others lost the fight and been *killed*. *To kill is to immobilise*. This is all the child understands about death during the anal phase and at the beginning of the phallic one. That is why a child can play at killing, out of ambition and omnipotent sadism, nothing more. To reduce what is animate to an inanimate state, this is what killing means to a child.

This is why, when a child is asked to keep partly or completely still, it is experienced as sadistic, and even more so if he is told to keep quiet by an adult, hypersensitive to noise. Chattering is a sign of both bodily and mental health in all children under seven. Mental concentration on a school task or in play, without accompanying noises or body movements and a running commentary, is a sign of a morbid lack of energy. Being made to keep still, when he has to concentrate mentally, can only be developed gradually and needs to be punctuated by moments of noisy bodily letting go. This training is more often damaging than useful; it is, unfortunately, too often synonymous with the well-behaved child, who gives every satisfaction to obsessed or hysterical adults whose thoughts and fantasies are disturbed by the child's vitality.

The silence and immobility of the well-behaved child are rarely anything more than a mutilation of vitality, a reduction to the status of faecal object, an enforced death to which the child submits. Before sinking into "mental retardation", which is the effect of this "death", he develops sadistic fantasies, which can become phobic hallucinations, the source of perverse erotic pleasure at all stages of the libido which is being blocked of active expression. Rhythmic masturbatory compulsions, twitching, stuttering, insomnia, encopresis, enuresis, are the last refuge of the libido for this socially inert child, tortured by a perverted upbringing.

As to the real meaning of death, he needs to see an animal or a loved human being die to understand the meaning of absence with no return, of the definitive loss of the object. Even the adult cannot prevent death or bring the dead back to life, in the way that he can so often mend things, this plunges the child back into the mystery of birth. Let us remark—and we will discuss this later on—*the importance of this chronological coincidence, of the appearance of castration anxiety with the discovery of death.*

The little despot in love, be it girl or boy, feeling neglected by the mother makes him aware that he is not the only object of interest to his mother or her only purpose in life. *He has a rival* in the person of his father and more than that, sometimes brothers and sisters.

For a long time, the father is part of the world of the mother, and provided father knows how to scold or praise when need be, he is invested with great affection and prestige. Furthermore, when something is difficult, Mummy says: "We'll ask Daddy". He is the one who carries heavy things and quite often snores. For the child, he is a strong being; but little by little, he becomes a rival, with whom the mother remains willingly, without paying attention to the demands of the child, to whom she is less subject than during his early infancy. He comes up against: "Go and play, leave us alone".

This rivalry will be the same towards brothers and sisters, and, depending on the extent to which he attributes responsibility to them, rightly or wrongly, for the lesser affection shown to him by his mother, he will experience conflicting feelings towards them.

For this reason, we will not discuss family conflicts, the mechanisms of which can be practically and fundamentally superimposed on conflicts between the parents.

One can say that in the great majority of cases, if the parents are psychically healthy, the girl is more docile, less aggressive and less noisy than the boy.

Right from the anal stage, as far as toys are concerned, girls are more likely to be interested in dolls, while boys tend to prefer cars. She likes playing with water and washing and bathing her dolls, whilst the boy throws stones into the water, playing at fishing and boats.

At the phallic stage, she plays at tea parties, with her doll, putting her to bed, taking care of her, rocking her, dressing her, and so on, whilst a boy, if he loves a doll (and it is not that rare), does not know how to "play with dolls". She is already interested in her appearance, in clothes, she dresses up, she steals her mother's make-up, and likes to stroll about with mother's handbag on her arm. In short, she identifies as much as possible with her mother, mimicking her acts, gestures, and words. This is gendered behaviour, consonant with the "genius" of her sex, still at an intuitive stage, at the genital level.

The boy at the phallic stage embraces aggressive games, plays at being a despot, armed with a stick, turning it into a gun or revolver, he loves to be scary and commanding. When he can, he struts about with his father's hat and umbrella. In other words, he identifies with him as much as possible and with men whose behaviour he has been able to observe, as the roles which govern masculine norms are beginning to be felt within him.

Everyone has seen children play at being Daddy and Mummy and how the roles are shared, already, as they will be in life. The boy naturally takes the role of the father and the girl that of the mother. (The reverse is symptomatic of neurosis.)

Around four, four and a half at the latest, the boy embarks openly in an emotional battle with his father; he plays at killing him, tries to totally monopolise his mother's affections, tells her that he is going to marry her, that he is going to take her far away to his house in a plane and that they are going to have children. He enters the Oedipal phase.

The little girl has an analogous experiences. Perhaps the attitude of the father, who, ordinarily, loves the girl more than the boy, contributes to awakening her earlier? The fact remains that around three and a half, four years old, a little earlier than the boy, the little girl will behave

at the time when the pleasure in these zones was the chosen aim of activity.

Intellectual interest is indeed awakened at these successive stages, through emotional attachment *to substitutes* for the sexual object, in proportion to the frustrations (oral, anal, urethral) imposed by the parents and the external world.

Intellectual interest flowing from the libidinal drive, requires that the subject tolerate this drive at least for the time needed for the formation of substitute interests and *until such time as* these very interests can bring emotional satisfaction, as well as the approval of the adults. Only then will the corresponding sexual interest be able to disappear of its own accord through a harmless repression: the possibility of sublimation has been acquired.

Over-development of "intelligence" in relation to the rest of the psycho-physiological activity of a subject appears to us worth being called "a neurotic symptom", which is to say a reaction to anxiety and suffering. Intelligence, defective, normal, or superior, can exist as much in a neurotic as in an emotionally healthy subject. Given the same capacity for sublimation as compared to the neurotic, the healthy subject has, intellectual faculties better adapted to reality and the capacity to be more creative. His interests being more numerous, without being disparate, they contribute both to his satisfaction and personal enrichment, as well as being objectively useful to society.

In such subjects, the phallic and latency stage, as well as the beginning of the genital stage at puberty, are marked by emotional involvement, and spontaneous and successful engagement in all activities.

With the maturation of genital sexuality, the individual will deliberately sacrifice (not repress) those of his interests which are obviously incompatible with the path of life he has chosen. This will happen without any residual bitterness towards the objects he has renounced which, without anxiety, he can observe being chosen by others.

What we have just said about the blossoming of intelligence is only a part of the satisfactory conclusion of libidinal genital development. This would be characterised by "vocation", and commitment, to what is chosen, which when complete reaches down into the unconscious, and is accompanied by a psycho-physiological blooming, with the libido other-directed, towards the love object, work, and the child.

(Dolto used the term "Oblative" to mean other-directed, giving and receiving of the self in the love between a man and a woman, involving a total reciprocity, denoting the total maturation of the genital stage of libidinal development, in contrast to 'Captative' which refers to a self-directed, possessive earlier stage.)

Thought process at the genital stage

We saw how, at the beginning of the Oedipal phase, thought process was still located in the anal mode, triumphantly captivating or triumphantly rejecting, tinted with ambition. It is only with the dissolution of the Oedipus complex that thought can be put at the service of other-directed sexuality, which is to say that which goes beyond the pursuit of narcissistic satisfactions without invalidating them.

At the genital stage, thought process is characterised by common sense, prudence, and objective observation. It is rational thinking.

The objectivity towards which the individual *strives* will be that of appreciating all things, emotions, people, and himself for their true value, which is to say at an intrinsic value without losing sight of relative value with regard to other people. The subject will only be able to aspire to total objectivity when, on the one hand, he has settled neurotic conflicts in himself, and if, on the other, he has not kept kernels of archaic fixation in his unconscious.

Furthermore, totally objective conscious thought, a prerogative of the completed genital stage, seems incompatible with introspection. Such was, but for other reasons, the narcissistic thought of the oral stage, preconscious and incapable as it was of objectivisation. The other-directed genital stage is characterised by libidinal fixation on the heterosexual object, for a life together and the protection of the child (or its substitute).

This genital sexual fixation can lead, in the adult, to the deep (as deep as the unconscious), true renunciation of instincts of self-preservation to ensure the protection, the conservation, and the unconstrained blooming of the physical, psychic (emotional and intellectual) life of the child. This is an other directed fixation onto an object outside the subject himself, whose survival and success are more important to him than his own. ("Oblative" must not be understood as ideally virtuous, but as a way of loving the other, the loved one, the work, the child with an instinctive, protective love, often equal in libidinal intensity to the instinct for self-preservation. This is the adult displacement of narcissism on to their descendants.)

With a mode of thought totally and constantly at the service of the genital libido, it is impossible to carry on simply thinking about the "self".

In order for such a thought to be formulated, a minimum interest in oneself (autoerotic) is required, intertwined with an "oblative" interest in the object, therefore it cannot be a driving force of the genital stage. Attempts at reflection around this thought process reach towards the ineffable; they do not come from the domain of rational human thought. Introspection therefore always stands for, even at the genital stage, an anal way of thinking, it is never rational nor objective.

The way of thinking which is totally genital, "oblative" is out of the subject's control. This is perhaps what accompanies the total psycho-physiological upheaval of genital orgasm during intercourse with a "loved" sexual partner, for the adult who has arrived at the conscious and unconscious duality, of the oblative, other-directed genital stage. The essence of orgasm is precisely that it brings with it unutterable, unthinkable emotion, ineffable feelings that are uncontrollable and incommunicable.

The "oblative" genital mode of the thought process can still regress after it has been reached. Failures or errors in the choice of the selected other, worries arising from a child or from work creatively conceived, can induce a neurotic regression through castration anxiety always associated since the Oedipal stage with the narcissistic ethical values of the individual. The modes of thought and reactions of previous stages can re-appear. These are the cases of traumatic neurosis whose symptoms translate into negligence towards the object, leading to the loss of the taste for life and a relapse into a critical Oedipal emotional situation transferred onto objects felt again as counterparts.

But, up to old age, libidinal drives structured by the Oedipus complex can recover their creative capacity through the reprobate struggle expressed through Oedipus. In the same existential mode, the libidinal drive and the death drive confront each other through traces which have remained from the structuring of the castration complex. In the same way as sleep and its dreams of satisfied desire support, through the necessary rhythm of rest, the conscious vitality of a third of a person's life, in the case of a major test in the genital life experienced in reality, regression into illness serves as a narcissistic compensation. The genital libido, which was undermined by the failure of its creative achievements, finds a paternal castrating substitute in suffering which orientates him towards a dynamic re-launch of his identity, reconfirmed in his destiny, without residual bitterness, as was the case during the Oedipus complex.

Creative joy is the sign of the genital libido being productive once again.

The role of sexuality in the development of the individual

We have tried to cast a glance both on how everything the child does is connected and on how he apprehends reality. *The search for sensual erotic pleasure is not the only pursuit of the child*, even in the eyes of psychoanalysts, as some would like to believe.

But at each stage, from birth to death, there is no thought, no feeling nor act which does not include a search for pleasure, that is to say, a libidinal drive. There is no healthy life without a healthy sexual life, and conversely there is no healthy sexual life in someone who is ill or neurotic.

Sexual health cannot be measured by physiological erotic activity, this being only one aspect of sexual life. The other aspect is his emotional behaviour towards the object of his love (*objet d'aimance*) which in absence is translated into fantasies in which the object figures.

The study of these fantasies and of their symbolism is the only way of knowing the emotional age of the subject and the developmental stage which is causing the trouble. There is no action without an emotional correlation in relation to the conscious or unconscious aim of the action.

And the aim of all education (prophylaxis of behavioural problems), as well as of all psychotherapy (cure of behavioural problems), is to use the libido such that the individual *feels* happy and that this personal well-being is in tune with that of others, and even encouraging their well-being rather than impeding it.

Our aim is to show the clinical accuracy of what we have just said and to draw practical educational conclusions from the following clinical observation:

> It is the libidinal energy diverted from its sexual aims which animates all the individual's actions.

The tendency to rhythmically rub any part of his body in order to get pleasure exists in the child from the first months of life. During the oral passive phase, sucking without swallowing has no aim other than hedonism; during the active oral stage, to bite or to nibble is a pleasure in itself.

The beginning of the anal stage inaugurates the pleasure of pinching, hitting, squashing, and "pushing", that is to say, the pleasure of making an effort. Now that the child is physically capable of muscular effort, he knows how to "push" and to "hold in". You can give him the onomatopoeiac sounds to accompany this effort whilst putting him on the potty. This enables him to learn how to master his efforts, previously just a game, putting them at the service of his first conquest in life, as a social being, at the same time as his first opportunity to please the beloved adult.

Unfortunately, the psycho-affective organisation of the sadistic anal stage is very active and the libidinal tension of the child *doesn't always find a way of total displacement* onto the alternatives offered or permitted by the adult at this stage. This is why the period of the anal stage is simultaneously the time when the child chews his nails, puts his fingers up his nose, scratches his skin—although there is no itch—sometimes going so far as to puncture his skin which naturally becomes septic (see the observation of Gustave, p. 147). One or other of these habits can be prolonged beyond the anal stage, and there is not much the adult can do to repress it. This just goes to show that the libido of the subject is not entirely ready to move on towards new achievements.

It is here that we find the explanation for those gestures, apparently absurd in themselves and devoid of pleasure, which everyone of us makes (in day-to-day language, these are called mannerisms). They appear in spite of us, at moments of reflection, preoccupation, effort, or concentration. These are qualitatively of the same unconscious value as obsessional symptoms, because they have the same origin and only differ from them quantitatively. Affectively, they serve to support feelings with the same charge as those of childhood, and to support fantasies which unconsciously or symbolically go back to conflicts of the sadistic anal stage.

Proof of this is when we see someone put a finger up their nose, or pull the skin around their nails, or bite them or their lips, play with their keys or money in their pocket. In the first instance, it annoys us; on the other hand, if we remark on it, it is they who cannot stop, without feeling embarrassed and unable to think; in other words, the tension that reflection creates can be released more easily through the compulsive gesture.

Other than these gestures, which somehow correspond to a "downgraded" masturbation, there are peculiarities of behaviour which are part of "personality"; bouts of anger, resentment, envy, jealousy, vanity, are just as much symptoms, because, despite logical justifications (rationalisations), they are invariably repeated in all the subject's relationships.

It is the child's feelings for the parents, most of the time reflecting their unconscious attitude towards him, which do or do not enable him to put the drives to the service of good cultural aims. Thus daring, a taste for risk, when it is rewarded by the admiration of the mother; victory over the adult during play fights or games of skill; or when the child fails, the encouragement of the adult rather than a teasing triumph; hugs or compliments encourage the child to show that he is a "good sport", generous in the inevitable fights with others, while severe scolding aims at "bringing him into line" when he is naturally gifted with a libido richer than that of others.

The drives and their libidinal discharge do not therefore have as much importance in themselves as by virtue of the emotions that they engender.

For the child who hasn't yet reached the "age of reason", that is to say, a sense of morality (the superego), *experience is ruled by the raw principle of pleasure/displeasure.* What causes pleasure will be repeated; what causes displeasure will be avoided.

But the child's instinctual drives will come up against obstacles. Whether these obstacles conform to the "human condition" taken in its largest sense, or they are set up without any rational need by the family milieu whose values derive from a distorted ethical vision, the child is not qualified to perceive. If he realises this one day, at puberty or later, as his inclination causes him to reconsider the values erected to the rank of dogma in his educational milieu and by his own superego, then there will be conflicts created between his distorted moral sense and his ego. This reconsidering of values at "emotional" puberty is nevertheless indispensable. To reconsider values is not necessarily to destroy them, it is only to catalogue them, to sort them out, and to keep those that fit. Inevitably, this crisis at puberty brings about a more or less marked family conflict, *even* when parents are very understanding, but *especially* when they are not interested in the child. Indeed, for the adolescent, the internal anguish of this normal conflict between *his* instincts and *his* superego is difficult to bear. It is easier when the young person is able to make others take responsibility for his suffering. Parents can be the *living* superego, the "ones in charge".

Of course, there are parents who accentuate the intensity of the conflict at puberty, but this does not make it any the less, physiologically and emotionally, normal. This is why these conflicts of adolescence can trigger more or less acute neurosis, whether they occur at the right physiological age or later, if the individual was already slightly neurotic, feeling guilty about his sexual urges before puberty. These conflicts normally emerge between the ages of eighteen and twenty-five coinciding with the first attempts at love relationships outside the home and the guilty feelings that they engender.

The art of parents and doctors is to enable the euphoric development of the child's natural potential, both emotional and physiological, in so far as it is compatible with the physical and psychological demands of his social milieu. It is not by isolating the child to prevent the risk of illnesses that one will achieve this, it is on the contrary in arming him against them. Similarly for psychic health, one will be no help to the child if he is kept away from the risks of life. He has to accept the inevitable suffering, the human anguish arising from the prohibitions imposed by society on his uncontrollable libidinal drives, his pleasures. One can assist him by enabling a *free and spontaneous disinterest* in forbidden pleasures or those little valued in the milieu in which he lives. *This disinterest is achieved not through strict training, but thanks to the important libidinal and emotional compensations that submission brings to the child in exchange for his consent to restriction.*

The adult must never forget that the libidinal richness of a child can be equal, but also superior or inferior to, his own, that the personality which exists *in potential* in a child can be very different from his own, and that he must never compare the personality of the child to that of another, except from the strict point of view of practical success, of health, and of the subjective happiness of a good emotional adaptation.

A means by which one can assess the intrinsic value of a human being does not exist, and will probably never do so. All adults, be they parents, doctors, or teachers, must have a very lively sense of respect for the individual freedom of the child in whatever lawful activities he might be drawn to, and be careful not to add anything to the instinctive restrictions that complying with the rules of his *contemporary* social milieu already demands of him.

These restrictions are not always the same, and are often less than those that the adult imposes on himself voluntarily through personal *ethics* or through submission to the exigencies of life. These are sometimes painful, the child is not responsible for them, and he must therefore not grow up considering them as *normal*.

The child can just as well love and admire the parent without being obliged because of this to believe that he is infallible in all his judgements. From the very fact that he loves the adult and feels respected by him, he, too, will be happy to respect him and please him in his turn and to imitate him, as long as this attitude is spontaneously in agreement with his original natural development.

Growing up, he will then be free to choose for himself a way of life entirely different from that chosen by the educating adult. In choosing a divergent path, although that is always painful for him, he will still feel supported by the certainty of success and happiness even if his choice makes him grow apart from the adult who raised him, bringing his parent the profound joy of seeing his life's work come to a creative conclusion.

As long as the adult is not neurotic where the child is concerned, there is an art emanating from the heart, which as we have already said parents, doctors and teachers need, not withstanding any intellectual capacities they might also bring. In fact, a psychically healthy adult has reached the other directed genital level; therefore his own psycho-emotional development leads him to devote his libidinal energies to his work, the objectives of his "vocation" and to his child. Knowing that his child is happy brings him a *joie de vivre* and enables him to age without bitterness.

The art of education is to ethical behaviour what prophylaxis is to illness. This "art", of the good parent comes from natural *common sense* which doctors need as well.

Whatever the faults or qualities an adult may have, he can have an emotional attitude which is sympathetic and respectful of his fellow men whether or not he personally approves of them. This is the only possible attitude for a doctor when a child is brought presenting behavioural or physical problems or both.

Provided he has scientific knowledge, he can make a diagnosis and attempt a prognosis. This is only the beginning of his role. He must also treat the patient, both bodily and emotionally, helping the patient to heal, by stimulating natural defences in order to overcome or repair (with minimum loss of substance as surgeons say) disorders with or without organic basis.

All those confronted with behavioural problems as well as organic functional disorders, the educators, doctors in the true sense of the word, need to have a sense of the role played by libidinal life and to know about the significance of sexuality in the developing adaptation of the individual to society.

The importance of the phallic stage in the pathogenesis of neurotics

During the first phases of oral and anal sexuality, the adult does not have to totally suppress hedonistic satisfaction.

If the parent is not neurotic, she will aim only gradually to achieve the relative regularity necessary to the child's health and the rhythms of life: how to eat properly and how to progressively control one's digestive function, without becoming obsessed by it. Harsh and overly strict potty training is neurotic in opposition to its intended aim: to disengage the ego from the drive so that the feelings, which are linked to the drive, can be used towards new and socially accepted ends. But, if intestinal functioning becomes a worry, for the unconscious economy it is as if anal eroticism ruled in the absence of cultural repression, but it is not at all the same in terms of the whole of the personality and its practical adaptation. The individual no longer has permission to enjoy a pleasure which has been forbidden; he is not free of anal preoccupation. On the contrary, constipation or diarrhoea becomes the most important daily issue; a great deal of libido is utilised to repress the sexual drive, itself invested with an equal quantity of libido. The libido thus blocked in the unconscious is no longer available to invest in the ego's practical social activities, nor is it available to invest in the phallic erogenous zone which has to chronologically succeed the anal zone in the supremacy of pleasure-seeking.

During the oral and anal phases, the child finds, through his acceptance of partial renunciation of the satisfaction of his instinctual drives, a means to win the friendship of adults without, in order to do this, being obliged to totally repress his interest in his digestive functions, indispensable as they are to organic life. Furthermore, what is repressed of the affective interest which he bears to his excrement is used to invest in other objects of "love". The mother, to begin with, is its first beneficiary, as the child learns to present her with gifts; then new love objects, each day more numerous, are welcomed into the emotional world of the child.

The libido, coloured with sadism and masochism once diverted from its primitive erotic aim, can then be put to the service of the body and the mind, physiologically capable of using, separately or simultaneously, aggression and passivity in practical activities. Cultural acquisitions and personal experience, which teach the subject limits and rules imposed by the external world on his individual drives, serve to create the conscious kernel of a personality. The ego of the child manifests its free choice in all that is not targeted by the prohibitions of the educating adult; he comes up against these prohibitions in the same way that he comes up against the physical laws of the external world. These inevitable encounters give birth to a suffering, which is called *primary anxiety*. The repressed libidinal energy, once removed from its pleasure-seeking oral and anal aims, will be used to reinforce adherence to permitted codes of behaviour, which will become defence mechanisms of the ego against primary anxiety, at the same time as becoming narcissistic satisfactions and a means of promoting development towards the genital stage.

If the educator is not neurotic and has attained the genital stage appropriate to his own sexual development, and if, on the other hand, the child is physiologically healthy, there will be no serious "neurotic" incidents in the child's adaptation to social life. His defence mechanisms have proved themselves good enough. They act in the direction of the displacement of affects onto interesting objects, which are culturally significant. They give rise to reaction-formations in the form of character traits and to sublimations in accordance with the surrounding social milieu, with the educator or the family circle, which are themselves in tune with this social scene. This is what is called "normal" reaction.

The results of frustrations during weaning and potty training are therefore: on the one hand, to shape in the normally well-brought-up child an outline of a differentiated personality whose interests and sublimations are already measurable; and, *on the other hand*, to stimulate sexual evolution towards the primacy of the phallic erogenous zone, invested in slowly and gradually as the new libidinal pressure can no longer find its outlet through the oral and anal zones de-invested of sexual interest.

At the phallic stage, a new fact appears, which turns frustrated erotic urges into mutilating psycho-physiological traumas. It is the impossibility for the child of displacing (without regressing) onto another erogenous zone the libidinal investment devolved to the phallus, elevated to the rank of selective erogenous zone. If, for the girl, the displacement can and ought to be done from the clitoris towards the vagina, the anatomical proximity of these two zones will make it such that a prohibition aimed at clitoral masturbation will often be felt to apply to vaginal masturbation too (besides this is also very often the intention of the reproving adult).

For the boy as for the girl, the genital area becomes the centre of sexual interest, which is not for all of that entirely detached from its old erotic fixations (tasty treats, scatological jokes, touching sexual parts, auditory, olfactory, and muscular pleasure-seeking, dexterity, dance, sports, playful aggressive biting, scratching, hitting, and so on).

The culmination of infantile sexuality in the supremacy of the genital zone is physiologically of the utmost importance. Respect towards its *natural evolution* is culturally necessary for the normal adaptation of the child to its ultimate life within society, which requires the physiological and affective development of the individual, that is to say his libidinal blossoming. Unfortunately, it too often happens that the ignorant or neurotic adult sabotages the first manifestations of investment in erotic-affective interest in the genital zone for the child. This interest is nevertheless the proof of a natural instinctual evolution in conjunction with the biological development of the human being. To forbid the child masturbation, as well as his spontaneous sexual curiosities, is to oblige him to waste useless attention on activities and feelings, which are normally, before puberty, unconscious or preconscious. It is morally self-evident (and even a theological commonplace, proof of which is the idea of the "age of reason") that some behaviours do not have the same meaning for the adult as for the young child. A premature awareness in an atmosphere of guilt is thoroughly damaging to the child's development, because it deprives him of the right to use differently, on the genital level, the libido unconsciously enclosed in these spontaneous activities. The psychically healthy child who has arrived at the phallic stage has mastery over his own needs, is skilled with his body and dexterous with his hands, he speaks well, listens, and observes a lot, loves to imitate what he sees being done, asks questions, waits for truthful replies without which he invents magical explanations.

Common prohibitions against masturbation

What measures does the adult take when he catches the child in the "disgusting" action that so deeply shocks him?

First, there is the simple prohibition without explanation. If it is not accompanied by a stern tone of voice and did not come from the favourite adult, it is the least traumatising of all. Indeed, the child only pays attention to a prohibition when he is in the presence of the "grown-ups", or when he notices for himself the realistic and rational risk that his disobedience might bring upon himself. Now as this "real danger" will never manifest itself as far as masturbation is concerned, he will be able to satisfy society's arbitrary demands, because, in fact, and this is the reality, society does not tolerate masturbation in public, but does not forbid it in private.

Not only does the adult disapprove of masturbation, but *it is very seldom that the adult does not justify its prohibition*, when the innocent child asks him for a reason. This is where the embarrassment begins for the adult who generally answers: *"It is not nice"* or *"it is dirty"*, without realising that these explanations can create a gulf between him and the child, who, until now, trusted him completely. If, unfortunately, the child accepts and makes his own these false value judgements, his "common sense" will be definitively changed; we will return to this point later on.

When the adult uses means of intimidation, he speaks with his "superego" voice and not at all according to a rational morality, that is to say, a morality conforming to the real social demands of his milieu. This is why a neurotic mother or carer (who is frigid, for example) is profoundly damaging to the early education of a child, even though the child forgets this first carer completely.

"So, it will be said, you are among those who would leave a child in an untutored state under the pretext of not inflicting pain!"

Not at all, but there are ways of demanding renunciation of instincts, and this way of asking depends on the level of profundity of the carer. She can help the child develop happily or, on the contrary, under the pretext of education, hinder his progress.

In fact, it is very rare that the child does not repeat the action condemned as so "ugly" and "dirty" that the adult is trying to make him think about; the adult then resorts to coercive means or intimidation.

First, there is a series of corporal punishments already in use during the preceding educational phase: slaps, blows, the strap, withdrawal of treats, and so on.

In some refined milieu, where hitting the child is not permitted, mothers believe themselves kinder—when in fact it is the most sadistic

CHAPTER THREE

The Oedipus complex

In normal cases, a child of three is no longer a little savage; he is already "civilised", he already has a personality, habits, favourite activities, a way of thinking, and extensive emotional potential channelled into relationships within his family circle and when all goes well with a few children of his own age, both girls and boys. His libido is therefore already well employed.

The manner in which adults have responded to his demands for unconditional love, and have known how to react with properly considered tender affection, the reprimands and the deliberate compliments which have brought him emotional satisfaction, are, in "normal cases", compensation enough for the renunciation required of him and which he has accepted.

The ease with which he has separated from the erogenous anal zone comes from the fact that he has been able to discover the pleasure reserved for phallic excitation (penis or clitoris).

In other words, *he is no longer an "instinctual pervert"*, that is to say, an It, greedy for wild and instant pleasure-seeking gratification; he has an Ego. His personal moral sense does not yet exist, yet the need he has for others' company already leads him to behave intuitively in accordance with the code of his circle. The time he spends masturbating, will be when he feels "bored", or when he has nothing more interesting to do (in bed when he is not asleep and when he has to keep "quiet"). This is a time when his imagination is running on empty, has nothing to work on or to play with that might lead to the physiological sexual release (in the wide sense of the term) that the libidinal drive demands; especially if he is in a state of physiological excitement (erection or clitoral tension). *That is to say that in a normal child, in good health, masturbation will rarely be public*, or frequent, and that, in any case, *the adult should show no interest in it at all*. This need will be all the less pressing if the mother finds ways to motivate her child towards achievement in all the useful and playful activities of which he is capable. The choice should mainly be geared towards activities that promote dexterity, muscular and intellectual activity, in imitation of older girls and boys.

It follows from this that in the case of a "normal" child who is frequently caught masturbating, one is dealing with a child who is exceptionally gifted and who should be encouraged into more demanding physical or mental activities than those usually reserved for children of his age group. But more often than not, one is dealing with an already neurotic child, for whom masturbation has become an obsessive need. This child needs to be treated and not scolded. Measures of coercion, aimed at preventing masturbation will inhibit his development assuming he submits (little by little, he will look "moronic") and, if he does not submit, he will become unstable, bad-tempered, undisciplined, and in revolt. None of these outcomes, we believe, is the result sought by the adult; however, it is, unfortunately, what the adult gets, and what he has unknowingly done everything to achieve.

We have already spoken about the question of the usual prohibitions against masturbation. We call them "castrating" because they aim at suppressing the sexual activity of the child. Conversely, a lot of apparently anodyne adult interventions aimed at suppressing spontaneous elements of the child's behaviour characteristics of his normal sexuality, will equally take on the value of "castrating" prohibitions. For example, curiosity in children of both sexes, the fighting instinct in the boy or flirtatiousness in a girl, simply because these prohibitions touch upon components heavily loaded with values of an emotional libidinal nature.

Any adult intervention which aims not only to totally suppress masturbation, but also, whilst attempting to make the child see reason, causes the adult to be unnecessarily involved in the child's imaginative and fantastic projects (which always mask sexual fantasies) has to be labelled as a castrating intervention. The result will only be to increase the child's normal and inevitable anxiety in this naturally difficult moment of his development.

Let us admit for the sake of simplicity that, contrary to fairly widespread common practice, no remark is made to the child about his masturbatory activity, either because the adult is indifferent to it, or he does not notice it.

We will see that there is no need for there to have been adult intervention for the child to suffer from castration anxiety, against which he will need to learn to defend himself and not *yet* capitulate. This defence, as we will see, will inevitably bring in Oedipal rivalry which in its turn will trigger a castration complex.

It is this struggle against the successive modalities of castration anxiety that we are going to study.

Let us say that in the best cases, roughly, the child resolves the Oedipus complex before the latency phase, he will then be able to enter latency in full physical and moral health, such that he is able to embrace the cultural world in the best way possible. Later on this will facilitate normal emotional and physiological fulfilment, from puberty and adolescence, through to maturity.

However, frequently the child does not manage to negotiate the Oedipal phase before entering latency; he is therefore drawn—if we can be forgiven the expression—"to sign a truce" with the castration complex, which, *at puberty*, will regain its castrating role: the subject will still be able to get rid of it *at this time*, or never again (without psychoanalysis).

Castration anxiety

The unease that the child experiences when he discovers the absence of the penis in girls initially induces him to disregard the evidence of his own eyes. As we said before, he remains convinced that the girl has got a smaller one, and that it will grow, or that it is hidden between her legs; one of our adult patients dreamed of such a woman, which reminded him of his infantile fantasies. But, however much the child tries to comfort himself with these consoling hopes, the boy nevertheless feels the fear that something like this may happen to him, because he has seen that it "is possible".

This is because, as we know, the mode of thinking at this stage is under the sign of magic. According to his logic or his mental development, the child seeks to make sense of this law of nature which hits him consciously as being an anomaly. It does not seem to him to be the natural order of things; because he had not noticed it earlier, he concludes that "it fell off", or "that it has been cut off", or that "it got lost". From each of these explanations, he constructs a story, that is to say, a fantasy in which things are represented symbolically; the drawings of children illustrate these fantasies (see drawing 1, p. 136), where the animal has its nose and tail cut off; and cf. the case of Tote (p. 194).

Michel, a young patient who is in analysis with me, tells me the following story to explain his drawing (drawing 3, p. 138): "There is a Chinese man who has peeled a banana and who is happy with the banana, then he looks at a tree and he throws away his banana because he thinks that it is a stone; a woman catches the banana." To my question: "Is this a true story?", he answers, "It happened to me. I had an apple for my afternoon snack and then I peed against a tree and I wasn't concentrating. I believed that I had a stone in my hand and I threw it away without meaning to and then I didn't have an apple any longer and I didn't know how it had happened." We can see how the true story serves as a support to the fantasy. The apple, a fruit already forbidden from the earthly paradise, which Michel knows, is replaced by a banana, a phallic symbol and the story brought back to his peeing. Michel's mother is one of those mothers who sewed up the flies of his trousers, which of course obliges Michel to take off his trousers when he wants to pee—therefore putting on the floor whatever he is holding to free his hands—then he forgets to pick up his afternoon snack, probably due to a parapraxis.

When the child notices that it is only *girls* that lack the penis, the first result of this observation is to devalue girls.

But he still doesn't accept, for all that, that women, especially his mother, can be devoid of a penis. Girls and boys continue to imagine the mother as infinitely superior to themselves, therefore as having a big phallus. To this end, to have a penis is "to be stronger than girls"; but adults, both men and women, are still stronger than boys. The child feels in a state of inferiority in the presence of the adult and so he should, given that he is a child.

See the hat worn by the lady in drawing 12 p. 144. Cf. Observation of Claudine, p. 207: "She is *him* (sic) who has nothing" in the drawing 11, p. 144 in which "the boys and the men each have a big thing for looking at the sea".

See drawing 6, p. 140 (that of an enuretic eleven-year-old boy). This big tree, a fantasy of pure imagination in this Oedipal drawing, stands next to an exact reproduction of *The Normandy* (a cruise liner) which he had been to see; the symbolism is so obvious that I asked him the question: did he know that women weren't made like men? He did not, though he knew that his sister and girls generally were not made like boys. But when they became "mothers, ladies", he believed that "it all sorted itself out".

Once he has admitted the fact, the child asks himself "why?". He tells himself: this is because "they have been punished"—prepared as he always is at this stage to see sanctions on an aggressive destructive level because of his own sadism which he projects onto others. He is, in effect, incapable as yet of conceiving of others as feeling and thinking beings different from himself.

"Who punished them?". He will answer his question with familiar or invented stories, or by fantasies around a fact told by the adult.

In one of my little patients, the castrating symbols all appeared in drawings. Successively, there was the grandfather with his razor, "Madame Fichini", the bad fairy in *Snow White*, the wicked stepmother, bad mummy, *"père fouettard"* the ogre, the bogeyman, the policeman, the constable, the Pope (!), the officer with his sabre, the man of the woods with his snare, the fish-man, the man of the sea, the diver. All these magical powerful beings are abundantly endowed with extraordinary hats, sticks, and a big sack to put children in.

In all these stories, the child falls into the hands of devouring ogres, of almighty and nasty beings. Why are children punished by having their "willy" cut off, their explanation for the absence of the penis "inflicted" on girls? It is because they have not been quiet or obedient. The illogical severity of the adults towards a child, noisy and aggressive in his play and other activities, normal for his age, needlessly increases the anxiety. For him, the grown-ups are marvellous, fair beings, who are always right, and it seems that it is to their goodwill that the child owes his (very) being as a boy or a girl. It is the adult who creates a girl by removing a part of the body from a primitively intact being who otherwise, without this castrating intervention, would have remained a boy.

We therefore see that castration anxiety springs from a false interpretation of reality; but it is an interpretation which no child can evade, because of the very fact that the danger which he invents is motivated by the magic power with which he endows adults and by his actual inferiority with regard to them.

For the child, the discovery of the difference between the sexes has the useful role of stimulating his development. The child refuses the castration which he believes he is threatened by, wrongly so; however this refusal is not a danger to his sexuality, quite the contrary.

What is important in this conflict, is that it happens in the conscious ego. The child is conscious of his unease, and he knowingly refuses it. He interprets it as coming from outside himself and he wants to know the reason.

This is what castration "anxiety" consists of; it is to be distinguished completely from what we will call the castration "complex". The castration complex is an unconscious phenomenon—(to understand what is the most difficult part of this account, it is important that the reader keeps clearly in mind, each time it is presented, the difference between castration *anxiety* (conscious) and the *complex* (unconscious)). We will see that unlike the castration complex (unconscious phenomena linked to the Oedipus complex), castration anxiety (pre-Oedipal and conscious phenomena) is rich with happy consequences for sexuality, which it helps to foster. On the contrary, the castration complex is a source of suffering for the child, usually without any outcome other than the temporary abandonment of his sexual interests in the latency phase. We saw, nevertheless, that in some very fortunate cases, the child manages to resolve his Oedipal issues and his castration complex *before* the latency phase.

The struggle against castration anxiety

*Consequences: the birth of the Oedipus complex, which,
in its turn, triggers the castration complex*

From what we stated previously, we can say that castration anxiety derives from three factors:

1. The discovery of the phallic difference between the sexes.
2. The magic power attributed to adults.
3. An overall and actual inferiority in relation to the adult.

The first of these factors is the only immutable one; the other two can be moderated.

The second factor, the baleful and magic power of the adult, the child can disassociate from and screen out by reasoning. The adult deemed nasty becomes the castrating parent; as to the other, the nice one, the child seeks in every way to persuade this adult to help and protect him.

As far as the third factor is concerned, the actual inferiority of the child, it can be remedied. Either the child can deny it, categorically and consciously, but that subjectively increases it because it makes obvious the difference between how things are and how he would like them to be, or else it may be overcome given sufficient cultural development. The advantage of this last approach is that it confers more appealing ways to obtain the help and protection of the Oedipal object.

But in this struggle against castration anxiety, the attitudes of boys and girls will be different.

The boy

The struggle against castration anxiety: pitfalls

For the boy, the fact of being favoured by nature (meaning the mother, the phallic mother)—whilst the "poor girl" is at a disadvantage—makes his penis even more precious. The phallus, already invested with narcissistic libido because of the sexual satisfactions brought about by masturbation, now receives an added libidinal investment and the little boy grows in self confidence.

But since sexuality is still qualitatively sadistic, possessively aggressive, the boy's manifestations of triumph are an exaggeration of sadistic components: noisy and rough at home, and, outside, racing around, setting off on adventures, playing in the bushes, searching for stones to throw as far as possible (there is always an aggressive note and an adventure theme), warlike fantasies whilst playing at being a soldier. In his fantasies, officers have the right of life or death over soldiers and prisoners.

However, the true object of love remains the mother, the more adored by the boy because he attributes the fact that he is a boy to a special favour from her. He wants to win her tender and appreciative affection and the means at his disposal are aggressive means, asserting his sexuality, which from his point of view ought to make his mother proud of him and his father too but secondarily. "You were very right to consider me worthy of being a boy."

His actual inferiority as a child is less painful to bear when his mother appreciates him, and he is even able to feel—thanks to identification with his father—that he can participate in her magic potency. He is a horse, a lion, a tiger in his fantasy play.

But, as we saw, his attachment to his mother goes on increasing, at a time when she is freeing herself of the constant subjection which kept her bound to the child. He remains wrapped up in her tender maternal attention, she makes him proud of being able to make friends with little people and big people and of behaving the way people do in his social group. She shows pride and happiness in his physical prowess, his successful initiatives and his new intellectual mastery.

Then, in the outside world, the little boy finds things that attract him, friendships, games, interests to which he attaches himself with enthusiasm, intellectually and emotionally. This is also why failures or emotional disappointments hit him so hard.

All these activities are animated by the presence of his mother. The quality of their interaction gives shade and colour to the emotions with which he will establish contact with other love objects. This explains the sadness of children who feel that their mother is troubled or cross, even when they know the reason, because they do not understand its emotional impact, especially if the mother is so wrapped up in her own worries, he feels totally abandoned. The parents may not be aware but the child believes that he is responsible; the least of his misdemeanours worthy of a telling off acquires the status of a crime, and his internal sense of good and bad finds itself distorted by scruples. So it goes with his high spirits or indifference, for example, when faced with a bereavement, saddening the whole family, when for him the dead person was not one of his very own love objects or in any event was not someone he had identified with. A sorrow, which has no meaning for him and does not share, cannot sadden him, and furthermore, imagine if the departed person happened to be a rival for his mother's affections, or was an objectionable tyrant, then the child cannot pretend to be affected by their loss; quite the opposite, a heavy weight has been lifted from his shoulders and he lets it be seen in his behaviour.

Although he already knows how to "cheat", that is, to deny something that could be held against him, the child does not yet know how to "pretend" when it is about something he feels indifferent to. Education will teach him not hypocritical pretence but respect for the feelings of others. This is why parents concerned for the well-being of their children, should not hide from them the actual fact of death but respect their carefree attitude towards it, and rejoice that they are not yet living through the pain which they will soon enough know to be heartbreaking: for none of us can live without experiencing the internal dereliction that comes from losing a beloved being. Let him experience reality, but let us respect in him his immediate lack of feeling or his natural means of defence, unless there is a risk that his attitude may bring in its wake real suffering later on.

The little boy who we left confident in himself, full of healthy libidinal potential, is still not able to "play with" others, however much he enjoys the company of his peers. He gradually begins to leave behind his fantasies and solitary play, now sharing games and stories that he loves to listen to and tell. He loves all activities in which there is a mixture of risk and audacity; he takes pleasure in showing that he is brave and crafty.

Now he seeks the company of other boys of the same age or older and does not like to include younger ones or girls in his group of friends. Whenever girls want to take part in the boys' games, there is a general outcry: "No girls, go away"… "Girls "don't count", and so on. If one of the boys shows himself less adventurous than the others, if he does not like to show off about his bravery and strength, he is contemptuously called a "girl", and he becomes the butt of the rowdy gang.

Incidents wounding to his self esteem, bumps and bruises, occasional accidents, are the price to pay for masculine achievements. The boy puts up with these bravely, proud in front of Dad and friends; happy to cry, unashamedly in front of his mother, who, without humiliating him, takes care of him physically, minimising the importance of this defeat, urging him not to give up but take his revenge and think about how to win next time.

Thus, the boy succeeds in mastering real difficulties, without the need for magical rescue. For the boy "crafty" is no longer fiendish, but on the contrary is synonymous with intelligence and cunning used to good purpose. With his new-found cleverness, he sublimates his uncontrolled aggression, thanks to his ability to anticipate the consequences of his behaviour in relation to the demands of reality. This is the root of good practical common sense. His prowess in the symbolic register of play, or in the cultural, social, and scholastic plane enables him to sublimate his sexual desire. The primitive hedonistic aim is itself sublimated into an emotional aim (to give and receive pleasure). It allows him to grow in the estimation of adults as well as acquiring his own self-confidence, based, this time, not on fantasies of magic power, but on real objective worth. This is the *age of chivalry*.

This boyish and chivalrous behaviour will bring about important emotional consequences. The boy *overrates his father* and *that makes him jealous of him* because, if the father is what a father should be, he is his rival for the mother, whom he protects and supports—(to "support" has to be understood in the widest sense of the word. He is her life companion even if the mother works outside the home). The boy will therefore try to do better than the father by trying to be useful to his mother in every way and by "learning" all that is required to be like Daddy, writing, reading, getting a good school report, earning money to buy flowers, or a present which he triumphantly brings back to his mother. He will do his best to please her by making things with his own hands. In this way, the superego starts taking shape, that is to say, his inner self, his "conscience", which lets him know the right thing to do or not to do, no longer following the direct pleasure principle, but following the moral line that one needs to be valued by mother, to hear her say "you are now a real little man".

But the more the boy develops in the avowed aim of pleasing mother, of becoming like father, the clearer the Oedipal fantasies become. (Bearing in mind that in many cases, the Oedipus complex is "acted out" on an aunt, sister of the mother, or on an older sister, so as to avoid the danger of rivalry with the father. The danger is nevertheless there, because even when the child "acts out" his Oedipus complex on another, it is of his mother possessed by a rival that he thinks, and he reacts towards the other woman "as if Daddy had forbidden her to him".) In his imagination, the boy takes his mother on a trip alone with him, he drives the car, he flies the plane, he builds their house, he chooses a job to earn money for her, he makes her happy, they have children. These Oedipal fantasies constantly clash with an opposing reality, the inexorable age difference. The mother belongs "to Daddy". Daddy says "When you are old enough you'll have a wife too."

- "But it's Mummy I want."
- "No, that's not possible, because Mummy belongs to me and she will be old like Granny when you are old enough to become a Daddy."

The child cannot yet admit this painful reality. Since Mummy belongs to Daddy, if Daddy wasn't there, she wouldn't belong to anyone and we would be happy together. This is where the belligerent, aggressive, violent fantasies towards Daddy come from, the "we do not need you, Mummy and me", and so on.

Let us suppose that the father does not get angry, and that he remains totally indifferent when confronted with this attitude and the aggressive make-believe world of the child.

Now then, *even* in this case, the guilt feelings of the child increase, completely independent of any external intervention: these feelings are due entirely to the functioning of the unconscious.

By the mere fact that the father is present, an adult who has rights over Mummy and whom she loves, there is no normal boy who would not feel real fear and jealousy while affecting disinterest. He tells himself that his father is jealous of him because he projects his feelings onto him.—("to project" means "to unconsciously attribute to someone else what one feels in oneself"), and he complains to Mummy about Daddy's strictness. Beware mothers who play games with their little Oedipal children by accusing the father of being too strict. They will lose some of their status and get involved in real quarrels with the father, which will evoke even guiltier feelings in the child, because he feels he has provoked them (see Patrice case, p. 162). Furthermore, precisely what he admires in himself is the strength and superiority of his idealised rival. If the mother attacks the father and he gives in to the mother, it is as if the mother was only allowing her son to become her "little man" in order to keep him under her thumb. Non-neurotic mothers, who allow the man the emotional upper hand, know very well that if the father is strict, it does not mean that he loves his son less. And if by chance he does not love him or is unconsciously jealous of him, it is not through criticism that the mother might enable him to change, quite the contrary.

Little by little, a rivalrous aggressiveness emerges in manifestly hostile behaviour, in conflict with his father for everything and nothing, in open disobedience aimed at provoking paternal reprimands, about which the child then complains to his mother. Such behaviour always occurs at one time or another during the development of every boy.

If the father is virile, sane, and strict but fair, it will be easy for the Oedipus complex to develop normally, because the image of the father is "powerful enough" to bear the unconsciously violent aggressiveness of the boy, without his needing to seek self-punishment due to his guilt feelings.

If, on the other hand, the father is physically weak, too soft or too strict, which means morally ineffectual, it is much more difficult for a boy to become genuinely manly. Even his legitimately achieved successes are conceived by him as guilty and his superego reacts as if they were such.

In a normal family, in which the father is the one who is in charge and is linked in loving tenderness to the mother, the only way for the child to manage is to definitively renounce the primitive object, prize of the competition, and to sublimate the drives aimed at possessing his mother.

In the name of inner necessity, the subject is forced to abandon the fight with the father, or to sublimate the libido, primitively employed in emotional fixation on the mother, onto other objects. Incest castrates the libido. I will try to demonstrate this.

As a matter of fact, if the aggression towards the father did triumphantly succeed on the conscious level and in reality, the son would no longer be able to identify with him; in fact, a child needs to invest his father, the true male possessor of his mother, with passive libido. He not only wants to *take* his father's place, but also to *imitate* him. This dual attitude, rivalrous and passive, can generally only take place in a "normal" family, that is to say, a family without neurosis, in which the boy is allowed boyish behaviour, and where the inevitable and necessary altercations blow up with the father without maternal interventions: "let the men sort it out between them". This is because the Oedipal competition between son and father is not *real*, the actual fact is that the mother *has already chosen* the father. Without blaming the father, therefore, she can give loving maternal comfort, but uncathected from her erotic libido to the little man who needs feminine affection during the difficult process of his social adaptation. The mother contributes in this way, stimulating in the boy the formation of a true genital superego. The boy renounces his rivalry with the father much more easily if he manages to recognise the *hopelessness* of his behaviour; the absence of this *recognition* is a source of anxiety. Whatever he does, his mother only loves him as a second, no more, and this allows him to attach to other female objects. If the child successfully negotiates his Oedipus complex, he can be proud of all his achievements, resembling his father, he no longer experiences guilt feelings, allowing the advent of healthy puberty.

Competition with the father can then be freely targeted towards the conquest of displacement objects. The boy sublimates his genital libido,

life, financially speaking, it cannot be in the same activities as the father or in activities of which he would approve otherwise it is at the cost of his sexual virility. Getting married, that is to say, publicly displaying the conquest of a sexual partner, is also a source of anxiety. And if he does manage to get married, he is afraid of having children. Children awaken such anxiety in him that he cannot behave as a "father" towards them. He is jealous of them. He chooses to "ignore" them, if not to destroy them.

This behaviour is almost always linked to a "feminity complex" in men, or perhaps more to the point, it is imprinted with an unconscious passive and homosexual attitude derived from a repression of Oedipal rivalry and not from its resolution. (Psychoanalytically, one speaks of "latent" homosexuality (unconscious or repressed) to differentiate it from "manifest" homosexuality, perverse homosexuals, or active or passive "sublimated" homosexuality, which governs friendly relationships between individuals of the same sex, with no unconscious affective components other than oblative components of the genital stage; that is to say, without ambivalence or jealousy.)

It can be found in apparently virile men whose attitude towards their children, if they have any despite the emotional poverty of their heterosexual genital life, is "possessive" and not "oblative" or "reciprocal". The presence of their children around them and dependent on them neutralises their castration complex, but they suffer from regressive anal frustration. Being apart from their children provokes aggression in them or melancholia accompanied by painful feelings of abandonment, which, through the projection of their own ruthless aggression, can go so far as to make them feel persecuted by their children. These are wealthy men who stop supporting their children as soon as the children want to create a life outside the father's sphere of influence. Fathers such as these discredit their children, denying them any personal worth and any chance of "managing" on their own. This way of thinking is necessary to allay their own anxiety. In fact, if these ideas were rational and not serving unconscious motives, their sons' success, in spite of the obstacles that they often try to put in their way, would definitively reassure them and allay their anxiety. On the contrary, they appear personally frustrated, as if the success of their sons reawakened in them feelings of envy and inferiority dating from the castration complex. In fact, it is a truly anal castration, depriving them of objects belonging to them that they had invested with libido in the service of the possessive egotistic love of the archaic anal stage, still active in their unconscious. If their daughters leave them, they are less profoundly wounded and react with a disappointed acceptance, partly compensated for by the aggressive epithets they employ towards those whom the girls have gone off with.

When homosexuality is sublimated and not repressed, there is an attitude of sexual and social equality towards same-sex individuals (parents or others). This implies *real friendship towards both parents*, based on an objective esteem and reciprocal affection and in any case equal spontaneous understanding for them and others. This attitude is only possible (in its unconscious determination) when in his unconscious the son has renounced the aggressive pursuit of his mother and the passive seduction of his father. In his heart of hearts, he lets himself disagree with his father's point of view, without the need to provoke punishment through pointlessly flaunting subversive ideas. He feels free within himself. And, furthermore, he displaces the exclusive interest bestowed upon his father or the men in the family, onto other men and boys, either by, as a rival, trying to outdo them through scholastic achievement, sports, and fights, or, as a disciple, he objectively admires them, yet feeling free to think for himself.

It follows that, as regards the father, the inferiority of the son is acknowledged as a matter of course just as it would with anybody else, without reawakening sadistic aggressive rivalry, painful feelings of inferiority, and the refusal to admire him (even if objectively justified— quite the contrary.)

At the time of his Oedipus complex, at six years old, the boy really is inferior to his father in strength and he can't win; the boy has to accept this and *abandon once and for all, and not put off,* competition for the maternal love object; that is, he must sublimate his Oedipus complex. Boys who do not resolve their Oedipus complex are not able to see their father as he is, and still love him with his faults and qualities, without reawakening the anxiety of the castrating superego.

It is obvious that the child, when he enters latency, cannot take up a completely objective position, but he can give up *all unfounded feelings of inferiority and all aggressivity towards his parents.* Accepting one's genuine inferiority, since anyway it is unavoidable, at the same time struggling to overcome any limitations possible at his age, living for others and working towards his own future, that is the only attitude compatible with entry into the genital-oblative mode of sexuality, for both men and women.

This complete resolution of the Oedipal conflict, which frees the boy's sexuality all the way into his unconscious, is accompanied by a separation. It is neither a conscious protest against one of the parents, (or against them both), nor a destruction, ("each man kills the thing he loves") *it is to use the same libidinal energies previously invested in his loved objects, to further his own development*; it is to "mourn", to accept the past is past, in the name of a present as rich, if not richer, in libidinal satisfactions, and to look forward to a future full of promise.

Clinically, this resolution of the Oedipus complex manifests itself in well-adjusted social behaviour, at school and at home, and in the ability to play, characteristic of a good adaptation. The child is in a normal "nervous" state, *no instability*, no anxiety, nightmares, or night terrors, and all curiosity, preoccupation, and solitary sexual activity has disappeared. The affective life of the boy will mainly take place outside the family. There are no conflicts worth remarking with the father or the mother.

Social life is marked by numerous investments, the aggressive or passive ambivalent drives previously bestowed on the father are displaced onto peers and teachers, while with girls, friends sisters, he likes to behave like a little hero, enjoying being admired.

From now on, games are communal. If the child is busy on his own, it is with objectively pragmatic activities, like complicated constructions or reading true stories. Games with complicated rules prevail: war games in which he is always decorated, full of bellicose authority, with the right of life or death over his subordinates and over prisoners from the enemy camp; games of cops and robbers, boisterous and noisy games and, if it is outdoors, there are always rules of the hunt in the games, running, chasing and adventure-seeking. The rules include "regulations", the attribution of administrative grades, penal sanctions. Girls are included in these games, but always as "understudy" to the boy; they build the camps. It is the beginning of mixed friendships, and "the girls" are there to be in goal, to keep watch, to play the nurse. He calls those who attack the girls cowards, and so on, whilst he plays at intimidating them himself. He terrorises them, consoles them, protects them, he gives them sweets, in short he uses his seductive and triumphant power with a type of love, which is still chivalrous and jealous and coloured with infantile sadism. Puberty will mark the arrival of tender reciprocal relationships between boys and girls.

The burden of castration on the boy

We have seen how a boy responds to castration anxiety whose defence mechanisms have been treated with respect.

We saw in the preceding chapter the usual prohibitions against masturbation. Simple disapproval of excessive onanism, that is, sexual sensuality, if not accompanied by magical threats or voiced by the loved adult (the mother) is not particularly traumatising. (Few children escape it, if not the mother nannies, teachers or the other children will take it upon themselves to inform the child.)

The true *"castrating" mother* is the one who systematically opposes anything that asserts the physical manifestation of boyhood (trousers with flies, short hair, masculine clothes), opposing as well the emotions and activities typical of boys (audacity, strength, pretend toughness, boyish bragging, pride in both intellectual and physical success, even accompanied by risk-taking).

If the mother forbids or belittles characteristic male activities, for "fear that he will hurt himself", if she constantly compares him with a younger or more passive child: "look at how good he is", if she sighs to see the child growing up: "you are no longer my little one", or regrets that he is not the girl she had wished for before his birth. Coming from the mother, the most important person in his environment, this is tantamount to making the boy feel guilty about the least of his activities stemming from his phallic sexuality. This is to tell him implicitly, even though prohibition of masturbation has never been formulated: "I would love you if you had no visible maleness".

To please mother, the boy attempts to submit his libido to this mutilation, the result of which is over-activation of his castration anxiety, because the second factor on which it depends (the magical power attributed to adults as described above) is being reinforced.

In other words, everything that thwarts the child's *natural* defence mechanisms against castration anxiety brings about harmful emotional reactions, rebelliousness, apparent or not, characterised by the refusal to make any effort and to submit to rules. In the erotic sphere, one witnesses regressive displacement of the libido onto erotic zones of previous stages. There will be enuresis, lack of appetite, or gluttony in the best of eventualities; or if this erotic unconscious regression has brought about scolding from the parent then gastro-intestinal troubles or nervous tics force the adult to take pity on the child and look after him. The means justify the end. The means (the illness), which is unpleasant, justifies the end: "possession" of the adult, attracting her pitying attention if he cannot get her admiration. *These are masochistic reactions, about which unfortunately the doctor is consulted not the psychotherapist.* They are nevertheless regressive neurotic symptoms. The medicine treats the effect not the cause.

Such a mother or father, when the anxiety originates with them, are pathogenic and going against their parental role, which is to "bring up" the child. It is they who *oblige* the child to regress to the urethral, anal, or oral passive stage, with the emotional behaviour concomitant to these long-gone stages.

The systematic prohibition through mockery or "rationalisation" of the infantile day-dream of being super-powerful can have a castrating role similar to that of the threat of sexual mutilation. If the child *needs* to imagine himself all-powerful to compensate for his inferiority, it is not by artificially suppressing this compensation or its expression that he will be helped; it is in allowing him to achieve genuine small triumphs and praising them. Besides, the credulity feigned by adults when they play at actively collaborating in the construction of fantasies, or when they pretend that the mythological, imaginary play of the child is real, are just as much castrating (for example, pretend "marriages" during the Oedipal phase), because the child will be forced to notice one day that he was tricked, and that he was laughed at. He will lose his confidence in adults and will no longer even be able to seek their approval, which will have showed itself as having no real value. Negativity, sulkiness, aggressive rebellion, inhibition of the capacity to love, emotional retardation may follow.

Later on, the castration complex will come into play on the plane of intellectual and social activity; the interest of the child derives from his sexual curiosity and from his ambition to equal his father. This remains as unhealthy curiosity and guilty ambition for as long as the Oedipus complex is not resolved.

Above all, *in the school domain*, we will see an *aversion to work*; the boy becomes unable to concentrate. This is the kind of *instability* that is so common in the schoolboy and the cause of so much scolding.

Maths, in particular, feels difficult; maths is associated in the unconscious with "sexual relations" (resemblance, difference, superiority, equality, inferiority)—and problems in whatever domain. *Spelling* is associated with "observation", thanks to which one can "see" clearly (cf. drawing 1, p. 136), about the relation between words). (Pages of maths in one of my little neurotic patients who was averse to arithmetic are scribbled over with knives and with scenes representing a chap sticking his knife into the sex of another smaller chap who is lying down, swaddled; when, for the first time, this child talked to me about his father, it was to tell me that he was always busy with accounts at home).

At the period when he was interested in parental relations, where children come from, applying himself to the problem was impossible by virtue of his guilt feeling. This impossibility carries with it, together with the repression of the libido which fuelled curiosity, an unconscious association: *attention* = *curiosity* = crime = punishment = frustration in love = *anxiety*. In order to avoid more anxiety, the superego now forming, triggers an unconscious defence mechanism: *inattention*, in its turn insurmountable without *anxiety*.

In these cases, *private tuition* can—without resolving anything—help the child in his school work because the usual element of rivalry with other children is no longer there to add supplementary anxiety. But in all these children, one will find a *determined babyishness*, a persistently infantile demeanour (aggressive one moment, cuddly the next), a lack of independence or its opposite, the independence of the unstable, of the aggressive rebel. This is an independence which does not liberate them nor does it allow them to attach to new emotionally interesting objects outside the family, nor to engage in practical activities. In all these children, masturbation is a "preoccupation", either hiding it away, or resisting its temptation. *The eroticism fixated on themselves, their feelings strangled by internal family conflicts, signifies the neurosis.*

The real inferiority of the child grows, because it is no longer just that of all children *in relation to* grown-ups. *He is not as strong, nor as clever* as the boys of his age, he reacts by being jealous of them, or else avoiding them, or both. He externalises this feeling through the only aggressive attitude available to him, with the least risk, he becomes a show-off and *mythomaniac*. He becomes wary in order to maintain the unconscious ambivalence. The boy is scared of others, he is unable to enter into competition with them. If masturbation has been strongly forbidden as being dangerous, he develops phobias and nocturnal terrors balancing the repressed aggression he projects onto others. If he succeeds in completely renouncing the libido of his sex, *he avoids children his own age* and seeks younger ones towards whom he is dictatorial or submissive, depending on whether his mother "indulges" him or not, that is to say, whether or not she permits the neurotic regression. Acting out his ambitious fantasies on the magic anal-sadistic level, he "pinches" money or objects that are like treasure to him.

Inevitably, the castration complex comes into play each time the child tries for success in the domain of masculine activity. Especially if he loves his castrating mother, the *boy will fail*, he will harm himself, for example, which is the symbolic equivalent of showing his mother that he is already castrated and he doesn't need to be punished in the way girls have been. In fact, his failures, accompanied as they are by wounds and bumps, if the boy complains instead of bearing them in silence, will fulfil the role that they were unconsciously intended to : *punishing the child by increasing his feelings of inferiority.* The beloved adult humiliates and mocks him: "I told you so, you shouldn't have disobeyed"—which is equal to a withdrawal of love—or else they feel disproportionately sorry for him, nursing, and consoling him. The adult will use this failure to suggest to the child that there will be even greater risks in the future if he carries on with his sporting or fighting activities, while passivity and unresisting obedience will earn Mother or Father's love. This is even worse for the child.

Sexuality of the girl as compared to that of the boy during the libidinal phases which precede the phallic stage

We have already described the development of sexuality in girls in parallel with boys up to the phallic stage. For children of either sex, the seeking of pleasure in the libidinal relationship with mother and the libidinal relationship with the inanimate world outside are initially the same. As long as the gonads have not reached maturity, libidinal hedonism is an aim in itself. This *fundamental egotism* determines behaviour being the most economic means for the psyche to achieve the satisfaction of the drives.

One can say that at the oral stage and at the anal stage, the ego is "neutral"; not yet capable of objectivity, the child projects onto the outside world, his own emotions, his own drives, his own way of thinking and of being. The adult is conceived of as being genitally undifferentiated because the child does not yet know the morphological characteristics of the sexes.

The girl, however, during the course of early infancy starting from the active phase of the oral stage, manifests less aggressive drive than passive drive. I do not think that the girl is born with less active drive than the boy, but all we know about this activity is what shows on the outside. From the outside, the boy is more visibly active than the girl because his drives are externalised and less quickly exhausted than those of the girl if they do not immediately achieve their hedonistic aim. As far as what shows on the outside, this means the girl is more easily discouraged actively which doesn't mean she is giving up the passive fight. Whether passive drives are predominant in the period of normal ambivalent loving, or whether the active drives carry less aggression, the end result in the girl is that *her practical and emotional demeanour is*, at a corresponding level of libidinal energy, definitely *less dynamic than that of the boy.*

At the anal sadistic stage, characterised by monopolising, the boy uses his muscular aggressivity to *grab*, the girl uses it to *catch*. (For example: the natural way of throwing a ball is "overarm" for the boy and "underarm" for the girl.)

At the phallic stage, characterised by ambition, the boy *goes in pursuit of* his ambitions while the girl *waits ardently* for what she desires; both put into their respective attitudes all the libidinal aggression at their disposal. Within the same activities and with apparently similar behaviour, even during the "neutral" phase of their sexuality, the girl clearly differs from the boy. The very manner in which, for example, children behave at a Punch and Judy show is characteristic of this difference. One knows that Punch is going to be hit, the boys become agitated, impatient, shouting and stamping their feet, the girls are watchful, stay still, don't take their eyes off Punch, are ready to say something to warn him, but they never lose sight of a single blow of the stick. Later on, playing with sand, for example, girls make all sorts of pies and shapes, decorating them with shells and leaving them on the beach, taking care not to destroy them. Boys love to dig deep holes and make castles, which they later demolish with gusto.

When it comes to group games, the girls play hopscotch (following their stone step by step and taking it back), or juggling balls, while boys play at seeing how far they can throw stones, chasing each other, ball games, or playing at hunting or fighting.

This predominance of passive libido and aggressive/attractive drive, which characterise the positive attitude of the girl's ego, has its corollary in the manner in which she shows herself negative. Boys keep going, come what may or are aggressively resistant, whilst girls, unless they are neurotic, stay put and passively resist. One finds the same characteristics in the fantasies of grown women: they "see" themselves rich, famous actresses, and so on; boys imagine themselves "starting" at the bottom and heroically climbing the ladder, "becoming" powerful, and triumphing over their rivals, who come and ask them for favours.

The girl

Struggling with castration anxiety: pitfalls

At the phallic stage, at around three and a half, the girl discovers that some children have a "thingy" that she doesn't. The boy hasn't noticed yet. She begins with denial then becomes jealous, while remaining convinced that *it will grow*. Most of the time, especially when there is a brother at home (older or younger), the girl will try "see" this famous "thingy", and to play with her little brother's, because for a libido which is predominantly passive, seeing and playing is a bit like "having".

Nevertheless she feels deprived and attributes this to sexual mutilation by the mother, just as the boy does. The desire for a penis becomes the theme of her masturbatory phallic fantasies when, with an ambition characteristic of girls, she "waits" expectantly for it to grow.

It is unusual to find a little girl who does not go through a period of exhibitionism lifting her skirts, wanting to be seen naked so that everyone can admire her. As if the fact of being admired allowed her to identify with those who are looking at her. If they show no surprise, then there is something to " be seen", meaning the sex of a boy. If there is nothing to "be seen", it's her way of "denying that she has nothing".

A normal three-year-old, taking the knickers off a doll I had just given her, said half mockingly, half scornfully, whilst looking at me as if to make me witness to this ridiculous situation: "She hasn't got a thingy", "She's not happy". Then dressing her again, said curtly a few minutes later: "She's horrid"; she dropped the doll in a corner and turned her back on me.

This little scene is a *normal and typical reaction of the girl's ego to the anxiety of phallic castration.*

She starts by trying to deny her inferiority by concentrating on the "thingy", she takes the doll's knickers off before even looking at it, a gift from the woman/mother. She is piqued and annoyed, projects her feelings onto the doll ("she's horrid") voicing them loudly turning towards the adult. Then, disdaining this gift from a woman, which reawakens the main cause of castration anxiety—the absence of the phallus—she loses interest in it, making the reason for her rejection perfectly clear. "She's horrid" means that at that moment the doll is just as bad as boys. (In the sense that, like them, "the doll reminds her of her predicament". "Boys are stupid, boys are horrid. I don't like them.") This is on top of deep feelings, of guilt,—which in girls always accompanies the anxiety of phallic castration ("She [the child] is horrible").

In other words, losing interest in the woman's gift once more shows how horrible the mother is, giving her a doll which has suffered the same fate, worse even.

Now the castration complex in a girl cannot be entirely parallel and inverse to that of a boy; because here it is a woman who plays the role of adult rival, phallic castration is no threat for a woman (which it is for the boy), but an actual fact.

From this lack flows a security, the girl can identify, with no threat to her sexuality, with "the one who hasn't got one"; the "threat" of phallic castration is an empty one—(as we will see, it won't be the same for viscero-vaginal castration. The castration complex in the young girl includes two distinct phases, the first one phallic, and the second vaginal; this latter is the only one involved in the drama of the complex rivalry with the mother).

Hence these important differentiating givens which are:

> If the boy's sexuality is endangered by the castration complex,
> on the contrary it helps that of the girl to develop.

In the boy, castration *anxiety* is a "happy" thing, which precedes and introduces the Oedipal phase.

The castration *complex*, on the contrary, is intricated in the Oedipal phase; if not resolved, it becomes dangerous and toxic.

In the girl, *anxiety* is dangerous *before* the Oedipal phase; *it* can prevent the Oedipal phase establishing itself normally.

(At the risk of repeating myself, but in other words, I want to come back to this relatively difficult notion, which is, together with the distinction *complex/anxiety*, the keystone of my whole argument; for the girl, "it is to her advantage" to be phallically castrated. This does not mean that later on she must be castrated viscero-vaginally. The precise articulation is: that if too great an *anxiety* of phallic castration prevents her from entering the castration *complex* (which is, as we have said, even in the girl, initially phallic), the vaginal investment will not take place. This is why we are saying, "that if the castration complex puts the libido of the boy in danger, it helps that of the girl". Or again, in other words, if you like: "the boy would rather ignore the castration complex; for the girl, on the contrary, it is what makes a woman of her.")

When the girl becomes aware of her phallic castration, she invests her mother with renewed passive libido aiming to attract her loving affection. She uses more of her sublimated aggressive libido to achieve grown-up knowledge. This could be the reason why girls are more articulate and have a richer vocabulary earlier than boys. The girl reacts to phallic frustration with analogous mechanisms to those which she employed at the anal stage to gain the caring attention of the adults.

But however patient the waiting may be, however propitiatory and passive (or aggressively demanding) the girl's behaviour, the fairy-godmother does not take pity and does not produce the wished-for gift; and furthermore, the girl discovers that she must renounce it forever; girls will never have a penis, her mother never had one either.

Reality coming in to challenge the clitoral masturbatory fantasies, the excitation of the clitoris now brings only disappointment: the recollection of an inferiority without hope, clitoral masturbation is abandoned. But we know that the unsatisfied libido needs to find another outlet.

For the girl, the withdrawal of the libido from the phallic erogenous zone cannot be done without compensation. In effect, the abandonment of clitoral masturbation is accompanied by a displacement onto the face and the whole body of the interest which used to be centred on the clitoris. There then appears, very markedly in the girl, the love of prettying herself, of hairstyles, ribbons, crowns, flowers in her hair, decking out with jewellery, unconsciously compensating for the conscious abandonment of the phallus. It is in the first place to "please herself" that the little girl adorns herself, frequently it is not terribly aesthetic from an objective point of view, but she finds herself beautiful and admires herself in the mirror.

This desire to please, gratifying in itself for her self esteem, allows her to renounce the "phallic prerogative" at the same time as reconciling her with the male sex. She gives up finding boys "horrid" because she had wanted to castrate them and stops getting her mother to castrate them (by "telling on them"); regaining self confidence she can now tell herself that boys and Daddies might want to share their powers with her. She will now try to win them over; it is the beginning of the Oedipal phase but it is not yet conflictual.

It is through penis envy that the girl orients herself towards men, towards attracting the admiration of those whom she deems superior and appealing to her mother. (This is assuming the parental couple is not neurotically inverse: weak father, annihilated at home by his wife. In this case, masculinity (which is not a question of anatomy for the child but a question of aggressive behaviourial domination) remains the mother's prerogative, even though she knows the physical truth). Her mother has lost some of her prestige now the girl has learnt that the mother is castrated like herself. She is no longer terrifying, but only more capable and bigger, she is a "lady". The intense guilt that she used to awaken in the child when she scolded or punished her, has lost its capacity to cause pain and anxiety.

It is of the utmost importance that the girl "stops mourning" her clitoral masturbatory fantasies and the phallic ambition that they hide, and that she definitively accepts, without bitterness, not being born a boy. Otherwise, however much she represses phallic sexuality for the sake of the prohibitions of her superego, she will always remain a painfully sensitive being, susceptible, prone to suffer guilt feelings and stinging feelings of inferiority together with ambivalent emotions never allowing her a moment's peace.

The libido, with its never ceasing flow of energy, will be forced to regress and re-invest in earlier erogenous and emotional positions, giving rise to personality problems, perverse or neurotic symptoms, according to whether there is a repression of sexuality or not.

The happy solution is vaginal investment. The little girl who spontaneously calls her clitoris a "button" (as many little girls call it), who remembers the voluptuous feelings that its arousal brought her, has also discovered, from envying her mother's breasts, the excitement of the erectile corpuscles of the nipple, more "buttons". In the course of

had known before, surely she wouldn't have become a nun and now it's too late!
- And as the mother and the Principal, very surprised, were not saying anything, the little girl carried on—only thinking about the young nun:
- It would be better if she didn't believe me; I'd rather she forgot all about it. If I had known that she didn't know, I wouldn't have told her, but the other girls were saying that it is disgusting to make babies. Oh, Mama, it's not dirty, is it? You told me that it was beautiful and Sister said that you were lying.

Once again, the Principal, very moved by the scene, intervened and comforted the child by saying:

- Your mother is right, my child, it is very beautiful to be a mother.
- And to the mother she was apologising:
- All the children are not as pure as your little one and many parents would be shocked by their daughters being told.

When, at puberty, she discovers with pride through her periods and through the growth of her breasts that she has become a woman, the rivalry with the mother will be settled by winning freedom of taste and dress, and through cultural sublimations. These will very often centre around children; *giving birth as a consequence of love* will no longer scare her, quite the contrary.

The predominately passive nature of the libido will not allow the girl to launch into a social life on her own. She can only prepare herself for being attractive by using the aggressive part of her libido to copy the women she sees attracting men, developing her seductive traits and waiting for the One, who, in her romantic fantasies, she sees as having the characteristics of someone or other she tacitly and ardently admires. Nevertheless, when that person comes along, she will hesitate to go out with him and will expect him to court and show himself worthy of her. If the boy is normal, together they will discover mutual pleasure through a blossoming relationship one with the other; it is a time of flirtation, preparing the stage for oblative genital love.

If there is a lack of paternal affection and masculine presence, the girl may either sublimate her unreciprocated emotions in active or contemplative mysticism, or else remain in perpetual expectation, unable to take matters into her own hands if no man, father substitute, comes to her rescue and awaken the sleeping beauty.

At the oblative stage, the way a man helps her to gain confidence in herself, making love to her without brutality, will bring her knowledge of her vaginal zone through the experience of orgasm. She will attach both sensually and emotionally to the man who has brought her this knowledge and through whom she has a child. Internally, unconsciously she now detaches herself from her mother having become her equal; although objectively she has reached the full genital stage, she still remains attached to her father with a very tender affection. Her activities, whatever they might be, are subject to the approval and encouragement of the man she loves.

The young boy, on the other hand, can, without hindering his normal libidinal development, choose a social path of which his mother disapproves and tolerate the pain of that disapproval. As an adult, he can lead his sexual life in a totally genital and oblative way without needing the approval of the woman he loves in the strictly professional part of his life.

For a woman, her life's work is essentially one with that of the man she loves at the genital oblative stage. So it is for the man, but he still has enough libido left available for other strictly personal activities, enabling him to give *more of himself* to their shared life's work.

In other words, in the most accomplished stages that we know, the emotional driving force in the man is to give "of himself" to the shared life's work of the couple, and the emotional driving force of the woman is to "*give herself*" to this task.

The importance of castration for a girl

One can see, therefore, that the real dangers of castration for the girl *precede* the Oedipus complex and can even prevent its proper formation.

Two things can happen: either the girl never accepts her phallic inferiority, she never rejoices in being a girl, and she always regrets not being a boy; or the defence mechanism (narcissistic investment in the body) which follows the devaluation of the penis is not made possible (by the adults—or through a manifest physical inferiority which prevents identification with the mother). This identification with the mother or with another *normal* woman is indispensable for vaginal eroticism to occur, and the only way in which the Oedipus complex can take place. This can signal the end of *vaginal frigidity in a woman*, *which in all the cases that I have seen is a vaginal non-investment, rather than impotence through regression.*

First pitfall: masculinity complex (lack of vaginal feeling)

In cases in which the vaginal erogenous zone has never been invested with libido, which happens if the defence mechanisms of the ego against the primary anxiety of phallic castration have failed, there will not only be vaginal frigidity, but also one observes possessive behaviour which can be *directed onto the mother* alone—this will always imply a certain degree of unconscious physical or psychological masochism—but also onto *both parents, or onto the father alone*, but *without* trying to rival her mother using her feminine wiles. This struggle is fought with cultural and intellectual means, considered the prerogative of boys in the social milieu of the girl. Freud named the neurotic syndrome that ensues, the *masculinity complex. It is a character neurosis.* There is always oversensitivity and, sometimes hidden, an aggressive envy towards those who "have more, an affective ambivalent attitude *with regard to* both sexes, and a conscious disinterest in genital sexuality. This is manifested in complete vaginal frigidity and, according to whether the ego is strong and more or less able to sublimate, there will be more or less marked clitoral masturbatory disinvestment. The clitoris will remain invested in cases in which aggression is prevented due to the passive use of the drives when there are strict or indifferent adults.

The masculinity complex can therefore give rise to various clinical situations, according to the tolerance of the superego for clitoral masturbation in infancy and for manifest homosexuality at puberty.

If the clitoris has remained invested with libido, its real morphological inferiority is a constant occasion for unconscious suffering, and conscious shame for the girl because she is what she is, she is "ugly". (This is the way young girls speak, even some who are very pretty and envied for their beauty. They find any aesthetic fault and become obsessed with it.) The girl reacts by denying the anxiety and "by a headlong rush" into an ambitious struggle, rivalling boys even in sports, in the same activities, in the same studies. It is a libidinal regression or a stagnation at this stage, during the latency phase, which draws these women towards "masculine" careers; during the surge of puberty, the libido must regress to the previous stage or satisfy itself with solitary masturbatory practices or, better, lesbian ones. (Later on, these will be the women who, if they do get married, will be frigid, vociferous victims sacrificed to the man. This is even more marked in their mothering; with their children, they will be castrating mothers, breeders of family neurosis).

If the superego does not permit masturbation, one sees these little girls becoming more and more "ashamed" at puberty, with a sickly shyness, phobic, lacking in self-confidence to the point of no longer being able to thrive in any of the activities in which they previously showed themselves gifted; the smallest of failures makes them inhumanly *uncompromising towards themselves* because of the feelings of guilt and inferiority inherent in phallic castration anxiety. This extreme shyness in public (or this extreme boasting, which is the same thing for the unconscious, the proof of a felt inferiority) is followed in adolescence and adulthood by an inability to rival other women. The narcissistic defence mechanism not having had the right to enter into play (because phallic masturbation had to be abandoned too early in childhood), their superego forbids them the possible use of feminine seduction which would make them enter unconsciously into rivalry with the all-powerful, magical, castrating, adored and abhorred mother of whom their superego has become an amplified echo. Added to which, there is a regression to the archaic erogenous zones, where the refusal of genital sexuality in the symbolic mode is played out (constipation, panic attacks, gastro-intestinal troubles, indigestion, vomiting).

In brief, the phallic castration complex is played out on the anal and oral level through the re-investment of previous erogenous zones. Each time there is a new instinctual libidinal surge, any prompting from the outside world (pre-menstrual excitement, sexual relationship, marriage, child) whether on an emotional and physical level, the woman, instead of investing in the vaginal erogenous zone, will react neurotically with negative symptoms at the level of previous erogenous zones: anorexia-constipation-pain.

Feelings of frustration, closest to phallic frustration, have their origin in fact, both chronologically and emotionally, in potty training, and it is probably the reason why the refusal of their sex, unconsciously felt by frigid women, is almost always associated with an obstinate constipation, which is the only symptom for which the doctor is consulted. Doctors are surprised that their therapeutic efforts remain unsuccessful. Some nevertheless notice that their patients "cultivate" their constipation through uncalled-for purging or by not taking their prescriptions. Once the doctor has been "dismissed", they go and see another one or change medicine constantly. This *anal exhibitionism*, this constant worry about their intestinal functioning, is necessary to them. It is a means through which they symbolically "masturbate" their anal erogenous zone and in this way withdraw their ego from genital libidinal investment, so painful to their narcissism. They submit with disgust to their husbands' lovemaking if they are married; only have lovers to gain material advantage—or deliberately make do without men by being in rivalry with them in the same careers. On the face of it, these women are "normal", but unconsciously they are homosexual without knowing it, strongly fixated on the maternal object contemporaneous with their anal phase, whose love they seek and whose abandonment they cannot bear. If they have children, they are the type of "dutiful mother" who is said to be "perfect", who "sacrifices everything" to these children (that is to say, their genital life, including the men and their happiness), just as they sacrifice their sexuality. But woe betide those who become attached to their children, and the children themselves if their development causes them to separate from their mothers, this is one more frustration that these women will have to put up with, the loss of the children they possessively love.

In these women, the ambivalent homosexual fixation to the mother does not allow open aggression towards their daughters ("as if the daughter were the mother"), as long as the daughter has not reached sexual development. At the moment that their daughters turn towards men, these mothers react by projecting their own aggressive feelings onto their daughters, the feelings they experienced towards their own mother during the anal phase, as well as the feelings of guilt engendered at the time. They suffer more from hurt and fear than jealousy, as some would believe. If their daughters move away from the family circle, the aggression of the mother, no longer having an object, will turn against herself in the form of melancholia, with feelings of abandonment, attempting to neutralise the need for punishment unconsciously linked to libidinal frustration.

Towards their sons, they are freer with their emotions and can express their aggression towards them without fear that it will turn back upon themselves. They love to tease them when they are little: the words they use for either scolding them or insulting them are, generally, and even in educated circles, borrowed from anal sadistic vocabulary: "swine, pig, disgusting, revolting". They love to threaten them with imaginary dangers associated with castration: "you will make yourself ill", "you are going to kill yourself", towards any initiative that the young boy decides to take. If he escapes the mother, she compensates for her frustration by publicly nursing feelings of overt hostility towards the woman who took her son away which protects her from a return of the aggressive drives against herself, such as that which happens with daughters.

All this concerns the masculinity complex, which has as a starting point an emotional stagnation of the girl through a fixation onto both parents (unconsciously considered as both equally phallic) or onto the mother alone.

If the girl is emotionally fixated onto the father alone, but without having ever libidinally invested in the vaginal erogenous zone, she cannot fight back against phallic castration anxiety through a general all-purpose facial and corporal narcissism. *The masculinity complex is then extremely marked,* the girl presents an ambivalent infantile affectivity with a good-humoured and boyish character, but she has a violent superego which forbids her any attempt at identification with her mother or any feminine seductiveness towards her father (because for the unconscious this would represent the acceptance of one's sex): and it is with ego-possessive loving (aimance) that she covets the phallus for herself and attempts to identify with boys. At puberty, there is an inverse Oedipal complex in which we see that sexual rivalry is played out emotionally exactly as if the girl were a boy experiencing his Oedipal complex. She avoids women and gets closer to men in order to try to identify with them, but her unconscious aggression causes her to behave in a castrating way that pushes them away. She is doomed to loneliness (cf. case of Monique, p. 221).

It seems that this only happens in cases of a strong pregenital anal fixation to a neurotic mother, herself somewhat masculine, and it also requires that the father, himself sexually incomplete and incapable of genital love, favours the emergence of manly qualities in his daughter. Unless there is physical infirmity, objectively painful to the girl's narcissism, such a character neurosis is always linked with a family neurosis.

In any case, if a natural inclination to intellectual or muscular sublimation serves her ego, she can attain appreciable social success, but she will continue to suffer perpetual anxiety and feelings of inferiority, arising from the anxiety of phallic castration. This is the case even where there is cultural and sexual success (sadomasochistic possession of a weak woman or of a man inferior to herself and whom she supports; perhaps especially in the latter example), because her unconscious guilt towards men, which results from her wish, which can never be satisfied, to really be equal to them on all levels, constantly reawakens an anxiety which takes the form of morbid jealousy towards her love objects.

I know that, in this case, many doctors and even the women involved believe that there is an added organic (hormonal) component. This is possible; however, psychoanalytic treatments of these emotionally hybrid beings may sometimes yield absolutely remarkable results. One must say that *the masculinity complex is perhaps one of the most powerful motivations that drives a woman to begin psychoanalysis.* In her eyes, it is seen as a new means of acquiring phallic power (penetration) for which she bravely accepts what seems to her a magical and sadistic operation.

If the ego has no inclination towards strong intellectual or cultural compensation then either in the area of manual dexterity or muscular skill, the masculinity complex takes a less obvious form. The girl, incapable of identifying with boys, presents personality problems, any feelings or activity are inhibited as the unconscious regresses to the anal stage, to passive drives in the service of a possessive and jealous libido, and also to aggressive drives entirely employed by the superego to be sadistic towards the masochistic ego. The girl's behaviour is always infantile, her social relationships are a weave of aggressive estrangements and tender reconciliations without any objective reality in the loss or attraction which plays out towards men in the same way as it does towards women.

One can see that if the little girl has not negotiated her phallic castration anxiety, if she sees herself "forced" to accept, or rather to put up with, her sex as if she were persecuted, emotionally this leaves her with an open wound, which flares up again and again every time there is an experience of real inferiority in life. Phallic castration anxiety, accompanied by guilt feelings, will inevitably be triggered on every occasion that she behaves "spontaneously", because this will engender a resonance of previous guilt feelings with regard to the womanly aspirations she doesn't share.

If, on the other hand, she overcomes her phallic castration anxiety, thanks to a reinvestment in her female narcissism and to the discovery of vaginal masturbation, she will be able to continue to identify with her mother. She will use the typical emotional aspirations of this period of her life in vaginal fantasies according to the normal development of female sexuality. In this way, she will be able to abandon what there was of the exaggeratedly passive (perhaps masochistic in a propitiatory way) which was previously superimposed on her natural passivity in her behaviour towards adults.

Second pitfall: frigidity through emotional immaturity

Once she has accepted her femininity, thanks to a defence mechanism, which consists of reinvesting her whole person with narcissistic libido, *a second pitfall presents itself for the girl. Narcissistic withdrawal must not get in the way of investment in the vaginal erogenous zone*, either because masturbation provoked severe reprimands from adults, or because the father is absent from the family (dead or divorced), or not interested in his children.

The girl, whose aggressive drives have little dynamic force, will then never find—whatever her efforts at seduction—the means to win the attention of men. Being at this stage *normally* "shut off" from the mother, she may remain in a narcissistic state forever, emotionally and culturally immature. But it could also be because the ego has not developed enough strength during the anal sadistic period caused by an inadequate upbringing or too strict an upbringing; this prevents the girl from displacing excremental libidinal and muscular affects onto cultural activities which could have enabled her to identify with her mother. (Mothers with a masculinity complex provoke emotional infantilism in girls. If these girls become mothers, they will engender in their children an early anxiety neurosis responsible for somatic or psychic disorders or both.)

One might ask if the narcissistic reinvestment of the face and body, a defence mechanism which accompanies the negotiation of the phallic castration anxiety, does not go through a global regression of the libido to the oral stage. I have twice encountered children who believed that boys were the children of Daddies and girls those of Mummies. For the girl, this return to infantile narcissism could be a means of participating in the phallic power of the father in a passive oral mode (from an emotional point of view), in the same way as the nursing female infant did with the mother. This would not be the result of aggression stemming from an Oedipal conflict (which has not yet taken place) but a total *disinvestment* from the mother through true unconscious libidinal negation: the impossibility of continuing to identify with a being who has disappointed, leads to a devaluation or negation of all the gains of the ego derived from the libido of which the mother had been the centre.

This possibility of changing one's pattern of identification could perhaps also explain the fact that women have less natural objectivity, despite the fact that girls, during the anal phase and the first school achievements from five to seven years old, show a realistic and positive spirit generally far superior to that of boys their age, a fact which is well known to the teachers of mixed schools. This could also explain why *the ego of the woman is most of the time weaker* than that of the man and would contribute an explanation as to why *her superego is rudimentary* (except in the case of neurosis). (It is for this reason "that they do not have a superego"—when they manage not to have one) that they are so attractive to men. "One can put everything into them"—"She will just take it all in". Conversely, the woman is fascinated by what this superego evokes of a boundless "civilisation". This bipolarity is without any doubt one of the givens of some couples, a sort of dialectic of the "nothing" and of the "all", which works better when they are differentiated as individuals.

It is because the woman does not have a superego—or because she has less of it—that her presence is "full of grace".)

Notice how children who don't have a superego are also so full of grace. This could explain the ease with which women during adulthood are able to adapt to an environment very different from the one which was theirs up to then, and, without difficulty, succeed in identifying with the image that their loved one demands they resemble. This could explain the numerous natural gifts, for languages, singing, the theatre, dance that are displayed by more or less all young women.

If, in this narcissistic position, which should normally only be a stage in libidinal development, the young girl does not find a father (Pygmalion) to shape her and make a woman of her, if there is a lack of masculine affectivity in the immediate surroundings of the child, or if the mother is very neurotic and denigrates the father, the young girl who renounced her mother because she could no longer invest in her libidinally *returns to emotional autism for lack of anything better*. That could account for an excluding mysticism at puberty with its total lack of normal romantic fantasies.

In this case, there may or may not be vaginal sensation but in any case not identified as such and women who could become sexually normal if they could centre their feelings on a man who would initiate them, otherwise would remain frigid or semi-frigid all their lives, with the many psychopathological problems which occur in response to instinctual libidinal demands, periods, the pre-menopausal phase, or the menopause. One also sees the appearance of colitis symptoms after the loss of virginity or the birth of the first child in women who had never suffered them before. These symptoms are probably a response to the awakening of female desire which renders them guilty in the eyes of the superego of the sexual partner. As a matter of fact, numerous men prefer that their lawful spouses be, or pretend to be, frigid. These are men whose libidinal development is arrested at the beginning of the phallic stage. This conflict between the claims of normal female sexual feelings and the prohibition according to the conjugal ethic of a "retarded" partner unconsciously reawakens, through regression, the conflicts of the sadistic phase and the feelings of inferiority of phallic castration anxiety.

If these women remain virgins, neurotic problems will only appear at the menopause and will be expressed by dream signs of oral frustration: fear of solitude, fear of emptiness, fear of the loss of narcissistic defences, of—growing old, hence the success of beauty clinics—anxiety, which provokes the reappearance of childish coquetry with the use of frequently unlovely little girl adornments. If they don't have a strong ego and can only use cultural sublimation calling for perfect physical health, these "old maids" will present psycho-neurotic symptoms of hallucinations and dreamlike states. (This is also found in those married to controlling spouses who, whether they become mothers or not, remain frigid and infantile.)

Conversely, if the first sexual partner of one of these infantile narcissists is an older man, chosen for being like her father, assuming he has reached the genital stage, the woman can work out her Oedipal fixation on him and only then engage in rivalrous confrontation with her mother-in-law and her own mother, or make jealous scenes with her husband about past mistresses. Her actual father does not come into play for her emotionally, he is barely invested with libido other than as a satellite of her mother. It is only after this confrontational phase, and if she renounces egotism in order to accept taking part in genital libidinal love (aimance), that she can achieve oblativity characteristic of the feminine genital stage from an emotional point of view.

Altogether we see that feminine sexual development differs enormously from masculine sexual development from the phallic stage onwards. The man's superego forms itself in order to resolve the Oedipus complex and entwined castration complex. Its aim is to protect the ego from the return of castration anxiety, that can be triggered by the interconnection of aggression and erotic and emotional passivity *towards* the love object, an ambivalence which does not allow either normal physiological coitus nor a masculine attitude in public life. Furthermore, the boy is underprivileged in comparison to the girl in the sense that in families in which phallic masturbation is forbidden too early, he no longer has an erogenous zone in which to invest, he can only regress to archaic stages which are castrating to his virility.

Thus the renunciation of genital eroticism in the emotional Oedipal situation which is often hidden by their social adaptability before puberty, explains the frequency of neurotic symptoms and personality problems. The dynamic strength of their aggressive drives causes their rebellion against castration anxiety to have an impact on the family, school, and social life.

Conversely, the girl can use inhibition and passive resistance as occult weapons in her struggle; if she arms herself with the neurotic reaction of a virility complex at the service of a powerful ego, she will never display social or personality problems before puberty. Her intellectual and cultural aggressiveness even earns her (before puberty) the admiration of adults and self-satisfying triumph over her contemporaries whose latency phase is spent in passive activity, or better still in feminine activity appearing less brilliant, which is often the case from a strictly academic point of view, as compared to the neurotically masculine girl. This probably explains why in consultation we have a proportion of seven boys to one girl! But later on, female psychopathology presents many more symptoms than that of men (frigidity, constipation, migraines, and so on).

One can then ask if the superego is not, after all is said and done, a defence mechanism due to a latent remnant of sexual castration anxiety in an individual who unconsciously has not fully resolved her pregenital conflicts.

The severity of the superego in the girl who fails to invest in the vaginal erogenous zone through non-resolution of phallic castration anxiety, compared to the absence of superego in the girl who has resolved it but who remains affectively infantile until the day she enters her Oedipal phase or her menopause (and therefore has not known vaginal castration anxiety), are clinical facts which would seem to validate this hypothesis.

It is still possible to be adult from a libidinal point of view, having fully reached the oblative genital stage, whose superego remains rudimentary or even absent, and whose libidinal energies all serve an ego motivated in its behaviour by the pull of an Ideal whose axis, firmly embedded in the genius of her sex, remains indestructible.

But this being, if such exists, has probably never been studied by psychoanalysts, because their absence of egotism allows them to accept that they don't have to solve problems which cannot be humanly solved, without necessarily falling into neurosis.

CHAPTER FOUR

Enuresis

One can wonder at the frequency of enuresis. This symptom, which we can be thankful for, brings children to us, whose neuroses would otherwise be ignored, has in itself more than one meaning. At the very least, it signifies stagnation at or the return to the sadistic urethral stage, which is the one preceding the phallic stage. *It is accompanied by an emotional regression* to pre-Oedipal fixations of one kind or another, itself complicated by guilt feelings, because, in the majority of cases, and even on a regressive level, the drives are not finding sufficient outlet. Enuresis can also indicate a regression to an even more archaic stage.

The persistency or return of enuresis is therefore the symptom of choice for those who cannot allow themselves either masturbation or ambitious fantasies, and who unconsciously live in erotised sadomasochistic dependency.

Faced with enuresis, there is not *one* psychotherapeutic attitude to be taken because then it would aim at the effect and not the cause.

It is only a study of the general emotional behaviour of the child, which enables determination of the stage he is in and the obstacle in the face of which he has regressed.

Also enuresis has, in some cases, to be *respected*, despite the demands of the parents, and the conscious desire of the child, *for as long as it takes* to help the libido of the child evolve (thanks to the transference) to the urethral sadistic stage, the dawn of the phallic stage. *It is only then* that one will be able, without danger for the future, to obtain bladder control. By demanding it earlier, the doctor takes up the role of the castrating parent.

From what we have just said, *there are cases where we can obtain immediate results* or at least speedy ones—cf. case of Alain p. 171, case of Claudine p. 203—without the repercussion of personality problems and where the suppression of enuresis in one or two sessions is without danger for the unconscious. These are symptoms of enuresis occurring in children presenting marked aggressive behaviour coupled with irregular school results (but which are sometimes good or excellent). It is therefore a situation that one sees *in the midst of a normal unresolved Oedipus complex.*

If, on the other hand, the Oedipal position is inversed—cf. case of Roland p. 167—(trying to passively seduce the same sex parent), we will first have to awaken a sense of entitlement in the right to rivalry with him, whilst helping our little patient (on the reality level) to gain Mummy's admiration (in this case, ours if we are women). We will have to stimulate our naughty little girl to try and seduce Daddy by encouraging flirtatiousness and confidence in herself (the right to hide things from us, if we are women), and we will begin to minimise the importance of enuresis, a symptom that all children find humiliating. Then, at the next session, when real behavioural progress has not achieved any results with the enuresis, we will have to reassure them and their parents. We will, of course, have asked for "several sessions"—which means, in this psychotherapeutic method, several weeks of weekly sessions. Let them trust us as well as the child!

It is only when the child has returned to a normal Oedipal situation that, in the name of Oedipal satisfaction (to please Mummy and ourselves, or Daddy in the case of a girl, or to show herself as a grown-up girl in Mummy's eyes who doesn't believe it possible), that we can ask the child the then easy auto-suggestive effort (to think about it when going to bed). If *the child succeeds*, an anxiety deriving from the castration complex will fatally ensue, although the child is consciously happy with the result. It will be translated either into *physical problems* (headaches, toothaches, tiredness)—which are so accurately put down on the ever open account of "growing up"—or into *anxiety dreams* with castration symbolism, or by *self-punishing mechanisms,* or by *personality problems* aimed at provoking punishment. But we will *then* be in a position *to resolve* this anxiety by attacking the Oedipus complex on a rational level and by supplying the child—whom we are discharging from his guilt feelings—with cultural substitutes, sublimation to which he will willingly apply himself, to please us as well as his parents, if he has regained confidence in himself, because the libidinal biological drive accords with the sexual satisfaction brought about by the sublimation.

If the child is at the passive anal stage—cf. case of Bernard p. 159—(total incontinence), the child should be allowed the freedom to be aggressive in his *general behaviour* before we ask him to sacrifice the local hedonism of the sphincteral erogenous zone. Once the physical symptoms have disappeared, we will only consider the child cured if he is under four.

If he is over four, despite the disappearance of symptoms (which is enough for the parents), he should not be considered psychically cured unless he is entering the Oedipal phase, he still needs to be seen in case of relapse; (an attack of anxiety several months after recovery can trigger the symptom of enuresis again due to the "fixation point" to which the child remains vulnerable until the Oedipus complex is resolved).

If he is six or seven, the therapist will have to guide him until the formation and the beginning of the dissolution of the Oedipus complex through its normal interconnectedness with the castration complex, disinvestment of Oedipal objects will follow and the libidinal drive will be transferred onto friendships and sublimated through schoolwork, play, and physical and intellectual pursuits, rich in the promise of eventual success in the world.

If the child is no longer a young child, but who has entered latency. more or less approaching puberty, that is, if the patient is past the usual age of the castration complex, we will have to study, in cooperation with the child's ego, the manifestations the superego has rendered unrecognisable, which in the eyes of the psychoanalyst indicate unresolved conflicts.

Thus, in young people who have not *resolved* their normal Oedipus complex, but who have *repressed* it in favour of the overly powerful castration complex, latent unconscious homosexual tendencies may be found. From the age of seven, such a superego, for example, only permits friendship between individuals of the same sex, to the exclusion of the other. Friendship between the two sexes being judged as guilty or boring, the reality being that faced with an individual of the opposite sex, defence mechanisms come into play: shyness and anxiety through inhibited aggression and feelings of inferiority. For the psychoanalyst this reveals a castration complex, still active and therefore the existence of its corollary, the non-resolution of the Oedipus complex.

Thus we have to study the symptoms with the cooperation of the ego and, thanks to the transference, modify the pathological superego.

Let us add that many castration complex anxiety neuroses *do not lead to enuresis*. This is because the achievement of sphincteral control was already well established when the first *active* threats of sexual mutilation occurred, that is to say the threats *linked* to the Oedipus complex.

These active threats could be, *in the first eventuality*, threats of illness or of mutilation *made by adults* and believed to be true at the time of secondary masturbation because they come from the people "who know".

But they can also be due, as a *second eventuality*, to *internal* threats, caused by the child's projection of his aggression onto the same-sex adult in the course of Oedipal rivalry, a parent with whom he had previously identified, whom he had "introjected" in his normal struggle with primary castration anxiety.

And lastly, the *third eventuality*, these active threats could also not be threats of mutilation of the hands or the genitals linked to masturbation, but (coming from educating adults or from physical or intellectual inferiority) restrictions of the *natural* defence mechanisms in the face of primary castration anxiety, from which, as one knows, no human being can escape, because his intrinsic libidinal drives are "ambisexual" and that practical adaptation to reality demands that he behave in accordance with his sex, be it male or female.

This is why the *enuresis may never have stopped*. The child unconsciously refuses to grow up so as not to renounce the prerogative of ambisexuality.

On the other hand, it could have stopped more or less from two and a half to four or five years old and have restarted at that age with the rise of the Oedipus complex. It is from this moment only that enuresis can be attributed to the activity of the castration complex. Indeed, for a normal castration complex to exist, it is necessary for *the threats to intersect* after the distress that follows from the girl's recognition of the absence of a penis and her feelings of inferiority combined with secondary castration anxiety, in the face of the taboo Oedipal rival. These threats correspond to those which we categorised in the second eventuality (see p. 56).

For a pathological castration complex to exist (prolonged, and not resolved after the age of eight), there has to be a reawakening of the threats of the first eventuality, or the threats of the third eventuality (see p. 56). Not only that, this absence of normal defences might bring about burning feelings of inferiority towards other children of the same age and of the same sex at the time of the onset of the Oedipal phase before it becomes a complex. Renouncing imaginary superiority over the rival will not be possible, and the child will necessarily be determined to refuse to *face reality* which would *resolve* his sexually castrating Oedipus complex and, therefore, he regresses when confronted with the biological libidinal drive.

One can now see that the symptom of enuresis has only a relative diagnostic role. In itself, with no knowledge of any accompanying emotional behaviour, it is impossible to make a sound therapeutic plan. Furthermore, once the symptom has disappeared, the child is usually not cured of his neurosis, but only on the way to a cure, unlike what the parents may think, alarmed only by the "symptom", the disappearance of which is enough to satisfy them. The parents are ignorant of the possibility of the mutation of this symptom into another more regressive one, for example, colitis, tics, stuttering, insomnia, or hyperactivity, with the possible onset in future of perverse sexual behaviour or social delinquency, both signs of an Oedipus complex not yet initiated, or in any case one that has not been resolved.

CHAPTER FIVE

Fear of death and castration anxiety

The fear of death is to be seen in many children.
To understand the case we are going to present, we need to keep clearly in mind what death means to a child.

For the child who discovers death, it is not "death" as such because he does not know what it is—and, anyway, death is "unthinkable" for all of us—it is a greater than usual frustration of his muscular and emotional aggressiveness, that is to say, in a way he can understand it: it is forced immobility, it is being still for a magically, very, very, very long time, and it is the absence of the loved being (therefore an emotional castration) for a very, very, very long time.

The *fear* of death is normal: death awaits us all, our inadequacy towards it is therefore real; we do not know what it will do with us, except that it will bring the disappearance of our being as we know it. Equally, the *fear* of death is "rational", but normally exists only when one is confronted with its imminence.

But *anxiety itself does not depend on external threats*. The proof being that these threats only become active when they meet feelings in the child which are not in accord with his imaginary aspirations.

Paul, a young boy of fourteen, was brought to Dr Darré's clinic at the hospital of Les Enfants Malades. Paul was sickly and backward, with the mental age and appearance of a nine-year-old. He had such a terror of death that a diagnosis of serious meningitis was made because of his alarming difficulty in breathing, stiffness, expressions of pain, and the stupor which accompanied these symptoms. The next day the staff realised he was a hysteric.

I managed to talk with him, and through his jerky speech, caused by the constant feeling of suffocation, he told me that he had been breathing like that for two days and that it was "because one day he might have been hit by a stone thrown by a big boy". He couldn't remember, but "it was a Sunday" certainly.

To my question "why did the big boy do this?", he told me that he had himself tried to throw a stone at the head of this "big boy" because he did not like him, and the other had responded. But it was a long time ago, and he wasn't sure that a stone had hit him, however it was a Sunday.

Now, the morning of the day he was brought to hospital (also a Sunday), "near the airfield at Orly, he had seen a plane crash into a telegraph pole and the pole had been uprooted". These last words were said with such breathing difficulties (and he mimed how he gulped with fear) that I said to him: "It is since then, maybe, that you are breathing in this way. You were afraid for the pole. You did not know that poles were not fixed very strongly in the ground." Immediately the breathing difficulty stopped. He then said that the soldiers in the plane had been killed on the spot and that the plane might have killed his little friends, some Spanish refugees who had come here so as not to be killed by the war in their country.

I later learned that the "big boy" was only a boy of the same age as him—fourteen years old—but that he looked like a man. They were together in a class provided for the school children of Orly to prepare them to become mechanics in the Air Force. Paul had attended "because one could play with planes", but in a few weeks' time all the pupils were supposed to begin actual flying, and he no longer wanted to follow the course, he did not want to fly, was afraid to go up in a plane, he only wanted to "play" with planes. But his mother had paid six francs per week for this training and had said that he had to continue.

During the first days in hospital, Paul would not eat anything, thinking that someone was trying to poison him. He suffered because his mother rarely came to see him and spoke all the time about how much he was costing her.

Mum "hit him" often. He had had "marks from being hit" (?)—Dad, "so that he did not get in a state" used to lock him up in the dark. The sister (younger by two years) "is very naughty, but mum never hits her".

The mother was totally indifferent, even hostile, to her son, put on a fake air of boredom with not the slightest gesture of tenderness towards him. She was an enormous overabundant woman who smelled of wine. Apparently, the father had a weak heart but had never received any pension. His wife thought that the doctors didn't know what they were doing when they said that there was nothing wrong with her husband. He "caught it" during his military service, he was discharged because of his weakness, he was a nurse and used to pass out when he saw blood: "it is his heart, but he is so stupid that he let the Doctor send him away" (sic).

The child remained on the ward, and I saw him for ten days; he was well, calm, eating, and it was decided that he could leave and that I would continue to treat him, but the parents did not bring him back.

Three weeks later, the child returned to my consulting room; he had not slept for a second for the last few days so as not to die, because he incessantly listened to his heartbeat in order not to die. He was very anxious and did not want to leave his mother. When he let go of his mother, he would grab his wrist to monitor his pulse. Instead of bringing the child back regularly, as had been agreed, the mother had, in the meantime, taken her child to several doctors, who had all concluded "that there was nothing wrong".

When I told her that I wanted to take care of him and to see him regularly, she told me in the midst of a torrent of filthy language that she would in the end find a doctor who would "see" what that child "had" in "one go". The doctors should know what they are doing. This child is probably now in a psychiatric hospital.

In this fragment of a case, one can see very clearly that death anxiety is caused by castration anxiety; inferiority feelings towards the powerful "big boy" are real; the stone that Paul tried to throw at his head represented a murderous fantasy.

Then he identified his enemy with the pilots who were killed instantaneously on a Sunday, uprooting a telegraph pole in the process, and it was this which was the unconscious trauma. (One really needs to have seen a lot of children in treatment, both boys and girls, to be convinced of the depth of their adherence to this kind of symbolism ("the uprooted pole") which appears to us as adults as shallow-minded, or even dirty-minded and laughable.

"This little song filled me with terrible sadness:

> *We'll to the woods no more*
> *The laurels all are cut.*

How can we explain the bizarre things of childhood!" said George Sand.[1])

The child was afraid for the telegraph pole. Later, he "rationalised" his symptom by giving it a motive through the fear he had had for the lives of his little refugee friends (unarmed) with whom he identified and the fear that the plane might have killed them while they were sheltering from the war (as he would like to do in imitation of his father).

The accident brought about the magic realisation of his murderous wishes upon the substitute of the castrating adult (the big boy, the officers from Orly).

One can see, through the intense emotion that Paul felt when the pole was uprooted, that unconsciously it represented his penis. His sexual inferiority towards the boys who had reached puberty provoked the scene of stone-throwing at the head of his schoolmate. This failed criminal attempt brought about its reprisal without action from the schoolmate (a stone "must have" hit him in the heart, a long time ago, but he was not sure). What was sure was that it was a Sunday and that the justifiable defence of the big boy had the effect of *forbidding once and for all on the level of reality a display of aggression by Paul towards him*—(it is this which constituted the highly and specifically traumatising event). He was left with only an imaginary weapon, the formulation of magical wishes of death, centred on the coming flying trials that this big boy had to do like him, and because of these wishes, Paul did not want to carry on with the course now that it was no longer a matter of making

---

[1]Quoted by Helene Deutsch (1928). "George Sand: A Woman's Destiny". Public lecture given in Vienna in German. Excerpt in *The Psychology of Women*, vol. 1 (New York: Grune and Stratton, 1944). Republished in full in Paul Roazen (Ed.) (1992). *The Therapeutic Process, the Self and Female Psychology: Collected Psychoanalytic Papers by Helene Deutsch* (New Brunswick, NJ). Poem by Theodore de Banville (1846). This translation by A. E. Housman (1922).

wooden planes and playing with them, that is to say, that it was no longer a representation but an acting out.

An intense feeling of guilt accompanied the magic realisation (displaced onto the pilots) of Paul's wishes; this is why the uprooting of the pole which followed this death reawakened the primary castration anxiety. (Let us not forget the guilt feeling has as its origin a defence mechanism against the adult and the external world conceived of as "all powerful" and "omnisexed".)

The actual impotence against the adult, conceived of as "all powerful" and "omnisexed", was brought about through an ego defence mechanism, the all-mighty magical power of thought.

The death wish having been enacted (displaced onto the pilots), the uprooting of the pole took on, through displacement, an intolerable intensity.

The actual death—("wished for by Paul")—followed by an actual castration—("feared by Paul")—(uprooting of the pole from the ground) brought Paul the immediate threat of libidinal death: this is anxiety. From this arises the symptoms of death: pained facial expressions, annihilation of the affective drives even to the depth of the vegetative passive oral stage, and the freezing of the respiratory muscles.

The syndrome was useful to the child "in his environment" where no aggressive drive, direct or sublimated, was encouraged. The proof of this is that after a few days in hospital, he had lost his pained expression, ate (was reconciled with the "good" mother), slept well, and smiled. He played in his bed, got up in the afternoon. From a schooling point of view (at the time, he was attending a class for ten-year-olds), his behaviour towards the others and the nurses was that of a three-year-old, capricious, unstable, undisciplined, punishment-seeking; but all that brought about scolding, nothing more. After ten days, he had become a little bit more disciplined, and one really had the impression that the child was blossoming. However, his guilt was increasing due to the fact that his mother told him, during the rare times that she visited, that he was costing her a lot of travel money.

At the hospital, then, a playful and emotional aggressiveness was permitted. During the conversations I had with him, after the first and sudden improvement, one day I had to endure a session of hostile silence, then a hate-filled session with pornographic insults, followed by tears which ended with a relaxed smile because I had allowed him to say all that without becoming "cross". The anxiety could be relieved through the release of the aggressive drives.

On the other hand, as soon as he was back home, his aggressive drives could find no (permitted) outlet, the deadly fantasies being too guilt-inducing and too castrating since the plane episode. And if he had expressed these fantasies, either through his behaviour or discourse, he would have come up against the deprivation of maternal and paternal love, and with it the deprivation of space, sight, and touch, of all basic activity in all domains, except that of the vegetative state.

He had rationalised the anxiety translated into difficult breathing and dyspepsia by attributing it to "the little stone thrown, possibly on a Sunday" by the hated and dangerous big boy, and which "may have" wounded his heart. All that was left to Paul was to fight against himself, by *negating "his" life*. Hounded within himself, the child could no longer live and was afraid that his heart would stop beating. (We need to add to this that the pseudo heart problems of the father, the reason for his being discharged from military service, rendered the hypochondriacal symptom valuable as a means of identification to the father and led to an overvalued masochistic passive-erotic position aimed at disarming his mother's real aggression.)

In the dreams of the patients whom we analyse, and in the fantasies, the image and even the "sensation" of death are often combined (as shown by the study of the latent content of these dreams and fantasies) with an anxiety linked to sexual drives. This linking of castration anxiety and death anxiety is a sign of neurosis, and I think that the exaggerated fear of death is always a symptom of castration anxiety, just as is the exaggerated fear of illness, when it appears in a living being—unless he is objectively at death's door.

Castration anxiety is a turmoil of *libidinal frustration*. It is triggered by a conflict between drives, aggressive and passive, at the service of sexuality, prohibitions coming from the external world (in early infancy) or from the superego (later). But the reason for the anxiety and the conflict remain unknown to the conscious part of the ego.

Therefore Paul's anxiety comes out of the castration anxiety complex, from the failure of the defence mechanism indispensable to the repression of the aggressive drives. These are forbidden because they would bring with them ambitious phallic fantasies, those which lead to sadistic emotional and physical castration inflicted by both parents. The father had been castrating through personal anxiety projected onto his son (so that he didn't become irritable), and the mother had been castrating with sadism and hatred of the masculine sex through an unconscious oral fixation to her own mother (bottle-feeding: alcoholism) which only allows her to tolerate aggression coming from her daughter.

When Paul clung onto his mother, unconsciously it was in order to be beaten, which would have relieved him, but his mother had unfortunately modified her aggressive objectives, which had become the "medical profession". (Before Paul's big crisis, she had never taken him to a doctor.) Now she seemed to identify with her castrated and backward son, who could never "get into aviation", which she had never allowed herself to contemplate consciously, and had stopped beating him.

When the masochistic position is allowed to the ego by the sadistic object, the subject may, through identification with the object, unconsciously become his own tormenter and the ego fears illness, a constraint on living, or death, the suppression of living. This is the true mechanism of hypochondria. It neutralises anxiety quite effectively.

But when the masochistic position is not allowed by the outside world within the object relations, the subject has to block his libido in himself, pitch his passive drive which do not have a substitute object against his own aggressive drive; there is no longer any way out. It is total libidinal frustration, that is to say, death as it appeared to the child the day he discovered it for the first time; and as there is no longer any free aggressiveness, even unconsciously, *the theme is played out on the oral level, where the absence of libidinal satisfaction is sleep. The patient consciously makes the translation sleep = death into the fear of falling asleep.*

Without *psychoanalytic* psychotherapy coupled with separation from the family circle, psychic peace can, it would seem, only come *through psychosis*; the dissolution of the ego then resolves the anxiety.

Anxiety which translates into "fear of dying" is not therefore *an anxiety about "death" but a "castration anxiety"*.

This neurotic anxiety is in fact a "magical fear" at the service of genital sexual drives, (repressed by a superego propelled by the castration complex), which are seeking, as usual in these cases, for an outlet on the anal or oral level. This is the mechanism of phobia, and one should always talk about *death phobia*, of *obsessional fear of death*, when clinically an organically healthy subject is terrified of dying.

CLINICAL PART

CHAPTER SIX

Presentation of a method

The children we will be talking about were, for the most part, sent to us for treatment at the Hospital Bretonneau by Dr Pichon, clinical director and himself a psychoanalyst. (Dr Edouard Pichon was the co-ordinator of the French psychoanalytic movement before the 1939 war and President of the Société Psychanalytique de Paris; he died at the beginning of the 1939–1945 war.) A special clinic—once a week—brought together abnormal children, retarded ones and those presenting neurotic or personality problems; this clinic became well known to the parents, and also especially to the schoolteachers, in the Eighteenth Arrondissement of Paris. (This was the first hospital clinic of its kind, which started a new trend.)

Besides the children who were brought to us directly because their disorder seemed to fit into the specific scope of this type of clinic, many others reached us through general medical consultations.

We would like to demonstrate that the treatment acts through helping the child happily resolve his castration complex and his Oedipus complex; it is not achieved through "personal influence or suggestion".

Free association is not possible with a child; in our analyses, we therefore employ a method of play, of spontaneous drawing, of "conversation", which is to be understood as having been triggered by various remarks made by the child. When the child asks us a question, for example, we never reply directly, but refer the question back to the child: "What do you think?" and our remarks consist of only a few encouraging monosyllables.

During our hospital consultations, we do not use play which necessitates equipment that we do not have at our disposal. What remains, therefore, is conversation, such as we have described above, during the course of which we will attempt to listen, watch, and observe without missing anything, gestures, expressions, mimicry, sayings, lapses, mistakes, and spontaneous drawings, to which we frequently resort. Through drawing, in fact, we enter straight into the subject's imaginative representations, his feeling states, his inner world, and his symbolism. This enables us, after we have tacitly understood it, to orientate the "conversations" we have with the child, to elucidate the meaning of his representations when they are aberrant. We never give direct interpretations of these drawings.

Symbols do not serve as keys to puzzles for psychoanalysts, as some would like to believe. The appearance of a symbol is not sufficient in itself to allow us to conclude that one is dealing with an unconscious this or that. One needs the context, the emotional situation in which the subject find himself at the time, the remarks he makes concerning it, the role the symbol holds in his play, the drawings, the dreams and the story he tells.

We use the same words as those used by the child. When he has made use of a symbol or a turn of phrase (which is laden with emotional unconscious meaning for us psychoanalysts), we adopt these same symbols and the same phrases in what we say to the child, whilst being very careful that the emotional state which is linked to it is moderated.

The psychoanalytic diagnosis is subsequently fine-tuned during treatment; the initial diagnosis is a diagnosis of symptoms.

If someone unacquainted with psychoanalysis listened to us talking to the child, he would often believe that we were speaking nonsense, pointless words, that we were talking "rubbish", that we were "playing" like a child ourselves with our little patient. He would probably partly be right, as these exchanges are not those we would have with an adult. We are not trying to instil our way of seeing things into the child, but only to present him with the true character of his own unconscious thoughts. Therefore, we do not speak a "logical" language aimed at the intelligence of the child, who is not yet logical (let's not forget this); we want to speak to his unconscious—which is never "logical" in anyone (something we must not forget either!)—this is why we naturally employ the symbolic and emotional language, which is his and touches him directly.

The ease with which the child begins to think, to live imaginatively with us, to release his internal world through his drawings, to recount his dreams, which he often tells his family he doesn't remember, to confess to mistakes, or to spontaneously tell us secrets that he never revealed to anyone before, this ease, this confidence are the basis of the therapeutic effect: this is what *transference means*. This is a situation in which there is emotional bonding to the psychoanalyst, who becomes a figure, of the utmost importance, within the inner world of the child for the duration of the treatment.

In itself, the *transference* is of no use. It is the use made of it which gives, or does not give, therapeutic power to the new emotional attachment of the child. The transference enables the therapist to study the affective reactions of the subject towards him and to infer a diagnosis and the therapeutic course to be taken. The therapy itself is only "conveyed" within the transference. Let's not believe that the transference acts through the suggestive behaviour of the doctor, because *suggestion requires something new, intellectual, or emotional in the psyche of a subject*, so in many cases, even in psychotherapy cases, we bring absolutely nothing new to the child.

In fact, if we give parents advice and if they accept it (in great part because of the trust that we try to generate in them and which—setting aside the voice of their unconscious resistance—therefore requires a certain measure of suggestion), *our attitude towards the child* is different. In most cases, he would be totally unable to report a single thing that the doctor has said to him. He comes to us all tense and anxious, spends some time with us, and leaves happy to have seen us, sometimes calmed down, sometimes quiet, sometimes cheerful, sometimes momentarily more nervous than on arrival; rarely does the child leave our sessions with "the same expression he came in with", and this is something we notice ourselves, and sometimes the child does too; in any case, the accompanying adult never fails to notice it. Often, the child simply speaks or draws and we simply listen. Sometimes we tell a story which sounds like any other story. Sometimes we "make conversation", and then the child remembers what we have talked about, but only dimly what the doctor said, because in most cases, we manage to make the child say what he knows without admitting it to himself. In short, we almost never contribute anything other than what is already on the child's mind.

If we do not act through suggestion, then how do we act? What is the use of this famous transference?

As we will see, we always proceed in the following way: first of all, we have *an interview with the mother* or the parents, always *in the presence of the child*, except in special cases when we ask for a one-to-one interview with the mother, sending the child back to the corridor for a few minutes. We never have this one-to-one talk *after* a private interview with the child.

Whilst speaking to the adult, we also take the opportunity to glance at the way the child is reacting. We generally have him settled at a table with paper and pencil in front of him, and we say: "Would you like to make me a beautiful drawing, anything, whatever you like?. The behaviour of the child (and that of the parents following the negative reaction of the child or the way in which he interrupts us to show us what he is doing) is already interesting subject matter for observation (quite apart from the drawing itself). Once we have obtained useful information from the parents, we give them some idea of our *a priori* opinion, of our way, different from theirs, of thinking about the responses of their child. Even without further information, we do not accept their proposed alternatives: illness or wickedness. We try to inspire their confidence and to extract their promise that they will bring the child back to us when we ask them to.

We then request that the mother leave us alone with the child; we do this during the first visit only if neither the mother nor the child are resistant to it. Should this be the case, we do not hurry things, and we say that we find their mistrust perfectly natural and we only ask that the mother remain as a rigorously silent observer during the initial interview which we are having with the child. Actually, mistrustful reactions towards these private interviews at Bretonneau Hospital are exceedingly rare because the routine is well known, and mothers tell each other about it in the waiting room. Therefore forewarned, the newcomers find it all quite natural. In any case, if at the first consultation the child seemed hesitant and the mother distrustful, I have never observed the mother or the child showing any difficulty in separating at the second session, quite the contrary. The mother usually suggests it herself.

So this is the practical aspect of our interviews. Let's add that *when one is dealing with psychotherapy*, no doctor can be content only to observe for as long as he judges necessary, in order to make a diagnosis; people demand care, and it is already a great deal that they accept leaving the clinic with no X-ray, no prescription, no remedies (for sedation or anxiety), without a special diet, in a nutshell without tangible proof that they have been to "see the doctor". One must, at the very least, talk to the parents, provide them with clear advice, which if applied, brings about some progress, however minor, in the child's behaviour, thanks to which trust in us is established and they will bring him back to us.

This means that we are *obliged to perform a therapeutic action on the very first day* even before we know the exact details of the case. Common sense is the major tool in our *a priori* therapeutic arsenal. There is nothing psychoanalytic in this. This is the basis of "conscious" psychotherapy, that is to say, methods used by our non-psychoanalytic colleagues.

To this psychotherapeutic method, which calls on the *conscious*, we add the oblique attack of the unconscious resistance of the family, when the ego of the (three- to four-year-old) child is merged with the external world of his family, and (after seven to eight years old) the unconscious resistance of the subject himself after the formation of the superego, as distinct from the ego.

Parents, in effect, have only two attitudes in the face of psychological or neurotic symptoms. They claim either that the child has an *illness*, a mental or physical "abnormality", or *has ill will*, is lazy, or is deliberately nasty. The first of these interpretations removes any responsibility from the child, and the second loads him with all the responsibility. These two attitudes *each as wrong as the other* have the consequence of fixing the child even more into the vicious circle of his neurotic symptoms.

The first increases the feelings of inferiority of the subject whilst in a way legitimising them, at the same time wounding his narcissism through the feeling of being "abnormal". Furthermore, in disabling the child's capacity for a healthy life, it allows the symptom to achieve its aim: flight, easier than fight, in the face of anxiety, and it initiates the neurosis that is characterised by a flight into illness.

The second attitude of the family, the withdrawal of love and the misunderstandings which it incorporates, *provokes feelings of conscious guilt* linked to the symptom, and the child tries to overcome it. But the symptom is a response to an unconscious need, it derives from a blocked or repressed drive whose energy has to find a means of expression at all costs. Therefore, after a temporary disappearance, the symptom will reappear proportionally strengthened by the way it has been attacked; all the stronger for a child with will power and sensitivity; or else we see another symptom appear, better tolerated by the parents and by the superego of the child.

Unfortunately, educators, doctors, and psychiatrists usually collude with the parents, either explicitly by trying to intimidate the child or implicitly by prescribing remedies.

Sometimes the doctor takes on a third attitude even more dispiriting than the others for the parents and the children. After having listened and given various remedies whose efficacy he doesn't believe in himself, he says: "And then, don't worry, it is nothing, it is only nerves", which is the equivalent of saying: "I don't understand what's going on and I don't care". Even when he does not understand anything, he does not humanely have the right to lose interest in a patient. He could, at least, confronted with the failure of a physical remedy, try to send the patient to a colleague who may be able "to understand something".

Let us illustrate through two cases—of children successively entrusted to two colleagues who knew nothing about psychoanalysis and then to ourselves—as we have just described. Let us compare the clinical results of these two attitudes.

The first attitude of the parents and the doctor—"the child is ill"—we demonstrated in the very simple case of Josette, which we recounted in the introduction to this book. In terms of illness, what was it all about?

The parents had decided to banish Josette from their bedroom. At least that was how the child saw it. This felt like a withdrawal of affection and, coinciding with the awakening of an interest in the facts of life and of the Oedipus complex, led Josette to put her development on hold because of this withdrawal of love. Of course, all this is not conscious, but it *is felt*.

The anxiety translates into disquiet in the face of the change she— the main character—had heard about without ever having been told directly "as if" she could not understand. In fact, she refused to pay attention to the buying of the sofa-bed; but the drive to revolt against the *displeasure* of being deprived of Daddy and Mummy is translated into symptoms of *negativity* (Josette turns *against* sleep, food, all previous interests and games), and *by a return to a previous stage* of libidinal evolution, which is exemplified by enuresis. The child deprived of love (at least in her eyes) is wasting away.

The understanding of the psychoanalyst (by asking the question: "Where does she sleep?") goes right to the heart of the subject—the burning question for a three-and-a-half-year-old child who is beginning her Oedipus complex. Then, her hypothesis confirmed and knowing that renouncing a pleasure can only be accepted in exchange for another, the psychoanalyst showed the child that she understood her conflict by allowing her to feel her pain and by translating it onto a normal plane.

Josette really suffered from the abandonment of the privileged position of "little baby". Taking the child's huge grief seriously enabled us to discuss its meaning with Josette's ego. We were offering her the possibility of accepting the imposed renunciation through promises of yet unknown pleasures, which coincided with the right to her own development instead of holding it back: "the sacrifice that reality imposes on you (your parents, your age) will bring you new advantages that you do not yet know: starting school and being loved like a big girl of whom father is proud".

We saw how the child abandoned her symptoms, *as soon as the unconscious resistance* to admitting suffering *became useless*, and how her development, for a moment compromised, resumed its normal course. Once healed, it is the child herself who asked her mother to go and tell the lady doctor, which the mother could well have done without.

To illustrate the second attitude of the parents and of the doctor—"the child is lazy, nasty"—I will cite the case of an eleven-year-old child, Jean, second and last of a family which comprised the father, the mother, and a sister of fourteen, all three in good health.

Jean is brought to Bretonneau by his mother, for his nervousness and severe personality problems.

With Dr Pichon, he is incapable of sitting still, fidgets constantly with his fingers and hands, makes faces and chews his lips. Furthermore, and still in the presence of Dr Pichon, he has great difficulty in expressing himself, difficulties for which, as well as psychotherapy, speech therapy has been advised. But then, this symptom disappears when the child is left with his mother and me, it only appears in the presence of a man.

Jean has presented with hyperactivity since infancy. He is always moving, sneering, teasing his sister, busy scratching himself, demolishing furniture, gnawing his nails, tearing at his clothes, and is unable to apply himself to his schoolwork. Seeing him growing up without being cured of this defect, and with the schoolmaster also complaining, the parents got fed up with telling him off. They bought a strap and, with this threat, they obtained half an hour of peace ("at last", they said) from time to time. The parents were satisfied with this result. The method of the strap took hold in the house: "as it is how you have to be treated". And the mother adds: "the father always has the strap in hand".

But before too long, another symptom made its appearance: Jean was a nice child and up until then only his hyperactivity was held against him. He became more and more anxious. Nervous tics appeared, then, in increasingly frequent bouts, Jean became provoking, lying, teasing, rude and impertinent. In parallel, the use of the strap became more and more common, it was no longer a threat but he was struck. More disturbing reactions started to appear, minor thefts, nastiness, and serious attacks on his friends, disobedience that could have been dangerous on scout outings.

The child has a charming sensitivity, and although he does not confess his remorse to the strict family circle, his continual hyperactivity, condemned by the parents, made him feel very guilty. Jean's family is very religious, and he himself is also very pious. His position as a wicked child revolted his conscience.

The symptoms against which he fought consciously were disappearing, but made way for silent twitching, less annoying for the parents; furthermore, his mastery of the aggressive drive translated into voluntary and temporary immobility, provoking a strengthening of the drive, which explains the sudden outbursts. Simultaneously they provided a beneficial discharge for the unconscious but were guilt-provoking for the moralising authority, the superego: "*I* do not mean to be nasty. *It* is stronger than *Me*."

In other words, how does Jean's ego get itself out of the conflict?; through seeking to be beaten up, which appeases the guilt anxiety. It is in the provocation of the "bogeyman father", of the intransigent mother, and—in the absence of strict parents—the worthlessness of the school results and the dangers courted with the equally indulgent schoolmaster and scout mistress. This means that when he cannot get beaten physically, Jean tries to get psychologically beaten by the other pupils in the classroom and risks an accident, which would weaken him physically.

One can see the endless chain of neurotic symptoms.

A well-known doctor and child psychiatrist, whom I will not name, was entirely of the opinion that the parents' interpretation was correct. After having sharply reprimanded Jean, without managing to get a word or a tear out of him, he seriously advised the parents, in front of the child, to put him in an asylum or in a private institution for abnormal perverse children. Maybe he did this in good faith, or maybe he wanted to intimidate the child; whatever it may have been, and without saying another word to the parents, he sent the three of them away after pronouncing his verdict. It was Jean's scout mistress, a medical social worker to Dr Pichon at Bretonneau, who advised the very worried parents to consult Dr Pichon again before making a decision. And this is how he came to be entrusted to us.

All of the above was told us by the mother. We listened dispassionately, and our first words to Jean were, at the end of questioning his mother: "Is all that true?", and as, stubborn and mocking, he did not respond, we added: "Poor Jean, I really pity you, how unhappy you must be". To the stupefaction of the mother, Jean, the "indomitable pervert", burst into tears.

Faced with such a picture, what attitude should we adopt? First, we must try to understand what it is all about, try to make sense of the symptomatology, much more complicated than in the case of Josette.

In fact, for Josette, the threat came from the external world against an ego in agreement with the id.

For Jean, the conflict with the external world is completely reworked through a supplementary conflict with the superego. *And this is always the case beyond six to seven, the age after which the superego is forming.*

Behind the recent secondary reactions referred to as wicked, one will therefore have to find the original cause of this more ancient hyperactivity, which triggered the introduction of the paternal strap.

Jean is ten years old. Before entering the latency phase, *had he resolved his Oedipus complex?*

He probably made the attempt, but has not resolved it, and the proof of it is in the symptom, that is, his difficulty in expressing himself in front of a man, substitute for the father, which provides evidence for the repressed aggression which is unconsciously projected onto all men who become magically dangerous in the eyes of the child.

Jean had reached the phallic stage, but, in the face of the threat of castration which emanated from the father and the castration anxiety intensified by the grandmother, the mother, and the sister, *Jean must have then regressed to the anal stage.* This is the meaning of the alternating aggressive outbursts accompanied by rude comments, followed by passive and masochistic repentance towards parents and schoolmates.

This behaviour is characteristic of the ambivalence of the sadistic anal stage.

And he told me that he liked to draw ships, especially warships, but that he cannot draw the canons, the masts, the cabin of the commander, and the searchlights (phallic symbolism). He also tells me that his sister forbids him to swing on the chairs but that she does it herself when Mummy isn't looking: this is symbolic of the prohibition of masturbation.

And the mother herself admits that she forbids her son to hide any of his thoughts. To do that "would be the greatest grief he could cause her".

One day he had surreptitiously brought back some illustrated magazines lent by a friend. What a drama it was, because she "found the stories in these filthy magazines, of bandits, guns and adventures, horrible". You can imagine her sorrow one day recently when Jean stole ten cents from the mantelpiece to secretly buy himself one of these magazines. Several times he hid his bad school marks from her.

After several conversations with Jean, I asked his mother if he had what some call "bad habits". The poor woman blushed with shame and replied: "Not any longer, luckily I managed to rid him of that, but two or three years ago, we were really concerned. It was then that we noticed that he was highly strung. But he understood and is not doing it any more. Sometimes now, he has a sort of tic of fiddling with himself by jigging up and down in his trousers, which makes me feel ashamed, maybe this is why you asked me this question?"

It was during one of the sessions, the one in which Jean owned up to not being able to draw what I knew were phallic symbols, that I alluded to the forbidden masturbation. He replied, "yes, when I was little ..." (and carried on immediately): "but grandmother is so afraid of everything, she believes that I am a baby and does not want me to cross the road on my own, she says that I am going to be run over".

We can now clearly see what happened two or three years ago at the time of the violent repression of the masturbation.

Jean, at that time, in the middle of the phallic stage and his Oedipal fantasies (warship on the sea), saw his masturbatory fantasies as well as his ambitious and aggressive fantasies forbidden, in the name of a risk of death (crossing the road) and of the withdrawal of mother's love (if he hides something from her). Stinging feelings of jealousy and inferiority, permanent and not resolved towards the father, whose organ he cannot imagine (commandant's cabin, canon, searchlight), gives him this *hyperactive* attitude towards *all* problems and *all* activities.

If at least the family circle had tolerated the peaceful establishment of Jean in this more or less regressive phase whilst allowing him the satisfactions linked with it: earning a few cents, being free to spend his hoard as he wishes, being free to play with toy guns, and to get passionate about war stories or police adventures. Jean would never have presented as a neurotic child from the point of view of making a social adaptation, even under the influence of the drive towards puberty. The Oedipal problem, which would certainly not have been resolved from what we know of his milieu, would have, without any doubt, presented itself again and under a form which would be very difficult to resolve.

The family neurosis demanded, on the contrary, that even satisfaction in a regressive mode should be refused the child. Therefore, there was only one way out, that of neurosis. We have just used the term "family neurosis"; this is because we encounter in the case of more than fifty per cent of neurotic children, *neurotic behaviour on the part of the parents or one of the parents*.

In the case of Jean, we are dealing with a *mother of the type "dutiful woman"*. The material situation is very modest. The mother does not work but looks after her house. From the mother and son's behaviour, one gets the impression that they come from a bourgeois background, more than from the working class. The mother denies herself all pleasures, all weakness, all temptations. She is of course *frigid* and willingly banishes all interest in the question of sex, which disgusts her; *Jean's grandmother, who appears as very anxious*, spoils her daughter and her grandchildren, but, worried about everything, panics at the sight of the smallest risk inherent in living. "When my mother comes to our house, we are all thrown out of kilter in the evening, including my husband, who becomes so, just from seeing us in this state."

As far as *the fourteen-year-old sister is concerned*, the mother tells me that she went through an aggressive and rebellious second infancy, then, all of a sudden and for the last two years, she'd changed completely. She became very nice, but she is very fearful, has a *phobia about going out alone*, has a morbid lack of self-confidence and has a veiled vindictive attitude towards her brother. "She will not let him get away with anything, in an unrelenting way, although he is just the same as she used to be herself."

The *father* is also extremely anxious, says the mother, he shouts all the time and, as we know, he "always has the strap to hand".

In a case like this one, when we have understood it, *what can be done?* The best would be to *psychoanalyse the mother*, but we are not even considering that. She is happy with her lot. *Should Jean be separated from his family?* This would be very painful for him, as he loves his mother like a baby, ferocious and cuddly in turn, even when the occasions on which he seeks cuddles are very rarely recompensed with a hug, because virtue doesn't allow the slate to be wiped clean of accumulated grievances. Furthermore, separation *would not resolve anything*.

We will establish a *very strong active transference*, thanks to which we will shake the resistances of the *superego*. This will allow the ego to consider an attitude of ambivalent response towards us, for example to think very unpleasant things, make rude remarks about the female doctor, a phallic mother, after having thought just the opposite. This we will allow to be thought of as something natural, which will not alter the cordial relationship which exists in reality between Jean and us. When he owns up to a lapse of effort, we pity him: if he forgets something he had promised us and shows how affected he is by this, we tell him that in fact we were half expecting this to happen and that opposing us is not that bad.

If we are talking about family incidents, we try to show him *the part which he has projected onto it and the part which is objective* in his interpretation of the others' attitudes.

One day marked huge progress, the one when he told me: "Now when I feel that Mummy is very anxious, I say nothing and I think: it is the same as it is for me, it must be out of her control Then it is not her fault but before, I always thought that it was because of me, of the worry that I was causing her. As a matter of fact, my week has been great at home and at school. The schoolmaster praised me and told Mummy that I had changed. Then I understood that Mummy was sometimes anxious about something other than me." That day, Jean spoke to me about his drawings and asked me if I could show him how to draw the things he did not know how to on the battleships? Unconsciously, it was extremely important. I replied: "You will certainly know how to do it on your own, when you know how to observe *how it is in reality*"— "well then, I'll bring it to you and perhaps with you here I'll be able to do it". To which I replied: "those are things which interest boys. You will draw them much better than I could, but you do not dare believe it, as if you thought that a child has to be less clever and skilful than a grown-up because he is younger! If I was your age, I would be a little girl and it is you who would show me how to do things".

Naturally, as one might expect, as soon as the symptoms *annoying the parents* disappear, *they stop bringing the children*, and for Jean, despite the favourable advice of the schoolmaster, the mother made the excuse that the consultation made him miss a morning at school so as not to send him to us anymore; everything was fine in her eyes, he had "calmed down".

Jean, nevertheless, although better, is far from being cured. The proof is that a good day spent entirely with his father, for the first time in his life, was to trigger an aggressive reaction the next day.

Another significant event in the unresolved conflict between the Oedipal and the castration complexes: his schoolmaster, as a reward for his efforts at school, gave him a pocket-knife as a present. What joy!— Yes, but the very next day, Jean lost it. Despair, he returned to the places where he was walking, but impossible to find the knife! Jean was low, discouraged, and actually trembling at the idea that the schoolmaster would get angry when he discovered that he had not been looking after his present properly. (This was the unconscious guilty intention.) The schoolmaster, on hearing it, instead of scolding Jean, told him: "Well, if you earn good marks for another month, you deserve another one, I will give you another one".

Luckily, the father and mother had not scolded Jean for losing it, too shocked by the violence of the sorrow which had overcome him.

Jean, through the new attitude of his family (the parents are hopeful again), and mainly through the self-satisfaction obtained at school and at scouts, managed to find some compensation for the inferior state and strict supervision under which his family kept him.

This detailed example should demonstrate the goal we set ourselves: which is to be impartial and to help the child find a means of expressing his repressed drives, adapting them to the reasonable demands of his circle and to his own ethics, appeasing his guilt feelings as well as satisfying the legitimate demands of his libido, in the best possible way.

One can therefore see, through both cases, one of which is very simple (Josette) and the other extremely complicated (Jean), on what our attitude depends, which is different from that generally held by parents and general practitioners.

In Josette's case, the hypothesis of an organic aetiology did not fit in with the absence of fever and the complexity of the symptomatology. In any case, the reappearance of the *enuresis* itself signalled an actual serious affective regression.

In Jean's case, the simple fact of having a "sympathetic" attitude towards him was enough to throw into confusion his defence of imperviousness, aimed at challenging the moralising attitude that he expected us to take.

When parents tell us about the misbehaviour of their children, how nasty, vicious, lazy, impertinent, and so on they are, we do not criticise them, we just content ourselves with listening attentively, asking them to give us the precise circumstances without echoing their complaints, or reproaches. Our benevolent attitude towards the child never falters; each of our reactions, our expressions, our words, our gestures is deliberately neutral or oriented in the therapeutic direction, which we believe is indicated. We never apportion blame. We seek to understand the "economic" reason (that is to say, "that which is the most advantageous for the pleasure principle") that pushes a human being to rebel and to live on bad terms with their immediate circle, which is not in the *a priori* logic of the human being.

If the child is conscious of having acted badly, either he does or does not feel appropriate guilt. In other words, there can be an exaggeration of *scruples* or, conversely, *a lack of judgement.* Therefore, we try to relive with him the socially unacceptable episode and to appreciate his view on the matter, in order to understand why his reaction did not fit. Then we can explain why unconsciously he is unable to take responsibility for his act, or, conversely, why unconsciously he judges himself with such severity, out of proportion to the moral code of his milieu.

In this way, little by little, *we lift the neurotic barriers and the defence mechanisms* which were primitively aimed at protecting the child, but which in fact now keep him prisoner.

Because this is what happened: for a momentary subjective "feeling better", the individual was obliged to make an abnormal distribution of the libidinal drives according to a schema which risks being incorporated into the construction of his personality, which then becomes a neurotic personality.

But for an individual, this risk of an attack on his original rich complexity is the risk inherent in living, and begins at its very origin, from the moment when he comes into being with the fusion of two germinal cells born from the father and the mother, and which bring with them-selves—potentially—libidinal drives and the hereditary potential to externalise them. First come the conditions for intra-uterine life, the nourishing quality of the food right from birth. Next come the thou-sands of influences, acting through their presence only and by the com-plex role that they play in the formation of the material and spiritual elements with which the young physical and psychological being will be constructed; climate, diet, living conditions, comfort, environment, ethnic characteristics, sonority and rhythm of language, religion, beliefs, folklore, national and local art and crafts; in brief, a complete *prefigured* set, as independent of him as of his mother, and that we could call the collective superego.

It is also important to notice "that a certain kind of health", a "certain equilibrium", is not especially the prerogative of beings who have arrived at the furthest stage of human libidinal development, the oblative genital stage. Everything depends on the family circle, which forms the emotional atmosphere of the subject, and of his own libidinal possibilities. The common principle of psychological health being an *attunement* between the sensibility of the subject and that of their sur-roundings. But it is obvious that a human being who has reached the oblative genital stage, or is approaching it through unconscious libidi-nal development, preserves his equilibrium more easily than another, whatever the affective level in the environment, because he reacts in a rational way to felt disagreement. *From a psychoanalytic point of view*, one cannot therefore say that psychological suffering is in itself either a cause or a proof of neurosis, it is only a cause or a proof of emotional *discordance*. It is the *practical* way in which a subject reacts to it which will be called a normal reaction or a neurotic reaction, the normal reac-tion being that which allows the personality to preserve *the wholeness and the free play of their life drive, as a consequence of their finding a creative way out*.

Psychoanalysis allows us, therefore, to understand the affective com-ponents in all individuals, be they psychotic or more or less neurotic or sane, and the "subjective logic" of their behaviour, *so often, for all of us, not logical at all*. Further, it allows us, with the help of transference in the therapeutic situation, to study the unconscious mechanisms of the subject, his behaviour towards the psychoanalyst, similar to the one he naturally has towards anyone.

The bringing to light of the archaic determinism and the out-of-date reactions which characterise his non-adaptation to reality, allows the subject to remake a different and better-adapted synthesis for himself with the elements which were in him without his knowledge, and which he becomes conscious of through the analysis of the transference (that is to say, through the advanced study of the reasons for his emotional behaviour towards his psychoanalyst).

A psychoanalysis in itself has never rendered a being saner than before; it only puts him on the way to becoming so after the treatment, through a work of personal synthesis, which he still has to do after the disappearance of the unconscious elements which kept the patient bound, during the duration of his psychoanalytic treatment, to all that was surrounding him, and in particular to the person of his doctor. This work of synthesis can be more or less begun during the course of the treatment, when the psychoanalyst is gifted with an appreciable quantity of genital libido, thanks to which he does not feel anxiety at feeling his analysand to be blossoming emotionally, even if this might surpass him.

In any case, the analyst cannot lead his analysand to a point of psycho-affective development which he has not himself reached. Equally, the doctor cannot, in many cases, bring the patient at the end of the treatment to full psycho-affective development as a consequence of a lack of fundamental libidinal possibilities.

One of the objections often raised is that treatments are extremely long and, because of this very fact, costly. This is true, and all truly psychoanalytic experiences, that is to say, treatments based on the rebuilding of one's personality by the subject himself, in which the doctor only lends her actual presence as a sensitive, "responsive witness", that of a contractual and temporary impartial mediator, are necessarily long. It is only among these treatments that one can count perfect and definitive cures, whatever happens later in the subject's life.

Nevertheless, during the course of the treatment, and often right from the beginning, the subject feels happier, some of his symptoms can even disappear very quickly. Let's not fool ourselves: this cure is only apparent. It is the effect of the "transference". The important place that the psychoanalyst and psychoanalysis take in the life of the analysand, and which is a "means" of the treatment, lessens some neurotic reactions of the subject because his very attachment to the doctor monopolises an amount of the libido, diverted from its previous fixations. This attachment itself is of a neurotic order, that is to say, not rational, because it is not based on any valid reasoning, except for the *a priori* trust in someone who is supposed to cure you. This trust can rest on convincing clinical facts, on a firm intellectual base, but this cannot explain the "mode" of the emotional relations, which come into play right from the first contact in the attitude of the patient towards the doctor. This is only an "advance" on the cure, if we can be permitted the image.

One can admit that there is a *virtual cure*, therefore a possibility of stopping treatment when the old neurotic has rediscovered a new equi- librium in day-to-day living, and when the study of his unconscious mechanisms shows that his instinctual drives—the part which cannot be sublimated—are accepted by his conscious personality, that is to say, that his unconscious mechanisms are at peace.

A cure is only assured when the analysand, apart from the lasting dis- appearance of the symptoms, "is internally at peace with himself". That is to say, that he reacts towards real difficulties in life without anxiety, through a spontaneous attitude adapted to the demands of a moral code that is in accord with the milieu in which he chooses to live, and with his own; whilst allowing his instinctual drives adequate expression (libidinal discharges in sufficient quality and quantity) which ensure the conservation of the acquired equilibrium.

This work demands long and slow preparation. *It is only definitive when the subject has reached the adult stage*—not only in actual years—but in emotional and psychological age. *In the depth of all beings, the analyst can find no more than what was already there.* This is said as much for those who imagine finding a panacea in this new science and in its practical application, as for those who believe psychoanalysts to be blind enough to believe this.

As we said before, for the sake of simplicity and clarity in this piece of work, we will only present cases here that have been cured not through pure psychoanalysis, but by a method of psychotherapy derived from it and which addresses beings in the process of becoming, and offers considerable practical advantages of speed in return for minimal inter- vention on the part of the doctor.

This method, apart from the appeal to the patient's consciousness specifically stemming from psychotherapy, refers back to psychoana- lytic experience point by point. Our internal attitude is absolutely the same as the one that we have in real psychoanalytic sessions.

Therefore, we put ourselves in a place essentially different from that of the moralist. However, our action does have unquestionable educative value: it suffices to read the following observation. It is that in any psychotherapy, from the moment we abandon rigorous psychoanalytic technique, we are, *whether we wish it or not*, acting in an educative fashion. (Anna Freud maintained the legitimacy of psychoanalysis being educative, in opposition to Melanie Klein.)

This attitude follows from our personality, therefore from our unconscious. But of two psychotherapists, the one who has been psychoanalysed has more ability than the other in getting close to the ideal of objectivity.

In fact, what does the term "objectivity" mean when we are talking about observing the behaviour and the psycho-affective mechanisms of an individual? It means that the doctor must not position himself either on moral grounds or on cultural ones, that he must not pass any value judgement, and that his aim must be discriminating the elements (drives and what opposes them) which are at the basis of apparently normal and abnormal reactions in the person he is examining. But, because we are dealing with the reactions of a living human being towards phenomena which are equally in play in another living being, one who is the patient and the other the doctor, it is obvious that numerous possibilities for error exist, *to begin with the influence of the unconscious of the doctor.* Let us make a comparison again here: if one observes a landscape through a red glass, it eliminates all the red rays from one's field of observation. The same applies to the psychotherapist who is himself a synthesis adapted to society. The specific way in which he succeeds, influences his objectivity without his knowing.

We only have one way to compensate for this which is not *to practice psychoanalysis until we have been psychoanalysed ourselves*, as deeply and for as long as possible.

This is the major argument against psychoanalysis, and indeed it is not a small one. Nothing is weightier than psychoanalysis or more painful to bear for an individual even in good health. The energy and perseverance required is perhaps found more easily in beings who have the courage and simplicity to recognise their difficulties and seek a remedy. When those are doctors and they use knowledge acquired at the cost of their own experience to cure others, I do not believe that one can humanely reproach them for it.

One sometimes hears witticisms which are not entirely ill-founded: one of them consists in saying that all psychiatrists go mad sooner or later, and people add that it comes from living amongst the mad. We are not saying that this is true, but it is certain that the taste for working with mental illness will never come to an individual whose attention has not been drawn towards conflicts that he did not understand. If such an individual sees his condition worsen after some years of psychiatric practice, the cause does not need to be sought in his daily contact with psycho-neurotics; it is enough that his own neurosis has developed, as it would have done whatever his work.

Another challenge to psychoanalysis which has some value in those who wish to rationalise their unconscious resistances (as if the attitude towards psychoanalysis, which is a science, could depend logically on the opinion that one has of one or another of its practitioners) is that "all psychoanalysts are former neurotics".

To this, we reply: the infantile psycho-affective determinants which lead an individual to the choice of a medical career are the same for psychoanalysts as for all other doctors. We are not talking about psychoanalysts who are not medical practitioners, because, apart from medico-psychiatric treatment, psychoanalysis, which is a science, attracts, in different ways, teachers, sociologists, criminologists, historians, in general all those who are interested in what it is to be human.

Human sympathy for those who suffer is at the basis of the choice of a medical career, and is a sublimation deriving directly from disquiet in the face of our own suffering, which is felt unconsciously during our development if we are gifted with a sensitivity which makes us more vulnerable than others. Of all the defence mechanisms employed *in relation to* this suffering, one of them and the most successful is the interest given to relieving others of their suffering. This interest can only originate from the projection onto others of what one feels in oneself, a mechanism contemporaneous with the sadistic anal stage. This interest only applies to beings towards whom, for unconscious reasons, we can compare ourselves quite naturally, those who experience the same suffering as we do or onto whom we can project our own.

But true oblativity, when it exists, in some doctors, researchers, surgeons, translates into the comprehensive development of their affectivity into the fully realised adult stage of "vocation". Only this enables the splendid universal devotion and inner serenity, the admirable example of which a few provide us with, without even noticing. Let us not mistake this true devotion with the masochistic attitude of the false martyr. It sometimes happens that a devoted doctor becomes the butt of others' attacks; he gives the proof of his true equilibrium by continuing, despite the difficulties encountered, with the useful work which is his *raison d'être* and aim in life.

It seems to us that Freud was an example of this type of doctor and it is for this that he has our profound admiration.

Any doctor with an interest in mental illness should undergo psychoanalysis before practising. In effect, his interest could be merely a neurotic defence mechanism, in which case he would not be able to give the psychiatric field the service to society of which he would be capable were he to use his genuine capacity to sublimate. If, on the contrary, after his psychoanalysis, his taste for psychiatry proves itself to be based on real intuitive gifts and sensitivity, and his emotional and sexual behaviour demonstrates that he has arrived at the oblative genital stage of his own development, he will then, with the minimum of risk to himself and others, specialise in psychotherapy.

Some people would want all psychotherapists to be wonderful and innately balanced. Can they not realise the impossibility of what they are asking? That such beings exist, we cannot deny, but we can also affirm that there are very few of them amongst doctors, and probably even fewer amongst those interested in mental problems. If we ourselves had not had our attention drawn by emotional conflict, not only around us, but also within ourselves, we would probably never have studied in detail the questions we are talking about here. Those who are reading these lines, from the very attention they are kindly paying us, prove that these questions are not foreign to them.

There is nothing pejorative in the epithet "neurotic". Our "will" can do nothing about neurotic symptoms, apart from aggravate them; our "intelligence" acts in the same way. Intelligence and will which are used to hide one's emotional difficulties from oneself or from others, negating them whilst we consciously try to overcome them, are weapons unworthy of a sincere human being. This unfair attitude, not only towards others, but mainly towards oneself, is perhaps, for intelligent men, the ultimate moral wrong. Stranger still—except for those who have an idea of the vagaries of the unconscious—is that people who have this attitude take pride in being ethical. If they are not doctors and this attitude helps them to suffer less, we cannot reproach them for it, but he who is a doctor does not have the right to take a subjective stance, in the face of illness and suffering. The patient is in pain and asking for help.

However naturally well balanced, a doctor who wants to become a psychotherapist and especially if he wants to be a psychoanalyst, must—let us emphasize this—must know himself through and through. He cannot do this through introspection for in that case he is only judging himself through his own unconscious mechanisms and therefore cannot be totally objective; and if he is somewhat objective, he will be even more so once psychoanalysed.

It may be that after psychoanalysis, a psychiatrist reaches perfect emotional equilibrium, which is more or less lasting, but that he should possess this equilibrium spontaneously and durably without psychoanalysis, is demanding the impossible.

None of us can undertake our work without a sublimated libido. We well know that sublimations are mechanisms of defence against anxiety, that is to say, against mental suffering, and the difference from a symptoms said to be neurotic is only a difference of social worth.

Everybody knows that one did not have to wait for psychoanalysis in order to do psychotherapy. But it remained in the empirical domain, reserved for doctors naturally gifted with qualities of perceptiveness, sensitivity, common sense, and one has to say, above all, intuition. The method of non-psychoanalytic psychotherapy varied with each therapist, and their therapeutic experience based on individual starting points was incommunicable. It was in fact based on the transference, which they used without knowing, and which helped them to have a personal influence on the patient, therefore it worked mainly through suggestion. The negative aspect of the transference was manifested by the refusal of medication, in opposition to which the patient even became aggressive and contemptuous.

Some psychotherapists obtain excellent results in some cases and, therapeutically speaking, it is better to have a psychotherapist who is not a psychoanalyst who heals, than a psychoanalyst who does not.

But if necessary, we make our own the therapeutic methods used at all epochs by our colleagues. We employ them in our psychotherapy, especially in order to obtain the trust of the parents when we are dealing with young children, because the practical possibility of treating their children, or not, depends on them. (This is why it is necessary to know adults well and their emotional reactions through the practice of classical adult psychoanalysis, in order to prevent harmful reactions, or to ward them off as much as possible, so as to shelter our little patients, their children, from their unconscious reactions, which are often damaging behind their conscious good intentions.)

If, therefore, in the observations which follow, we sometimes use common-sense advice, which speaks to the conscious, and that would be familiar to all psychotherapists, it is because common sense is the necessary basis of all psychotherapy; but it is also the keystone, if one might say, of psychoanalytical interpretations.

A false interpretation—whether it be of resistances or conflicts in the drives—*will never modify the actual behaviour of the patient.* Even if it seems intellectually seductive, its therapeutic action will prove worthless and will sometimes aggravate the condition.

This is why we propose (to the doctors who are reading this) that they accept the therapeutic criteria, *"the proof of the treatment"*, as one accepts it in organic treatment.

I do not believe that, in all good faith, there could be a colleague who having read these case studies could say that the children, after treatment, are worse than before.

Such views, at first sight paradoxical, were nevertheless reported to us by a very likeable woman whom we did not know, but whom we later learned was one of our senior colleagues.

It concerned the case of a very abnormal child whom she had heard about and whose case we were presenting. The case of this child which needed full psychoanalysis is too long to speak about here. This child presented, amongst other symptoms, castration anxiety with death phobia and all its associations. This condition had made him, not only seriously retarded, but also so obsessed that no school could manage him.

All the symptoms have disappeared. The child, who is now eight years old, behaves more or less like the other children of his age, despite still having, in our eyes, marked emotional problems and learning difficulties. (From his psychoanalytic treatment, which lasted a whole school year of twice weekly sessions, I have extracted drawings 1, 2, 3, 4, and 5 (pp. 136–139)).

Recently, a serious accident occurred at his school, which cost the life of one of his favourite friends. There followed a clinical result that the schoolmistress, the mother, and myself found meaningful: instead of reacting as he would have done a few months ago with neurotic symptoms of physical anxiety, with fainting and muteness, our little patient reacted to the accident as most of the children from his class did, not as the most unstable ones. On his return home, still distressed, he told his mother what had happened in a natural and detailed way (of blood, etc.). For the first time in his life, he asked his mother to teach him to pray for his little friend (one has to say that the Church and all that is linked to it formed part of his phobias). At night, and to the great astonishment of his mother, he slept without nightmares.

The behaviour of this child, faced with this tragic and unexpected event (although, personally, we know that he is not yet cured), denotes, for his family and ourselves, (and I believe for all who are sincerely concerned, especially those who know the grave problems he suffered before the treatment), considerable amelioration of his symptoms. (Since then, this child has led a normal school life, done his military service, got married, is the head of a family, and has succeeded professionally.) (note added in 1971).

In spite of this, the afore mentioned doctor, shocked by the detailed account of the accident the child gave his mother, declared with an aggression which would astonish anyone apart from a psychoanalyst: "Your child has become more disturbed than before. That is what it means " (sic.). I did not reply. Then, a little while later, a mother who was there who happened to be one of my friends asked a question, and before I had time to reply, my female colleague, announced with tension: "Come on, all this is not for little girls." (In this friendly little group, apart from our female colleague, mother of one of the young women, there were only men and women of thirty or over, most of them married, fathers and mothers of families.)

If we recounted this little anecdote, it is because of its general interest. *It is very difficult to follow a psychoanalytic case objectively.* It is not, let us repeat, a question of intelligence; it is a question of feelings. Psychoanalysis reawakens serious anxiety in many adults because of repressed drives.

Without knowing it, this female colleague gave us an interesting example because it was so typical:

1. Facts are negated.
2. One attacks the one who provides the reason for anxiety (the psychoanalyst); she attacks me, whom she doesn't know, with "castrating" comments, which, without any doubt, remind her of those that her own superego, speaking like her mother, made in the face of her murderous Oedipal fantasies.

It is obvious that if I had spoken about treating a fracture, for example, through a new bone-fusion system, this same doctor would have been interested or not, without her emotional reactions being brought into play.

Let's note that the attitude of the young nowadays, in medical intellectual circles, is rarely as emotional or as resistant, and this is easily explained.

We hope that this work, in which we discuss clinical observations taken day by day, will show the therapeutic interest of psychoanalysis. (Now, in 1971, we can see the extent of the ground covered since the publication of this book in 1939, the book which was my medical thesis.)

CHAPTER SEVEN

Observations

Firstly, we are going to present some drawings collected during treatment of the cases which we will be speaking about. We will begin with two examples of dreams demonstrating how the conflicts expressed look alike, regardless of the shape in which they are expressed, and especially regardless of the age of the subjects.

Dream of a twenty-five-year-old impotent adult

"It was night time, I was in my room, I heard a noise in "Mummy's room", I was scared and I didn't want to go in there. I grabbed a revolver, although I don't have one, and I decided to go in. The door was open, but it was impossible to get in and I could not see the rest of the room, as is the case when a door is open. I think that there was a man there in black, hidden. The door was like a guillotine. If one entered, there was a click and it unleashed a blade, which cut off heads. I woke up sweating."

(This is an anxiety dream connected to the Oedipus complex and to the "primal scene" of the parent's coitus. see drawing 4, p. 138, from a seven-year-old child.)

Dream of a ten-year-old child with enuresis

A ten-year-old child with enuresis dreamt two days after his enuresis stopped that he was fighting with giants and killed some.

The next day, the dream starts again and he kills all the giants except one. Then he kills him too, and with his sword cuts off his feet, then his wrists, and he tries to cut his head off too "but it was too hard and my sword broke, never mind! I had to let go of it."

These dreams, far from being nightmares were marvellous. He felt so happy, proud, and strong that ever since his schoolwork has seemed interesting and easy, especially maths, "as if a curtain had been drawn back".

This same child had done drawing 6 (p. 140) during the previous session, which provoked a question from me which allowed him to complete the drawing.

Drawings

Castration anxiety (boys)

The horse (a boy who has had a phobia of horses and of butchers specialising in horsemeat since the age of three; just a glimpse of them in the street sends him into a cataleptic sleep). Nose, legs, and tail are cut off.

2.

"The child-lantern-who-can-see-in-the-dark" is led away by "a mer-man" like the cat who had a broken leg and who had been taken to the vet, and the dog whose tail had been cut off. "And the vet also cuts the cat's thing off" (same child).

3.

Drawing of the story of the Chinese man who loses his banana, which is taken away from him by a woman (see p. 54) (same child).

Castration complex (boys)

4.

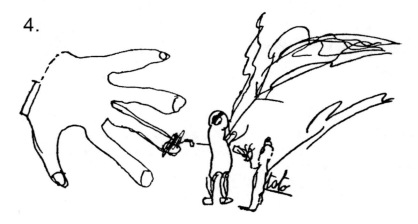

Same child at eight. First appearance of the complex shape, that is unconscious, and lived out, of the castration complex. During the week, he caught his finger in the door of his "mother's" bedroom (of course, it is that of "both" parents), following an argument with his elder sister (a symbol for him of the "wicked" mother). During this argument, he took refuge in his "mother's" room, supposedly to "look out of the window", because his sister always prevents him from "seeing everything". The "deep-sea diver" is a "Mummy's boy" (*homme-de-la-mer*), but the little boy Toto is "a clever boy who is not letting the others get the better of him", he has a sailor's beret with a red pompom on it "I am going to be a sailor too" says the child. The father was in the Navy for military service and during the war. The black pencil mark on the head of the diver is found on all the drawings that the child makes of his grandfather, "who has a big razor" and who sometimes cuts himself shaving.

5.

Symbolic drawing of the "primal scene". Sadistic possession of the mother (same child; drawing which preceded the previous one by three weeks). "The whale is really giving him a hard time. You have to *see* how she jumps, but he plants his thingy in her and in the end he wins and it's bleeding." "He" is a "merman" (*homme-de-la-mer*).

See p. 31

6.

Ten-year-old boy, with enuresis. Symbolic drawing of the phallic mother. At first, the child had only drawn the ship on the sea (frequent Oedipal representation). To my question "Did he know that women were not made like men?", the child added a tree in the sea "because there was something missing, but it is not a real tree" (phallic mother) (see p. 136).

Castration anxiety (girls)

7.

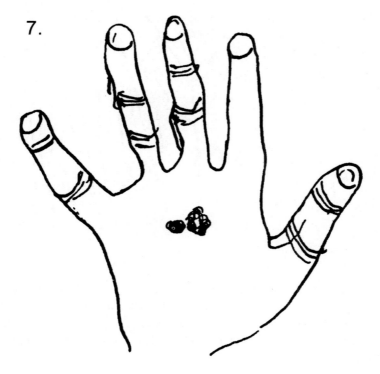

Drawing by Mauricette, eight years old. She had wanted to be a boy since the birth of a little brother a few months ago. Initially, this drawing did not have anything in the palm of the hand. She added the two dots after my analysis concerning her suffering from jealousy relieved her guilt.

8.

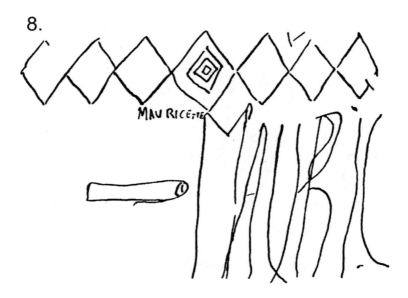

Second drawing by Mauricette. One can clearly see the symbolism: if there was not this "cut finger", Mauricette would be Mauric (pronounced "Maurice", taking into account the spelling mistake; Mauricette is just beginning to write). "It's a matter of decoration." (She thought herself ugly.)

See p. 85

Drawings by Claudine

(see p. 205)

9.

I   II

The two drawings made on 22 February.

10.

Claudine, 1 March

11.

Claudine, 8 March

12.

Claudine, 22 March
(See observations of Claudine, p. 208.)

One should not be surprised not to find specific graphic representations of the girl's castration complex.

Take note that often a serious drawback occurs at this stage, exclusively experienced in the body—appendicitis—death of the child—death of femininity. This is not the case with Claudine, who negotiated this stage in favourable circumstances.

We have seen what a difference there is between the castration complex of the boy and that of the girl.

CASE STUDIES

Gustave (aged three)

Child in good health—(according to the notes made daily by his mother).

Gustave is not yet three. His mother is pregnant, he notices it, and asks questions, he is interested in his mother's answers: she is going to have a baby.

He had already seen little girls naked, but had never appeared to notice any sexual difference between them. At this moment, he sees a little girl who is having her nappy changed and looks at her attentively without saying a word. Four days later, Gustave becomes unbearable and revolting. Four days after that, he dreams this anxiety dream: the folding ironing board got into his bed to pinch him, to hurt him. Nightmares, screams. His mother arrived. Still distressed, Gustave tells her his dream:

- The ironing board? asks his surprised mother.
- Yes, it really was, but not the same, maybe it was as tall as you, maybe as tall as Daddy. (He cannot explain.)

Mummy reassures him, showing him the ironing board, which is a "thing", it cannot do anything on its own, and Mummy says that she will always protect him. In short, "it is spoken about" for an hour that very night and Gustave falls asleep. The next day, Mummy asks him if he remembers his dream. Yes, and they speak about it again for a long time, Mummy says that she will never allow anyone to hurt him. Gustave's good behaviour is restored, and he becomes as nice as he was before.

A few weeks later, Gustave begins to scratch himself all over; at first, the mother thinks it might be a skin disease, but there is no sign of one. She nevertheless puts some soothing powder on him, but nothing seems to work, Gustave scratches himself more and more, even sometimes breaking the skin. But surprisingly, he scratches himself everywhere except the genital area. His surprised mother points out to him that he is not actually scratching everywhere. Maybe somebody told him not to play with his "winkle"? Yes, says Gustave, he was scratching himself there too, but the maid got cross with him one day and said that if he touched his "winkle" he would be peeing all the time, and Gustave does not want this as he would have to wear nappies like the little girl. Mummy speaks to Gustave about all this, she says she knows better than the maid, that there is no danger, and she adds:

– "It is *your* "winkle" and you can do whatever you like with it, it belongs to you."

This explanation got right to the origin of the obsessional scratching, because it disappeared in a few days (and masturbation did not then become more evident).

Furthermore, the day after this talk with Mummy, as his grandmother, seeing Gustave scratch his face, was telling him off and ordering him to stop, Gustave said to her:

– "Granny, this is *my* face and I can do whatever I like with it."

Scratching his skin after the threats made by the maid was due to the diffusion of the libidinal tension originally located in the phallic zone to the entire cutaneous surface.

Some time later, Gustave became fearful of everything, shy. He told his mother that he kept on having the same dream: he sees a dangerous man, who looks nasty and who has a large spade. "A bit like mine, says Gustave, but much bigger." The man does not do anything, but he could hurt him with this large spade, he is strong. Gustave will never be able to carry a spade as big as that.

– But, of course you will, says Mummy, when you are grown up. All men are little boys before becoming big. Then Gustave detailed all the extremities of his body: nose, fingers, hands, feet (except for his penis), comparing himself to his mother, and adding: "Daddy's is even bigger." Mummy affirms that Gustave's will grow too, and that later on he will be the same as Daddy, "even your winkle", adds Mummy.
– But there are some people who do not have one any more, it has fallen off.
– Do you think so? Is this true? Who did it happen to?
– I saw a little girl, she didn't have her "winkle" any more.
– But of course, says Mummy, girls have never had one, and when they grow up they will never have one. Mummy does not have one, women don't have a "winkle", girls and boys are not made in the same way, and because of this Daddies and Mummies are different. Gustave thinks, and says:
– Eyes are too sunken so they can't be pulled out, but feet and hands, if one pulled hard, they could fall off, couldn't they?
– But of course not, says Mummy, the body is very sturdy, it is not possible for such things to happen.
– Pull on them, to see, very hard. (And he wants his Mummy to pull hard on his fingers, on his hands, on his feet.)
– There you see, says Mummy.
– But my "winkle"?
– It's the same, replies Mummy.
– But if it was a nasty man, very strong?
– Nobody could. It's attached too strongly. It could never come off. And then Daddy and Mummy are here so a nasty man could not get near you.

Thus we see that Gustave, having noticed the absence of the penis in the girl, explains it through a loss. He associates his genital organ with his extremities, the small size of which seems to preoccupy him, and he reports his inferiority feelings towards strong men like Daddy and even towards women. The fear of sexual mutilation is sustained by mistaken interpretations. His ambition of becoming strong clashes with his true inferiority as a child. The resentment which he feels awakens his vengeful aggression, and he projects his feelings onto a "strong and wicked" man, substitute for the father, hence the anxiety of the dream. In the conscious, the symptom appears: shyness, pusillanimity, and a "girlish" attitude. We can see, in the raw, how primary anxiety and the nascent castration complex begin, which in some cases affect the entire development of a boy.

The girl, who (according to his view) possesses a tiny hidden phallus, is envied, she does not risk anything. (The eyes are too sunken to be pulled out.)

The object relation towards the mother is played in the passive mode. This is what is translated by the symbolic game of making Mummy pull on all his extremities. Clearly, he would love it if Mummy also played with his "winkle", which would be equal to a successful passive seduction.

The advantage of such an emotional attitude towards the mother, when it is encouraged by her, is that the boy remains loved by his mother without having the need to enter into rivalry with his father; on the contrary, he also manages to seduce Daddy. (It is not rare to hear mothers say of their son with pride: "He is as good as gold, he does not give me any more trouble than a girl", or for them to forbid their sons to play roughly at risky boys' games for "fear that he would hurt himself".) This passive pregenital attitude, if it is prolonged, gets in the way of the full development of a normal Oedipus complex, which at this point is just beginning.

Just another word on young Gustave which will prove that the symptom really has a propitiatory function, and which will confirm the interpretation that we gave of his passive feminine behaviour which, of course, had as its aim the magical suppression of the threat of sexual mutilation.

Some time after the previous incidents, Gustave started being terribly afraid of the threat of war that he was hearing about. Indeed, Gustave's family is in Austria and there is the threat of the *Anschluss*, and the atmosphere of war, the troops, and so on. He is afraid of the war, "he might die". His mother explains to him that he is Swiss and that he has nothing to fear. Simultaneously, Gustave began coughing all the time, but the doctor who examined him could find no cause for the cough; one day, they spoke about going to the cinema and Mummy said: "Yes, we can go when you have stopped coughing". Straight away, Gustave was no longer to be heard coughing. Mummy took him to the cinema. But a constant sniffle developed after a few days, despite Gustave not having a cold, and led his mother to say: "But don't sniffle like that", to which Gustave replied:

– If I don't cough, I have to sniffle.
– Why is that? The doctor said that you were not ill.
– But I have to do something, you understand, so that I can stay in Switzerland forever.

Sebastian (aged ten)

Brought by his mother from a neighbourhood close to Paris. Very nervous child, impossible to discipline, a liar, a bully. He is not learning anything at school, the teacher can't bear him any longer. We administer a test (5th October).

12 October:

The result of the Binet-Simon test (Miss Achard) gives the following results: a mental age of eight years and six months (probably very disturbed). During the test, the child appeared very pleased with himself, unstable, answering without thinking, convinced that he is right, adjusting badly to a succession of different activities. The mother complains that the week has been bad, temper tantrums, pathological lies.

He got up one morning at 5 a.m. to cut the buttons off his trousers (he was caught in the act, but nothing was said to him and he went back to bed). Several hours later, he said that somebody else had done it when he was at school. He regularly cuts the buttons off his trousers, and he always says that a friend did it. The mother is wondering whether he is lying or if he is mad. One could have killed him without him admitting to anything.

I quite quickly have a good rapport with the mother, who gives me the details of her grievances, the unbearable atmosphere that Sebastian creates at home, his tempers when he breaks everything. Nothing daunts him. The mother cannot work regularly (she is a cleaner), because Sebastian cannot be kept at school, and no one can stand him. He is always late for school. He does not do his schoolwork, despite being reminded by his mother, who finally helps him to do it or does it herself.

During our conversation, the child is anxious and obstinate, he does not answer any questions and shrugs his shoulders when his mother speaks.

The mother appears gentle but not very intelligent. She says that the child in general obeys his father more than her. The father is a nurse in a neighbouring locality and only comes home once a week. He earns little money and the mother really could do with the freedom to work. She asks us, in short, on the advice of the schoolteacher, the address of a specialised boarding school which caters for difficult children.

We ask the mother to change her behaviour towards Sebastian, for the coming week, in only one way: not to tell him more than once to get up to go to school. If he doesn't get up, it doesn't matter. She must promise not to show any interest in the matter. Sebastian is old enough to know that school is not a threat, and if he prefers to feel guilty, it is his problem, he will not know more or less for having missed school and he will have learned that he is free to learn or fall behind the others.

We explain to the mother that if Sebastian is unpleasant, it is because he prefers it that way. He is free. The doctors are not there to scold him but to understand. We will try to help him, if possible. If not, it can't be helped, and we will give her addresses of boarding schools for difficult children, where of course he will be fine, but it is a pity to be definitively classified as a difficult child when one's heart is good.

The mother promises to take our advice, a bit worried about the consequences. We tell her that even if he doesn't go to school at all this week, she will have to remain indifferent, but to bring back the child in eight days.

During the course of the conversation with his mother, Sebastian's attitude had changed and he was listening.

He and I stayed alone together for a time. General conversation on his lateness for school and his "babyish" behaviour in life. Maybe mother bores him when she thinks she is doing the right thing and it annoys him. Now then, at ten years old, one is big enough to know whether one wants to learn or not. If one does not, what is the point of turning the house upside down?

– Yes, I will be good, he replied, I will be good, it is not nice to be like that, I'll be nice (this said with an agitated delivery, with a critical and self-important air).

19 October:

Sebastian went to school every day, his behaviour was good at home during the week until yesterday, the mother tells us. Yesterday, a terrible tantrum at lunchtime, Sebastian refused to come and sit at table and escaped into the countryside.

On my own with Sebastian. A general rambling conversation starts. I praise him for his efforts until yesterday. *"But what happened yesterday?"*

– Yes, it's not nice, it's not nice, I won't do it again. Oh no. I know perfectly well that it's not nice, etc … .
  I ask him:
– When do you see Daddy?
– Thursdays.

Then, they spend the whole day together gardening. Daddy is nice. He showed Daddy his exercise book. It was better.

His delivery is still agitated, anxious, with a condescending tone, as if he were speaking with the voice of a moralising adult.

– Does he dream, does he sleep well?

Anxiety dreams, nightmares. He always has them. He cries and this wakes Mummy up, and even awake he is scared. Flames, burned-out planes, burglars.

About school, Sebastian begins "telling tales", as if he were outraged by the behaviour of others "who do terrible, dirty things".

– It's not right! They lock themselves in the toilets so that no one can see them.

I ask:

– On their own?
– Yes—(*sic!*) Isn't it disgusting! (and with a wealth of detail, he describes masturbatory activities with bits of cloth, "because they don't do it without anything!", descriptions aimed at making me pass judgement on such scoundrels).
– Worst of all, I tell Mummy about it, she tells me that they are filthy beasts, and that I must never do anything like that. But, of course, I am not dirty. Oh, what does it look like, and the worst of it is that you can see it on their face afterwards.

I listened to him (anyway his agitated delivery didn't let me get a word in) and at the same time, I was thinking about the trouser buttons, which I had never spoken to him about. His mother had told Dr Pichon, but not myself. Without any doubt, Sebastian did not think that I knew about them.

As it seemed to me that his breath smelled slightly of acetone, I asked for a urine sample to test for diabetes; the nurse happened to be free, and I entrusted Sebastian to her and told him to come back afterwards.

The test was done showing no acetone present, but an interesting scene took place. When it came to urinating in a glass, there was despair and tears. His mother came running. Sebastian hid his head in her skirts, prostrated, and he was still there when the nurse came to tell me the result. He did not want to come back with me. His mother smiled whilst saying:

– See, he is ashamed to do it in a glass, he is not used to it.

I took Sebastian by the hand again.

– Come, don't be afraid, you see Mummy thinks that you are ashamed because you did it in a glass, but there is nothing to be ashamed about. And also, you were not ashamed; when one is ashamed, one does not kick up such a row, and if you were ashamed, you would not be afraid of coming back to see me as I asked. You were not ashamed, you were scared. Maybe a bit of what you told me about the others earlier on, it is you who does it, maybe even all of it. Perhaps you believed that it would show in your pee?

Then, distraught with tears and sobbing, Sebastian owns up and tells me that I am right. I let him cry, and then we speak of this masturbation, which I call "doing it" using his own words. I tell him that he is not the only one, many little boys are unhappy about it. I reassure him about his fear of sexual mutilation, the threats of illness, imbecility, madness, and prison.

I tell him that it cannot be much fun when one is afraid of so many things, therefore it must mean that he really wants to do it if he is willing to risk so many dangers despite his fear. And of course, none of the stories he has been told ever happen. Simply one's mind is filled with guilt.

I ask him if maybe he is itching there? Does he know how to wash himself? "No, he never touches it" (*sic*: this explains the bits of cloth).

Then I tell him that he must wash there as everywhere else and I explain how to do it. On this occasion, as he is embarrassed, I tell him: "But I am like a Mummy, a Mummy Doctor." He has well-developed genital organs for his age, and the end of the penis is irritated.

I tell him:

- And there's Mummy who still believes that you are a baby! But you are a big boy and I am sure you know many things which would surprise your Mummy.
- You won't tell her what I told you.
- Of course not, it's your business and yours only. These are personal things. Everybody knows them, but you don't talk about them. If your mother has told you all the stories you told me earlier on, maybe she believes that it will make you ill.
- Yes, there is an idiot in the village.
- Well then, idiots "do it" all the time because they are idiots, but they are not idiots because they "do it". I am a doctor and I know this better than your mother. All boys, all men do it sometimes, but not all the time. And then, even if it was bad, it would be better to admit one's doing bad things, even if one is not proud of them, rather than inventing stories blaming others.

And I add:

- I am not even saying that you are lying. It looks like it, but as soon as you start to tell stories, then you start believing them, don't you?
- Yes, and then it is as if it was not me.
- Yes, but it is you nevertheless. Are your schoolmates doing it as well?
- Oh no. Oh maybe … .
- Why maybe?
- I don't know, I haven't seen them. But sometimes they speak about things … and I don't listen to them, I don't want to listen, it's not nice.
- What things?
- Well, like … babies … married people.
- But it is not ugly. One says that it is not nice to little children, but when one grows up, everything is interesting and these things too, naturally. Daddy and Mummy were little once and they grew up.

I let him think about this and I add:

– Do you want me to tell you if what your friends are saying is true?
– Yes, perhaps they don't know.
– What do you believe?
– Oh, I think that they are right, I agree with them.
– What do they say?

There followed a vague description of sexual intercourse. The man puts something into the woman. I ask him to be more specific. There is a notion of the absence of a phallus in the woman, but not of another organ apart from the intestine. I explain the physical attributes of a woman.

I say:

– It is the man who puts the seed in the woman, and sometimes the seed starts to grow in the woman's womb. It is natural and it does not hurt her. The baby grows in nine months and then it's the birth: how?
– Some of them say through her side, and even worse, one of them says it's from lower down. But it is an operation, "one" goes to hospital and "one" (sic) is lying down.
– Yes, it is lower down. You have seen how a flower opens, well it's the same thing for the mother. And it is natural. She is in a bit of pain, so she says to herself "well, he is about to be born", and she goes to hospital so that everything can be very clean, because a baby is born very little and he can do nothing except cry and the mother is sometimes very tired. It is easier to be in a hospital where everything is done for her and the baby. And then soon there is milk, which is made all on its own in the mother's breast and the baby only needs to suck. And the Daddy and the Mummy are happy because the baby belongs to both of them and he looks like them.

Sebastian thinks for a while and then says:

– And if Mummy knew what we have been talking about.
– Well, she would be surprised because she believes that you do not yet know how she became your mother, but she would be proud to know you have grown up.
– Yes, but her?
– Her what?

– Does she know all that? … Oh, I am stupid, of course because I was born myself (fantasy of the taboo mother).

After this discussion, I tell him: "So you see that you have to work well to pass your certificate and learn a trade so that you can earn money and become like Daddy."

And as I knew the scenes he made every evening about his home-work, I told him to hurry up and do it as quickly as possible on return from school so that he is free to go and play all evening.

Taking him back (calm and smiling) to his mother, I tell her:

"He is a big boy and soon you will be proud of him."

I ask her for a last effort for this week: to leave his homework to him. He will do it or not. That is his business. She can check the exercise book once a week, the day it is marked, but she must leave Sebastian to the complete daily control of the schoolmaster.

26 October:

Sebastian is *transformed*. His mother tells us that she does not recognise him. We have changed him for her. She is even more surprised by the change at night, because he was always talking and crying in his night-mares every night, without even waking up. He now sleeps peacefully. He has not made her cross this week.

She followed my advice about his homework, and Daddy checked it on Thursday. He got 10 for behaviour. She is so happy that she would not have brought him back given the distance they live from Paris, but Sebastian insisted he was brought back so that this good news could be brought to me. Now that he is nice, could he be put into a boarding school so that she can go out cleaning?

I ask to speak to Sebastian.

He is calm, speaks slowly or, rather, normally, in a simple and natu-ral tone. He tells me what his mother has already told me. The marks he got for schoolwork and lessons: 7 and 8. The schoolmaster says that there is a marked improvement, and that he had never had 10 for behaviour before. He is doing his schoolwork on his own, he feared that he wouldn't manage, but Mum told him: "I won't ask you to show it to me and I won't speak to you about it, but if you need my help, you can ask me." And he adds: "But I didn't need it."

He speaks to me about his father, about his bicycle, which he rides. I am surprised (because he is small) and ask him how tall his father is. "Oh, he is up to your shoulders, a lot smaller than you. Mummy is also much taller than him." And after a silence: "I would very much like to be taller than him."

Whilst I am taking a few notes on his session, Sebastian draws silently. Previously, he chattered incessantly. His drawings: a beautiful *Normandy* (a liner) with flags, drawn quite childishly, and some decorated capital letters. These are the initials of the first names of his uncles, his mother's brothers, of whom he speaks with admiration. "They are tall", he would like to look like them, "and they have good jobs". Now the father had been unemployed for two years before finding this low-paid job as a nurse in a hospice. The mother says that he is "not strong". (In fact, he must be on the borderline of dwarfism.) Sebastian says that he would like to do the same jobs as his uncles. We speak about the boarding school and he agrees to the idea.

2 November:

He is still doing very well. The mother says that he has definitely changed. He is no longer anxious, does not get cross. He is good but not too good. He plays, he is happy, and no longer has either nightmares or nocturnal terrors. At school, he is unrecognisable. The schoolteacher is pleased with him.

19 January:

Sebastian writes to give me his news. "I am good with Mummy and Daddy, I work a little better in class, and I won some stars. I think about you."

30 March:

We write to the mother to find out if she has sent Sebastian to one of the recommended boarding schools and to know how he is doing. She replies that she has kept him at home, because he has become so easy. She can work locally and leave the house because he is good on his own at home. She is very happy with him on all fronts.

Conclusion

It was, as we had thought, a castration anxiety case. There was a touching clarity to the symbolism of the trouser buttons. Excellent prognosis.

The self-satisfied behaviour, being the moraliser, while his pathological lying projected his faults onto others—what did all this signify?

Sebastian projects responsibility onto others and really manages to believe them guilty. His superego speaks like Mummy and his slanderous stories allows the mother to go even further ("filthy scoundrels") but in the end, it is Sebastian who accumulates guilt feelings, which added to his castration anxiety, lead him to seek appeasement, which he finds through the punishment provoked by ridiculous scenes of childish disobedience and systematic negativity.

The exceptionally rapid resolution of this case is certainly due to the fact that Sebastian interpreted the urine test wrongly, which happened, by chance, after his lying narrative and his words "It can be seen on their faces".

Bernard (aged eight and a half)

The child is brought by his grandmother, who was entrusted by the parents to take him to the hospital for continuous enuresis which only stopped for a month and a half when he was six years old during a stay in the countryside. However, she has brought him largely because of the recent onset, initially episodic but now daily, of double incontinence during the day. These problems do not respond to punishment.

The grandmother says of Bernard that he is "like all children, stubborn, violent if his brother is annoying him, scatterbrained". She says that the parents are quick to react and that Bernard is slapped "more often than he should be because he annoys everyone, he does not pay attention to anything, but it is not serious, he is well liked". As far as school is concerned, the grandmother cannot give us any information. Bernard says that he is twenty-seventh out of forty-five.

He was with a wet nurse from twelve days old until he was four. He has a brother aged four, René. The parents took Bernard back in order to send René to the wet nurse, but they only left René for two years.

The physical examination yields absolutely nothing. The child is chubby, babyish-looking; seated, he seems slumped in his chair; expressionless; he still has a milk tooth.

On my own with Bernard, I cannot get anything out of him except for a drawing, which he does for me, very ashamed of not knowing how to draw. It represents a fellow driving a lorry (his father is a lorry driver).

In short, very unstable child, scatterbrained, refusing to make any effort, not aggressive in himself, but putting up considerable inert resistance.

Given the fact that the enuresis stopped when he was six years old during a stay in the countryside without his parents, at a time when the little brother was not with them either, and that it restarted immediately on his return, I think that the jealousy towards his little brother plays a part. Also, Bernard is only violent with his brother when he is annoying him.

Then I talk about other children like Bernard who are jealous of their brother, I explain that in his household, there is a reason to be jealous, because he had himself been deprived of his parents for so long, and I say that envy may not be a very pretty feeling, but that it exists and that perhaps sometimes he would truly like to hurt René. I add that thinking and acting are not the same thing, it is better to know that one is envious and to try to find a way to make the other envious from a position from which one cannot be dislodged. For him, who is tall, for example, it could be by becoming a strong fellow, "a tough nut", a good pupil; then Daddy and Mummy would be proud, he would make them take notice: "Our eldest, here, our eldest there". It will not happen immediately, but I will be here to help him, and, whilst waiting for the family to notice, I will bring him back a reward next week if he has worked well. As far as what he does in his pants goes, I don't think that it is important, or rather that it does make him look like a baby and it doesn't smell nice, but if he enjoys it and if there is nothing more enjoyable than that, I won't stop him from doing it (8 March).

22 March:

The child refused to come last Wednesday because he had an end-of-term test, the parents did not object because he had already made progress, but *it is mainly since the* day of the test that the biggest progress has been made. As far as the symptom which interests them, the enuresis, he wet himself only once, and there was a small discharge in his pants, also only once, during the day.

The grandmother tells me that he has changed a little, he is less quiet and more offhand than before with his brother. René has been obnoxious with his big brother, especially for the last eight days. He takes his exercise books, hides them, and won't let him work in peace. In order to have some peace, the mother backs the little one, "then, everybody is shouting". Before, Bernard would be slapped and give in.

Bernard is very happy to tell me that he was seventeenth out of forty-five; I encourage him and show him that his little brother is jealous of him going to school. If Bernard is a little bit envious of René because mother spoils him more, he probably is right, but Grandma seems to prefer him to his little brother (Bernard confirms this for me) and it is a compensation, and then René, try as he might, will never be the eldest and will always be four years behind him, if Bernard doesn't let himself fall behind in school. He will begin his apprenticeship four years before René and will earn money four years before him.

29 March:

Bernard stopped being doubly incontinent during the day and at night. He is making good progress, says the grandmother, and the schoolmaster has told his father he no longer has any need to scold him, whilst in the past he was the one who was the most told off. I ask to see the father.

19 April:

Bernard comes with his father, a tall and gentle man, who we will later learn is only Bernard's adoptive father. The father is less indulgent towards Bernard, though he is very fond of him, than towards René, who is his son. He tells me that he is happy about the change in Bernard and about the fact that he is now clean. He also sees that his personality is changing. According to the grandmother, I had spoken of his personality and said that everything was linked. This surprised them, but the father tells me that he'd noticed since Bernard had changed that he was not really more capable than his little brother and that he was only just beginning to be. He describes Bernard's instability: his mother asks him to help clear the table, Bernard obeys but then afterwards, he starts touching everything and taking everything out of the cupboard.

His mother slaps him and tells him to do it again and Bernard cries. Often he forgets the shopping that he is sent to do.

I remain on my own with Bernard and he tells me that what is annoying him now is that his little brother is so scared at night that he does not want to sleep in Daddy and Mummy's room but wants to come and sleep in Bernard's bed.

– I don't sleep well, and sometimes I have bad dreams.

After a moment, Bernard adds:

– René has bad habits because he is nervy, maybe you could cure him of his nerves.

I ask:

– What do you think about his bad habits?
– Oh, Mummy says that he will become ill, she hits him, and tells him that the doctor will cut it off.

I reply:

– Well, this is not true, tell René. These are bogeyman stories and you also know that it is not true. Babies are told these stories to scare them. This is why René is nervy, bring him with you next time.
– One can clearly see that Bernard, through the stories about his brother, was talking to me about his own masturbation, which was provoking the anxiety dreams.

Conclusion

This treatment is still ongoing, but we thought that it would be of interest because of its very simplicity: a return to the passive anal stage. The re-estimation of his abilities (for example, his feelings of inferiority about his drawing) allowed the expression of envy, of ambition, of aggression, and allowed Bernard to move to the active anal stage. But the instability and the anxiety dreams indicate the castration complex, confirmed by the preoccupation with masturbation.

Patrice (aged ten)

Brought to a medical consultation because he is slow and very anxious. He moves ceaselessly, his teacher complains about him. At table, he eats very slowly. Dramas in the morning about getting up. So-called ritual scenes daily, supposedly because he has not finished his prayers. Sometimes obsessional worries at bedtime or about his clothes—other times, disorder, dirtiness, he "makes a mess everywhere".

As far as school is concerned, he is in the first year at the lycée, good at drawing, reciting, reading, very bad at spelling, mediocre at arithmetic. Bad marks for class work, irregular marks for homework, very bad marks for effort and behaviour. No problem as far as friends are concerned. Patrice is an only child.

With his father there are continual fights. The father is very anxious, says the mother, and cannot stand the child (?). The parents are constantly arguing about him.

In the course of all these family quarrels, Patrice appears cocky and impertinent, triumphant when he scores points, so much so that the mother, enlisted in the argument between father and son so as to defend the child, starts to scold him because he is taking advantage of the situation. And it is she "who gets it" as she puts it. In brief, perpetual scenes, a family atmosphere in turmoil about "nothing": for example, if Patrice eats bread or not with his meat, if he sits sideways on an armchair, if he fiddles about on his chair, and so on.

It seems clear that Patrice, an only son, exploits the tense situation of the parental couple, which is not of his making. It is therefore impossible for him to arrive at the Oedipus complex without inordinate feelings of guilt which are at the service of the castration complex and provoke self punishing defeat.

The therapeutic target to aim for is to dissolve the triangle by allowing Patrice real triumphs, derived from the Oedipal situation, but played out on substitute Oedipal objects, that is to say, outside his family.

But the mother works, and says that she won't be able to come back. Therefore one has to act quickly. (At the end of our conversation, she agrees that Patrice can come back on his own, if necessary.)

Without doubting what the mother has told us about the father in a rather passionate tone of voice, we only take into account what she said about her behaviour towards Patrice. "She will have to trust us, Patrice does not need medicine or a change of scenery."

Very simple advice of a general order follows, given in the presence of the child and aiming at bringing the family confrontations back down to their true proportions. We try to play down the role that the mother believes she has to play. Patrice is big enough to have quarrels with his father without her intervention, we tell her. He does not need to be defended. And to eat slowly, to eat bread or not, strictly speaking from Patrice's point of view does not matter. If Patrice has not finished his lunch at the same time as everybody else, he can take his plate with him, and finish it in a corner and then bring it back on his own to the kitchen. If he does not want to eat all that is on his plate, he can leave it, it is not putting anybody out. The day he feels hungry is the day he will eat more. Anyway, it would be better if he helped himself instead of being served. Then he will take what he needs depending on his appetite.

This common sense advice seems to dumbfound the mother as much as the child. This dispassionate conversation initiates the child's trans-ference and triggers this question from the mother:

– But then, what am I supposed to do? If you think it is that easy.

I know, I tell her, but from a distance one can see things impersonally. Do not worry and if you feel able to trust me, promise me one thing only for this week: in the morning you will tell Patrice the time once only and then you will not pay attention to anything else! Whether he goes to school or not, leaves late or without lunch, without washing himself, must not concern you. If he is put in detention, that's too bad for him, and if he manages not to be punished at school, good for him. It may not go without a hitch, it will be painful for him and for you. But stick to your guns, I am only asking you to do this for eight days. And if you really want to help me, don't be mean to him. If he has not man-aged to get up in time, he has punished himself, do not be triumphant. On the contrary, console him and encourage him for tomorrow.

Patrice remains on his own with me. A very good rapport establishes itself. He speaks to me of this and that and tells me of a recent inci-dent, with a triumphant air at the beginning and that of a victim at the end. It was about the purchase by his mother of a dinner set that he chose and advised on. His father was furious and he "scolded him and slapped him".

I go through his story with him again and show him what must have happened: he was flattered that Mummy bought what he found beautiful—which she did because her taste probably coincided with that of Patrice. But Patrice wanted to see a personal victory in this and must have bragged about it to tease his father, to "cock a snook" at him. Naturally, father, who is clever, understood his disrespectful intention. Patrice was looking for a slap and got it. In truth, Patrice knew very well that Mummy did not buy this dinner set to flatter him. He used an occasion, which presented itself to have a fight with his father and then after that adopted the air of the poor victim. Patrice is a little annoyed at this but he admits that what I say is true.

Then I explain to him that he is jealous of Mummy and that he is unhappy. He wants to show off, lie to himself, to tell himself that Mummy only loves him and to triumph over his father. But there is nothing to be done, his father matters as well. That is the way it is. His parents did not need him to be there to survive whilst he could not do without them. This is why instead of being happy when he wins a victory of being close to Mummy, it is as if he was doing something bad and he cannot benefit from it. He seeks punishment (7 February).

14 February:

A week after the first conversation, Patrice comes back on his own and brings me a letter from his mother in which she tells me that she is very happy with Patrice. She had started to despair during the first two days, which followed our conversation. He had never been so awful. Despite everything, she kept the promise she had made us about the morning and Patrice now gets up on his own and ahead of time too. For which, surprised and delighted, she thanks me.

Patrice has blossomed and is calm whilst telling me the content of the letter, which he is aware of.

He tells me that the situation was very bad with his father for the first three days. There were scenes at every meal because of his slowness and because he eats either the bread on its own and forgets about the dish or the dish, forgetting about the bread. Daddy got cross and Mummy said nothing. But for the last four days, there have been no incidents at the table, because—without meaning to—he does not forget and now eats his bread and the dish together; and he is the first to be surprised about this.

He has got 6, 7, 8, or 9, for his schoolwork, then yesterday ... 3! He is heartbroken because it brings down his average. He knew his work very well, he could have got 10. The question was about the tributaries of the River Loire and he recited those of the River Seine perfectly, and it is because of this that instead of getting 0, he got 3. He wants to raise his average. I encourage him and tell him that it is not that terrible; I explain the *psychological aspect* of this forgetfulness, *as if he wasn't allowed to get*

10. Patrice adds that he was afraid the teacher would be angry but he had said nothing. Three days ago, the teacher, noticing the improvement in his work, had said that: "Patrice was going up in his estimation", and yesterday, shortly after the incident in the geography test, as Patrice was the first to understand an oral maths problem, the teacher said "Patrice is going into the top set". Patrice is very proud, and I tell him the great pleasure this is giving me as well as his mother.

He also tells me that he hit a nasty boy who was bullying him all the time, and who, for a long time, had been showing off in front of everybody that he was stronger than him. Patrice had always avoided approaching him because the others were scared of him. He had already "beaten up" some of them. "But what the heck, this time I told myself "let's see" and he was the one who fell down. He was furious and annoyed and everybody was pleased. So you see, I thought that this boy could get me."

We can see how the ambivalence towards the father was displaced onto the external world. The passive homosexual component was displaced onto the master (who he is proud of seducing) and the aggressive component finds a displacement onto a "nasty big boy" which serves as substitute for the Oedipal object.

At the same time, the family situation is becoming easier. Patrice can be happy about pleasing Mummy, the libidinal energy has been displaced from the Oedipal rivalry towards the struggle for life on the level of reality: scholarly and other successes not only permitted but encouraged. And we see how at first castration anxiety is still in play, triggering self-punishing failures (the bad mark through absent mindedness) inflicted by the superego.

This case, with a complicated medical picture, was in fact very simple. A conversation with the mother in front of the child and two meetings with him on his own modified the symptoms.

But we must not delude ourselves. Our therapy has not cured Patrice. It has only allowed him to become aware of his place in life from a new point of view. It is the successful displacement, with satisfaction at stake, which allowed the child's unconscious to renounce his symptoms. The three first days, (worse than ever) showed the unconscious resistance of Patrice. Happily for the child, the mother kept the promise she had made us. Her silence, instead of her usual intervention during the quarrels of the first few days at table, allowed the castration complex to *"mature"* the Oedipus complex. The "charm", in the magical sense of the word, which kept the child in a sadomasochistic position in relation to his father, had been broken, and an enormous libidinal release took place, which could immediately be used to invest in potential sublimation. The role of the psychotherapist was only that of a catalyst.

Conclusion

Similar cases are numerous. One could even say that Patrice is more or less typical of the gifted only child in whom the castration complex is forced to be very violent, because the Oedipal situation has to be played out of necessity on the father, without the possibility of displacement.

The *prognosis* is good, but some work remains to be done, which his success at school should allow Patrice to do, we hope: it is the lessening of the severity of the superego.

Roland (aged eight)

Unstable child, brought by his mother on the advice of the Headmaster, with enuresis and anxiety at home and at school.

There are three other children, Jacqueline, five, Lucienne, four, Daniel, one year old, and the mother is pregnant. Between Roland and Jacqueline, a spontaneous miscarriage at four and a half months.

Roland was breast-fed until he was a year old, he has never been away from his parents. He was clean at two and a half years old and still remained clean after Jacqueline's birth, until the time when the mother, pregnant with Lucienne, sent Roland to sleep every evening close by at his grandmother's house

This is where he started to wet the bed almost immediately, and he has not stopped in spite of all the promises of presents or punishment.

Roland is very jealous of his sisters and mean and very teasing with them. He is teasing but affectionate with his brother Daniel, who is one year old. The personality problems—nastiness, indiscipline, instability, capriciousness, temper tantrums—mainly appeared during the last year. "Now we have to shout at him all the time", says the mother. I underline the coincidence: the little brother is a year old. Without any doubt, in his eyes, the birth of this boy has dislodged him from his mother's heart. He suffered less, as long as there were only girls.

At the beginning of the conversation with his mother, Roland was looking at us with a boastful and stubborn look. He had refused to draw and to sit down. At the end of the conversation, he is ashamed and sad and listens to what we are talking about.

I keep Roland on his own and speak to him about how sad it is for the eldest child who has had his mother to himself for three years to see others come along. Roland sheds big tears without saying anything. To my request "Do you want to be cured of wetting the bed?", he replies: "No I couldn't care less", and he appears sincere, "it's what Mummy wants".

I do not insist, feeling that the mother is "blown away" for the moment. I glorify the role and potential of being "the eldest" in a family. For Daniel, he is like a giant who knows everything. Later on, he will be able to work like a man.

Roland then talks to me about his uncle who works on the railway, and he wants to be like him. His father is a deliveryman. "He is strict", but from Roland's tone of voice, I feel that he loves him, and admires his strictness. Then I say to him that if he became a really big boy, his father would be proud of him. This seems to touch him.

We touch upon the hygiene of genital cleanliness. Roland acknowledges that he almost never washes and when he does it is only his face. His penis often itches especially at night. I ask him if he scratches himself even when it is not itchy. He whispers "yes" and hangs his head. I ask who told him not to do this, which had made him so ashamed. "It is grandma, she said that she would tell Daddy". (Observe that the enuresis started as soon as Roland slept at her house).

I minimise the importance of all this, insisting on daily cleanliness and especially more interesting things: work and the advantages of being the eldest (30 November).

21 December:

The mother only came back with Roland three weeks later. Eight days ago, Daniel was so ill (pneumonia) that she had to take him to hospital. His life was in danger. Now he has recovered.

Roland had been much less incontinent the first week after our conversation, but the incontinence started again in earnest during the second week.

During these same eight days (since Daniel became ill), he had played truant. At school, the teacher says that Roland would do whatever was asked of him if he could have individual attention.

And the mother asks me to get rid of him for her, because he is too much like hard work, and could I send him to a sanatorium or to the countryside (a number of parents come to ask the same thing for the same reason!).

I explain to the mother that in putting distance between herself and Roland she will make him believe that she loves him less than the others and it is what he already believes. He is already very unhappy about this and this is why he avenges himself on the others and is unbearable. And in front of the mother I speak of her pregnancy (not hiding it).

With Roland on his own, I continue to talk about this. He tells me, looking shameful, that he knew, but he pretended not to know, because they thought that he could not understand. I reply that one must not be ashamed of being intelligent, quite the contrary. I also tell him that he himself was in his mother's tummy for a long time before he was born, and after that she fed him her milk like all the others and when he was ill Mummy had also just looked after him, as she had Daniel last week.

He tells me that during the eight days in which he played truant, he ran some errands for a man who is a plumber. He wanted to give him four cents, but Roland refused. During the last few days, he would get empty crates in the market, and bring them back to Mummy on his back for the fire so that she could save on bundles of firewood (and therefore he would be forgiven for running away and share his guilt with his mother as well as playing at being "grown up"). I listen without answering and do not scold him at all for having played truant.

28 December:

He only wetted his bed twice during the two nights which he spent at his parents. The other nights, at his grandmother's, who threatens him with punishments, there was no enuresis, but nightmares and terror on waking.

To his mother, he says that he cannot remember his dreams, but he relates them to me. Someone wants to cut his head off. A crocodile swallows his hand and forearm. He has been locked up in a prison and he escapes with his friend. He often dreams of a man who cuts his head off.

At night in the prison dream, first of all he had been playing with his friend and a car. They had attached a gun to the car and were playing at killing the cat by pulling its tail. "It hurt him, but we were stopping him from running away and it was funny, wasn't it?" I replied "Certainly!"

10 January:

The mother tells me that he only wet the bed once and only slightly; it woke him up. It was after a particularly good day where he had played with trains and Lotto with Daddy. Roland looks better, he does not dream any more. He sleeps and eats well. He is getting nicer and nicer to his brother whom he no longer teases. With his sisters, there are no longer the same quarrels.

On his own with me, Roland starts to chatter freely. He is happy to no longer have bad dreams, which made him afraid of falling asleep. He tells me loads of stories in which he is the hero. He is going to the hairdresser on his own. He helps Daddy carry crates weighing 100 kgs! Mummy needs him. At home, they need a boy who helps with everything, fetching wood, carrying his little brother, and so on! He tells me that he will give all his toys to his little brother when he grows up, and "all he has belongs to Daniel too!". "And even … to my sister. You see, she wants to play with my train, so when I am helping Daddy or Mummy do things, I don't mind, I told her that she can play with it then"; at school, in accordance with the mechanism of projection "the teacher has started being nice".

Conclusion

If Patrice was typical of the only child, Roland is typical of the recalcitrant oldest child in a large family.

The symptoms, which aim to give additional work to Mummy, have at least the advantage of obliging her to pay attention to him in the same way she does to the youngest; therefore all coercive means aimed at suppressing the symptoms (the grandmother's threats) only have the effect of provoking anxiety and night terrors.

It was necessary to reconcile Roland with his mother, girls, women, to treat him like a big boy (speaking openly about his mother's pregnancy) and giving him the desire to achieve the respect of grown-ups. In this way, we could enable him to relinquish the infantile position.

The unresolved castration complex is symbolically expressed in the dream about the guillotine, which followed the sadistic games.

The resolution of the castration complex is expressed in the dream where he escapes from prison after having pulled a cat's tail and mainly because in telling his dreams (to myself only) he confided, on the symbolic level, his anxiety about sexual mutilation and because of my attitude to the cat's tale, he saw that I consented to vengeance on the cat (here symbol of the father).

Alain (aged eight and a half)

An only child, never been separated from his parents, intelligent (first words at 10 months), brought by his mother for enuresis. Alain wets his bed at least once a night, sometimes more. During his life, he has only stopped wetting the bed for a fortnight, at the beginning of the summer holidays.

He sleeps on his own. Nothing was found at the medical examination-genital organs normal. The child appears intelligent, is a good pupil at school, third or fourth out of thirty.

The father is a policeman (officer) and is very fearful for the child. He does not want him to play outside in case he will perspire, he cannot bear noise, he is always predicting illness if Alain goes out when it is raining or cold, and if he plays with others, he fears contagious illnesses. The two parents differ about this, the mother would like to get Alain into the cub scouts so that he can see other children (I encourage her).

On Thursdays and Sundays, Alain stays on his own with his parents or with his mother at home according to his father's wish.

On my own with Alain, a good rapport establishes itself, after he held onto his mother for a long time, because he was afraid that in remaining on his own with me "it would be cut off". Mummy had told him. He had been threatened with hospital for a long time. I reassure him and tell him that it has never happened. I tell him such things do not exist anymore than the bogeyman does. I tell him that wetting the bed does not come from masturbation. He replies "I did it when I was little, but I never do it now, because I understand that it is rude." "Yes, I said, it is not nice to put one's fingers up one's nose either, but it is not terrible and it does not make you catch a cold. People do it from time to time, but not in public. When children are bored, the wish to do it is sometimes stronger than they are".

He tells me about Daddy who is strict. "He is in the Police! So he's horrible" (*sic*). Things are difficult altogether with him. "He pulls my hair and slaps my face if I talk too loud. He doesn't want me to play with the electric train, because it's noisy, and it was him who gave it to me". I told him to play with it when father is not at home and to draw or paint when he is (2 November).

9 November:

Alain has not wet the bed once during the week, but he has been more disobedient and unmanageable. The mother is very happy about the result with regard to wetting the bed, but panicked that he has become undisciplined and answers back.

On my own with Alain, I show him the self-punishing function of his problems. He has allowed himself the right to be a real boy, and I am very pleased and congratulate him, but he does not need to get himself punished and scolded like a little baby, because Mummy gets disheartened and loses respect for him.

I advise the mother to enrol him in the cub scouts so that he can fulfil his need to be physically active and noisy and be with other young people, while at the same time asking him to make some effort to please her in return.

At school, he still has excellent results.

16 November:

Cleanliness has continued. The child seems proud of it. Alain is going to cub scouts and is very happy about it.

Conclusion

We can see in this very simple case, the economic role of the symptom: *Enuresis is doubly determined:*

1. Aggressive protest in the face of the threat of sexual mutilation.
2. Substitute, on a regressive sadistic urethral mode, for phallic masturbation.

The enuresis is therefore guilt inducing and brings about the fantasies and the masochistic attitude towards the father.

The assurance by the doctor that he will not be castrated and that it is not forbidden or "horrible" to masturbate—although it is not "nice"—brings about the suppression of the symptom, but the guilt in the face of the paternal superego causes him to provoke new threats of being disowned by the mother.

Becoming consciously aware of this mechanism brings about a calming down of this anxiety and allows Alain to be supported by his mother against his father (this is the significance of the cub scouts) and to grow up normally, which is also his father's wish.

In this case, it looks as if Alain's father is an anxious man and that the choice of his work betrays a violent repression of his aggressive drives which he forbids his only son (his alter ego) whose life he fears for so much.

Didier (aged ten and a half)

The child is brought to the clinic because he is considerably behind at school, and unable to follow the lessons. A good natured, nice child, but listless, he has a fixed inexpressive face. He is in very good general physical condition.

The child was born at 8 months, the midwife said that the afterbirth was as heavy as the child (?) no nasal mucus at birth no enlarged spleen. The mother is a healthy, sprightly, merry, noisy, intelligent, Mediterranean type, who"has only lived for her child" since her husband's death (pulmonary tuberculosis), "due to the war", when Didier was five years old.

An only child, he has always lived with his mother.

Didier has been at school since he was seven. Around eight years old, his schoolwork started flagging. He is at a religious school where being sent to another school is out of the question.

After the first examination, Dr Pichon writes: "one has to pull words out of his mouth to make him say that Paris is the capital of France and England is an island. About who came first out of Charlemagne and Napoleon, the child says the opposite of the truth and does not seem to care much about what is being asked of him and what he is being told."

A Binet-Simon test reveals an above average intelligence for his age and it is remarked: "The problems he presents with are personality problems. They only started after the father's death". In fact, the mother when questioned informs us that the change of personality dates back to the father's death; the child, five and a half at the time, threatened suicide. We decide psychotherapy is appropriate (30 March).

27 April:

The child's face is perfectly immobile, he does not turn his head, has lowered eyes, he is as still as a statue and his voice is as soft as that of a little girl; he only opens his mouth to speak and closes it again immediately. At the beginning, *entirely inattentive*; little by little, as I made him speak about his father, his mother, children at school, one can see that the image of his deceased father is that of a "superman", that his mother does not inspire confidence in him for serious matters, but that he loves her a lot. His mother appears to be understanding.

After having enlightened the child on sexual matters, the birth of babies, boys and girls and so on of which they speak at school in a fantasising way, I advise his mother not to interfere with her child's schoolwork, despite her fears.

4 May:

He is progressing at school. The teacher reported very good effort. (Lets note an anxiety dream: bandits who want to kill him; a pleasant dream: he was at Bretonneau hospital and he was speaking to me.)

11 May:

Making good progress. Better marks, 8–9-9, not yet a 10. The child asks questions such as these: "Why are there some people who can sing well and others who sing badly?" Details on types of snake. "How tall are babies when they are born?" The child reads his schoolbooks from cover to cover at the beginning of the year, then is annoyed that he has not found the answer to everything. Then, he loses interest in studying.

Next week, retreat and first communion.

Recommendations to the mother to let him read books by Jules Verne and a scientific magazine *Sciences et Voyages.*

25 May:

Didier made his first communion. He brings me a holy picture and a photo of himself.

He also brings me a dictation, bad, in which the spelling mistakes are underlined by the teacher, but not corrected by the child at the time when spelling is done aloud. Same thing happened in maths, also not resolved later on, because the teacher refuses to give the answers once the lesson is over.

I advise him to ask his schoolmates, who know the answers, for their exercise books after the corrections.

Dream: that he arrives too late, the others have already gone, he does not know where, he is lost. (Exactly reflecting the difficulties at school, he is now facing: always being behind the others).

I advise that he be given private lessons by a student, or in any case a *man* so that he can pass his end of year exam.

The mother saw her usual doctor again who warmly encouraged her to persevere in the psychotherapy treatment for at least three months. She was expecting him to laugh at the treatment.

1 June:

Today, Didier *looks me in the face* for the whole of our meeting. His mother has enrolled him with the Scouts of France. Didier is *very happy* about that. He went out on Sunday, dared risk climbing trees just like the others, at first with no success but then he managed despite a fall. But come the evening at home, he wanted to carve his Scout walking pole, and he cut his left thumb quite deeply.

I explain the mechanism of self-punishment to him, and I tell him that he has to carry on growing up like a man, despite these minor difficulties which want to frighten him just as the nightmares did at the beginning of the treatment.

We speak about his father who would be *proud* if he was here and who is, from where he is, (because Didier is very much a believer) proud to see his son his replacement, his continuation on earth, becoming a splendid person such as he was himself. He is not jealous. *On the contrary!*

After a few minutes of silence, Didier tells me: "At Scouts, one of the boys was amusing himself throwing his knife at a beautiful oak tree, his knife rebounded came back towards him and pierced his cheek right through." This anecdote associated to his father is significant.

Spoke to the mother. I praise her for her initiative regarding the Scouts. Then she tells me *how much of a sacrifice it is for her to let go of her little boy, to see him happy to prepare his bag with not a thought for her;* and she reproached him about it the other day. (Now, earlier on, I had broached

176 PSYCHOANALYSIS AND PAEDIATRICS

with Didier the subject of the mechanism of self-punishment and he had answered: "Oh no, I knew that it was Mummy who registered me herself.")

The mother tells me that when her husband died it took her a long time to be able to stand the child, "that he lived and that her husband had gone was, she said, terrible for her". They could have had another child to replace that one if he had died instead of his father. She could not bear his gaiety, his questions.

The mother adds: "It was about two years later, when he was about seven, that all of a sudden I noticed that the child had changed, he was not like the other children and so I took him to the doctors."

I had previously noted in speaking to her an obvious jealousy towards me, despite her pleasure in the improvement of the boy and the confirmation of the good influence of this treatment by her family GP (if he had not agreed she would not have brought the child back).

"And yet you are a woman, and it seems that you are the only one who is right and who knows everything, I find this difficult to swallow, I who always tried to live only for him and to have his trust; he doesn't believe a word I say."

Today, therefore, I emphasised what a wonderful idea she had had, enrolling him in the Scouts, and I said, in front of the child, that she was a *great help to us*. And that if Didier was becoming attached to the "chiefs", even at the risk that she and I were relegated to the second division, she should be delighted about that.

I tell her *that for herself too*, the freedom of the days when her child is camping and on outings would be very beneficial, that she had the right to live for herself and not always *for the child*, for whom it is rather a heavy weight to feel that he is the exclusive focus of all her efforts, fears, and happiness.

The mother says that what strikes her most about the child is that for the last few days, he looks everyone in the face when he speaks, which *he never used to do*.

8 June:

He spent the Pentecost holidays at the camp without any problems. This new life pleases him a lot. He looks up to the "chiefs", he admires his "nice, clever "friends, not like at school. Although he thought that it would be more comfortable to go by car, he did not say so and walked like everybody else. Only the strap of his bag broke. A happy accident, which meant that someone carried it for him.

During the night, sleepwalking, he got out of his sleeping bag and went to lie next to his favourite friend.

15 June:

Good progress. He now has little clashes with his mother, about arithmetic problems that she wants to teach him. Mummy is quick tempered and Didier is slapped. None of this is too dramatic and proves that family relations have entered a new era.

Didier complains of pain walking in the lower right limb, knee, shin, hip. I send him for a surgical consultation. (Nothing is found.)

Speak to the mother who is surprised by the change that everyone notices. Didier speaks more openly, he is more alive and so on.

– "But when it comes to maths problems his eyes become lifeless, he stops listening. *And he likes being slapped!*"

I explain to the mother that he lacks *basic* maths. He needs private lessons, which will start again from the beginning.

Asked about Didier's clothes—because I had noticed that despite his wearing different clothes his trousers always button up the side—his mother tells me that she always adapts them in this way even when they have a fly when she buys them, because *she finds this more proper and cleaner* (sic). For a long time, the child was dressed as a girl and she further tells me—at my request—*that until he was seven years old he had beautiful curls* and that it had been a sacrifice for her to cut them off.

The mother is *noisily* sorry, as "she now understands" that she did not do her son any good. From this moment on, she will give him the same trousers as the other boys.

– "Ah! If only someone had told me about this before!" But instead of being sorry about it, she seems to find it funny (?).

22 June:

The child is going to move school. Letter to the new schoolmaster to explain the necessity of going back to basics.

About the rule of three which I explain to him and that he understands for the first time, I show him: 1. that he doubts himself; 2. that when he sees a number, he completely loses the sense of that number (francs, measurements, apples, and so on.). It becomes a number outside the real which he does not know what to do with, nor how it has arrived in the calculation.

Today the child is tired and feverish. Due to an infected vaccination; swollen glands. Letter from the teacher who will soon be giving him private lessons.

29 June:

Didier's mother does not want him to go camping this summer. There is nothing to be done about it as she has made a vow to go to Lourdes with Didier, to pray for the maternal grandfather's legs to be healed!

It is very regrettable and significant that she made this vow three weeks ago. After that Didier will go to St Etienne for two months, where her cousin who is a teacher will make him work.

Psychotherapy on the conscious level.

To Didier: advice about life (during the holidays he is generally served breakfast in bed and then does not get up until 10 a.m.!). I suggest other possibilities for his mornings.
To the mother: during the holidays she should not concern herself at all with schoolwork. She should leave exclusive direction of the work and sanctions if it is not done entirely to the cousin; she should not try to impose homework times nor try to verify whether the work programme is being carried out.

6 July:

Didier talks about everything, especially the outward appearance of mature men (hat, size, how Dr Pichon looks English, bruises acquired during mock battles between the Scout chiefs). He tells me about sports, he wants to learn how to swim this summer and, on his own recently, he managed not to sink for the first time by moving his arms, but he does not yet dare move his legs: "it is too tiring".

He will write to me this summer and will come back in October.

Didier tells me that before knowing me he often dreamed and had many nightmares; now he almost never dreams and when he does it is never unpleasant.

28 December:

Didier comes back to me at the end of the first term; he is well, he is at the local elementary school. A letter from the schoolmaster is addressed to me.

The schoolmaster had read my letter addressed to whoever would be teaching Didier, and told the mother that it was what helped him to persevere with him at the beginning, because he felt that he was backward and his case hopeless, which now appears to him quite wrong. Didier has an enormous admiration and a real affection for the teacher, "as well as for you" says his mother.

He has gone back to Scouts and his chief says he is progressing. He talks to the others, and mixes in games. At school, he is friendly with everyone except for two or three and is an integral part of the form. He came twenty-seventh out of forty-two at the end of December (same place as in November).

Since December, I have had a note from the mother saying that progress at school and at Scouts was continuing. She does not want to bring the child back to us any longer because she prefers him not to miss his class on Wednesday morning.

Didier is far from being cured, but the mother is developing an enormous resistance beneath an appearance of goodwill; and as she is an image of happiness itself as long as Didier has a few good results and does not make *her* feel ashamed, she does not ask for more, (she who was good at arithmetic, spelling, etc., when she was young, she passed her 'O' levels, etc).

She could have gone back to work (nurse or teacher, I can't remember) but she has not done so, so as not to be away from Didier. In the same vein, she has never wanted to marry again. Anyway, she considers men like "children" and her child as a "thing".

The only policy I could employ in front of such a castrating mother, one should say *devouring* (she laughs a lot showing all her teeth which are long), is to flatter her through her weak spot, "intelligence", "a woman like you!", and so on. In the hospital waiting room, she always had a following when chatting with the other mothers.

She did not dare take the child away from me because I had told her that she was "admirable to have had the idea of bringing him to us". But, as one can recall, she had ingenuously admitted that she had taken Didier after the third session to the old family doctor to tell him all about the psychotherapeutic treatment; she was expecting him to laugh at it. If he had done so, I would never have seen them again. But the old doctor, on the contrary, finding the child much better had recommended continuing the treatment at least for three months (a pity he did not say a year!).

This is what happened, during this period, in the mind of this woman:

When she enrolled Didier at the scouts (after having learned from another woman that I had advised her to do that for her child), she wanted to compete with me in giving him this pleasure and I complimented her warmly. "One could see that she was intelligent, without her what could I do? And so on".

But she must have been furious later that the child was so happy preparing his own scout bag and leaving her behind to be with "people he did not know!".

This is why the following week, she made a promise to the Virgin Mary, without telling anyone, to go and pray *with Didier* in Lourdes this summer. Naturally, in getting God on her side through a vow, there were no longer any human weapons, even the persuasion of a scout chief or the desire of a psychoanalyst, which could compete with her! Oh irony, the phallic mother and the castrated son were going to pray to the Virgin Mary so that she could give back the legs, that is to say, the potency of the old paralysed grandfather! If it were not so sad and the future well-being of a man was not in play, it would be highly comical.

Conclusion

If only because of the mother's resistance, the case of Didier is interesting, because the position taken up by this woman derives from unconscious motives. She believes that she loves her child, and she is destroying him.

We can see how this child, happy, lively, noisy, and more advanced than his real age since infancy, is being extinguished, closed down after the death of the father. His outward display of unintelligence and scholarly incompetence would have had him mistaken for backward, if the schoolmaster had not been made aware by us of the huge gaps in his basic education and of his sharp intelligence, linked to great sensitivity, which did not show in his behaviour.

At five years old, Didier was in full Oedipal phase; an only son, although he had been disguised as a girl, he had a rival, his father.

The death of the father puts the feelings of guilt attached to the magical death wish onto the child, because at this age the child still reasons with the type of thought called anal sadistic, not rational.

Furthermore, the mother, instead of holding the little boy who is left to her in her arms, explodes with aggressive despair towards the child. Why did he not die instead of his father? She could have replaced him with a new child.

The suicidal thoughts which emerged in the child at the death of the father show how far gone were the feelings of guilt in the face of the loss. Not only was he guilty, but mother was disowning him. Furthermore, his feminine looks, his sown-up flies, the premature and vehement prohibition of masturbation, had established a pregenital sexless position, that is to say, masochistic and seductive towards adults whoever they may be, *men and women without distinction*, including the father; so therefore the child, at this time, forced not to be in the normal Oedipal complex, had regressed to the anal stage faced with the castration complex, and played out his Oedipal complex in the anal mode, which is characterised by ambivalence.

The anxiety resulting from the realisation of his death wish inhibited not only his phallic libidinal development, but also prohibited the aggression linked to the anal stage, magically responsible for the Oedipal murder—therefore, the impossibility of making the least effort, the smallest muscular activity, the slightest noise. Didier smiled at us, but barely (and without showing his teeth), he has never yet laughed with us (but I know that he does at the scouts). He cannot identify with his mother (she disowned him) nor to his father (Didier killed him and the father will avenge himself; cf. association of the knife in the cheeks after having spoken about the father during the 1 st June session).

He then regresses to the passive oral stage and, even at this point, he is not sheltered from the castration complex which is still in play, giving him anxiety dreams with an obvious symbolism (bandits kill him). Each progress will be followed by a self-punishing reverse with symbolic castration (cut thumb, pain in the knee). Didier is far from cured.

He is fond of us, yet doesn't feel guilt about preferring men—Dr Pichon—because we enabled him to become fond of his scout chief and thanks to us, his schoolmaster showed him a patience he was rewarded for. Didier can now obtain academic and emotional satisfaction in the outside world. At last, he no longer has nightmares.

At present, his libidinal attitude towards love objects is still at a homosexual stage, not in the way that happens in the oral phase or at the beginning of the anal phase, but at the time of the urethral phase with over valuation of the penis (men's hats, masculine voices) according to the mode which precedes the appearance of the castration complex linked to the Oedipus complex. *Didier needs to be left in peace to live through this out of date phase, as if he were three years old*, despite being eleven and with the build of a strong twelve-year-old. The sleepwalking episode at the scout camp where Didier got out of his sleeping bag at the risk of catching a cold and went to lie by his favourite friend, demonstrates this emotional state of affairs. So we made no comment about it. Luckily, for the moment, the mother finds this *very amusing*, and the scout chief was understanding enough to interpret it as a harmless display of boyish enthusiasm in such a pathologically closed off, sensitive child.

In our opinion, the social prognosis for Didier is good, but at the sexual level, puberty being close, Didier does not appear capable with the mother he has, of resolving that question in any other way but through manifest homosexuality. This is the most favourable outcome, because in him, homosexuality represents the only modality unconsciously authorised by his superego, replicated on the maternal superego.

Didier does not appear to us to be able to go further than the reclaiming of a negative Oedipus. That is to say, that his superego is perverse and thus will only allow him a passive role in homosexual relationships. In another possible outcome, his love objects will oblige him to repress his homosexuality during his adolescent years. For fear of losing their esteem, Didier will lose the greater part of his means of sublimation and will probably be obliged to live a sexually impotent life, dependent on a rich authoritarian woman who will in due course tell him about her affairs with other men. He will be more or less a voyeur and in any case socially inhibited and masochistic.

It is still nevertheless possible to hope, though rather feebly, because the mother has no longer any interest in having her son treated, now that he is succeeding in his studies, that we will be able to follow Didier in his adolescence and let the mother catch a glimpse of the necessity, for him, of a true psychoanalysis, with preferably, we would recommend, a male psychoanalyst.

Marcel (aged ten and a half)

The child is brought by his mother because of a patch of alopecia. It seems to have appeared following the failure of a catechism test. He is a big, fat child, broadly built, fair-haired, and flabby-looking. His features show no pathology. Round face, barely defined (hypothyroidism), genital organs little developed. Work is mediocre. The mother reports that the child often makes spelling mistakes through reversing the letters. He is flabby, indifferent, egotistical, and lazy. No previous clinical history.

Father in good health, he is a sales representative in the car industry. Mother very anxious, had St Vitus's dance at eleven years old and several nervous breakdowns. Her body is covered with patches of vitiligo (areas of depigmentation not affecting the face). She has an enlarged thyroid whose size increases at certain times and diminishes at others. Marcel has a brother, Maurice, fifteen years old, in good health (5 January).

12 January:

We administer medical treatment to the child: hormonal endocrinal treatment.

The test does not show any intellectual retardation.

23 February:

The alopecia patch is diminishing. The child is more focused at school. The thyroid treatment has been stopped since 1 February. No perceptible progress with the genital organs. Restart the tablets.

6 April:

The alopecia has nearly disappeared, but schoolwork is not satisfactory.

In summary, it is noted: "Child probably has hypothyroidism, but his laziness includes clear psychological aspects. He does not understand the need for schoolwork. He would prefer agricultural work, towards which it may be worth orienting him".

The child is then entrusted to us. The mother quivers with shame at the idea that her son could do such work, because she wishes her children to be educated and have honourable professions (sic). Her father was a doctor!

Contact is not good at all with the mother, who is in a rush and nervous, because we are asking Marcel to come to see us regularly every Wednesday. She does not agree with psychotherapy. Faced with her attitude, we give up after having told her that she is making a mistake, and that maybe she would be less anxious despite her thyroid problems if she had been attended to psychologically when she was young.

27 April:

To our surprise, she comes back three weeks later; she has thought about it, she says. She is more indulgent as far as Maurice's laziness and egoism are concerned. As a matter of fact, she adds, what I told her the other day may not be wrong. She had had depressive episodes throughout her life, which played on her nerves, and she even had the St Vitus's dance at eleven years old, following the death of her mother. Her father, a strict doctor, could not stand that one might be self-indulgent. She admits to being anxious in the extreme, and to feel a need to administer slaps indiscriminately, and it is Marcel who gets them, because he (sic) can put up with anything, whereas, his older brother is hypersensitive, a real girl. And anyway, only Maurice gives her complete satisfaction. The father is a man absorbed in his work. At home, he rarely speaks and never to Marcel except in "pidgin", "babyish" language as if he were still two years old.

I notice that Marcel has an open mind behind his frozen appearance. But there is a delay of twenty to thirty seconds before he reacts to what I have said. I follow his rhythm.

I tell him that it would please me if he worked harder and, another time, speaking to him as an equal, when I say that "the difference between grown-ups and children is not that the latter are inferior", his eyes fill up with tears. I revisit his agricultural vocation with him and ask him where his taste for it came from. I learn that it is from a schoolteacher whom he liked in the past and from his holidays, where a neighbouring farmer was very kind to him and let him do some gardening. The present teacher has made him supervisor of the class garden.

Marcel and Maurice sleep in the same bed, and it leads to rumbling disputes. Maurice is a boy with obsessional mechanisms, hard working, pernickety and brilliant in his studies. Marcel is jealous of him and I tell him that I understand him. But if mother compares them, it does not matter, because they each have a life which can be very different, two brothers are two different men without any need for comparison.

Given the relatively well-off milieu, we should be able to advise the mother to have the boys sleep separately, but this is an intervention which we prudently postpone until next session, because the session with Marcel on his own has already made the mother tense up a lot. At my request, she promises to let him work on his own this week.

4 May:

Vast improvement, "turned a corner" says the mother, after the first two days following the visit when he gave himself airs, a bit too much.

Instead of six spelling mistakes in dictation, he only has one or two. He does his schoolwork entirely on his own. Before that, his mother checked it and helped him, believing him incapable of doing it alone.

The child speaks a lot more openly with me, *and laughs!* He did not dare come on his own to the consultation, or stay on his own while his mother was going shopping, despite the encouragement given by his mother and her promise to come back and get him.

The mother shows herself satisfied on the whole, but the older brother, taciturn, conscientious, still wishes strongly for one thing: that Marcel leave him alone. Marcel is preventing him from working. I asked that they get separate beds, the mother answers that it is impossible. I insist.

(Marcel brought a drawing of apples and pears done especially for me.)

11 May:

The mother turns herself into our assistant despite her personal difficulties. She obtained permission to buy a divan for Marcel from the father. She finds him progressing not only from a school point of view but also in "resourcefulness" and in generally paying attention to what is happening around him.

The day after the last session, Marcel had a hostile emotional reaction to his mother and brother, after she had sent him shopping (for *pain au chocolat*) on his own for the first time and he failed, not daring to ask for one in the shop when there were none on display.

This time he had brought me a drawing, a copy, representing two cats surprised by another cat strutting about.

18 May:

In my absence, Mme Codet (my psychotherapy colleague in Dr. Pichon's clinic) sees him and notes: "The child came on his own. He sounds more self-assured-continuing to progress—very good impression".

1 June:

This time too Marcel came on his own without apprehension. He got 9 out of 10 in the recitation test (previous time 0). He got an average of 6.5 for the month in lessons (he had never had over 4). General behaviour clearly progressing, I encourage him. He risked going out on his own, taking a new route, despite his elder brother's worry, who would have liked the mother to stop him, under the pretext that he would get lost. Marcel was worried he would prove his brother right, he had got hot, but did not show it and he did not go the wrong way. There were no adverse reactions after the previous session. But for the last fortnight, he has been hiccupping several times a day between 2 p.m. and 7 p.m.

15 June:

Progress continuing. Sometimes he admits to being lazy: he is slap-dash with his work. Excellent memory, he does not read his notes, it is enough for him to listen in the lesson when they are being explained! But sometimes not everything is explained, and then he is "caught out". I encourage him to make the effort to read his notes every day. This will give him the proof that he deserves to succeed, on the days when he is discouraged by a failure.

The hiccupping has disappeared. The child reports another problem of the nervous system. When he is tired, his left ear is boiling hot and the other one cold. It is unpleasant. In the past, a doctor had prescribed something for this, but it did not help. I minimise the importance of these slight "nuisances" which do not worry me.

29 June:

The school marks for the month show a clear improvement. Marcel has doubled each of his marks in arithmetic and spelling, in comparison with the previous month, and got the top mark for application and behaviour. The schoolmaster is very pleased. And, contrary to the February forecasts he will move to the Certificate class in October. Warm congratulations.

Some conflicts with the brother, settled with fights that the mother more or less tolerates.

Marcel asked to learn how to swim and began to dive. For the last eight days, he dares to dive from the four-metre diving board. His mother encourages him with money.

The child has not had any organic treatment since February. A series of tablets is prescribed in August and they are told to come back in September, at the beginning of term.

30 November:

His hair has started falling out again.

During the holidays, there had been such a huge improvement that the mother had not thought it necessary to bring Marcel back at the beginning of term.

At the beginning of the school year, he appeared so different from before: serious, attentive, nice, big boy. He has a calming influence on her and on his brother, she says—some difficulties, a slacking off in results at school during the week of All Saints and then the reappearance of the alopecia.

I have not seen Marcel since July and I am struck by the thickening of his thighs due to fluid retention, Marcel's more obese appearance, his fat stomach, his dull look out of his swollen cheeks and his woolly, lustreless hair.

The child is despondent about the drop in his schoolwork of the last fortnight, he obviously wants to do well. His eyes wake up as he talks to me. Start a series of tablets again. Weigh him and measure him.

26 January:

Physically looks a little better than in November. Thighs less swollen, stomach reduced, face still puffy, but I am struck by his anxious expression, his furrowed brows, listening is an effort and understanding is slow. Hypothyroid appearance and sluggish functioning; genital organs still under developed.

As far as school is concerned, the schoolmaster is pleased. But the results are still mediocre, especially in spelling. Marcel often feels like an "idiot", he complains about feeling as if he has a lump in his throat. At home, mother needs to continually nag for him to do his homework, she says.

It looks as if there has been a regression. The mother has started harassing Marcel again from morning to night. Today she seems terribly anxious. She thinks he is getting fatter and fatter (but she has not weighed or measured him). I have the impression that it is the mother who is actually demonstrating that she is uncomprehending and resistant for two reasons. She is personally humiliated if Marcel's success at the school certificate is uncertain, and instead of trying to understand the physiological and psychological condition of her son and to help him, she makes it a personal issue and stuns him with pointless reprimands. She drowns him in words and defeatist forecasts.

The other reason (which she is ready to acknowledge) is that Marcel has started puberty. He is losing his childlike aspect, I find him better. He has lost weight, his thighs are less swollen and more muscular, and the mother says, in a disgusted and aggressive voice, looking him up and down—(in response to my saying that "he was becoming a man")—"Now then, you are easily pleased, I think he's getting fatter and fatter. I see him getting worse and worse on all fronts!"

Treatment: a series of multi-glandular injections. To Marcel, we only say that we are very pleased with him and his perseverance. Then, taking the mother aside, I try to explain to her why her attitude is damaging for Marcel, even though she means well. With a very hard father, even a venerated one, she had suffered. And perhaps she suffers to see

Marcel becoming a solid man, strongly built, the opposite of Maurice, whose sensitivity, female softness, and delicate complexion she values.

8 March:

The child has been transformed by his injections. He has lost weight, is nice again, hard-working. The schoolmaster is pleased. Marcel no longer has a lump in his throat. Spelling remains the only weak point worrying the child. He has abandoned his ideas of agriculture and is thinking about a commercial school.

Conclusion

This case study is interesting because of its complexity both in terms of the hormonal imbalance and the psychology.

From January until April, the medical treatment improved Marcel physically, whilst the personality problems came more into focus and the bad school results became even worse.

From April until November, without medical treatment, there is a transformation in the child's school results and personality, but despite all this, from October, new hormonal symptoms appeared without altering the psychological progress. The child is only brought back to us at the end of November, when the hormonal imbalance is very obvious and its impact on the schoolwork brings back difficulties with legitimate inferiority feelings—without superimposed self-punishment. The medical treatment is enough to re-establish the balance.

At present, the boy is starting puberty. He does not have personality problems any longer, gets on with his family and at school, he still lacks some self-confidence but has won the respect of his schoolmasters.

Marcel is on the way to a recovery that perhaps he will never fully achieve; in any case, the happy adaptation to his neurotic family circle, whilst allowing him a normal social life, is a compromise towards which we tried to direct him, the only possible actual solution of conflicts, as long as he has to remain with his family.

The essential difficulty in this case is, the mother. Despite her conscious good will, she is deeply neurotic and physically unwell. Marcel has difficulty in letting go of a masochistic attitude towards his mother, the more so because his older brother (whose influence is now much reduced) makes his emancipation difficult.

In order to continue Marcel's treatment, diplomacy has to be employed with the mother, to restrain her when she goes to extremes, without hurting her feelings while also neutralising her castrating influence on Marcel as much as possible, to allow him to love his mother despite all this. The favourite in the family, let us not forget, is Maurice "who is really as good as a girl". As far as the father is concerned, there is a total failure to take any responsibility. He plays no part in family life except that of a mute and preoccupied banker.

Under such affective conditions, a normal Oedipus complex in Marcel could not take place. No identification was possible with the father; the rival at home was the feminised brother, no fun, fussy and finicky, always worrying about Marcel, whom he considers more or less *moronic*. The castrating mother plays the role of the phallic mother. The Oedipus complex had by necessity to invert itself and Marcel, with a strong constitution, had to use passivity to rival the delicacy of Maurice, the mother's favourite—hence the inhibition of aggression at all levels and the formation of a superego forbidding effort of any kind.

It is through cultivating his masochism that Marcel could keep the maternal love object—hence the slaps of which he was willingly the permanent beneficiary, while not allowing himself to leave his mother's skirts.

This attitude is that of a child stagnating at a passive anal stage, that is to say, repressing his sadism.

The child needed to substitute his interest in excrement with a taste for gardening. With this agricultural career, he attempted identification to the "fathers" by whom he had felt loved (farmer, schoolteacher). It is on the level of this identification that his mother was castrating him: this choice appeared to her dishonourable.

Deprived of the right to sadistic anal aggression, on the one hand, and of the object of libidinal interest, on the other, he experienced all effort not only as useless, but as detrimental to his unconscious emotional comfort. The school results had to be hopeless. But this increased the inferiority feelings that Marcel had towards his brother, brilliant in all his studies. So as not to suffer these feelings, Marcel neurotically regressed to a pre-anal stage.

What his mother called his *egoism* was only an *oral passivity*, which, as we can clearly see, Marcel was unconsciously compelled to regress to.

In this placid attitude of indifferent Buddha, greedy for love in the captive mode, incapable of bearing the absence of his object, he sought with a certain vigilance—and knew how to provoke—the nagging, the reproaches, the slaps, the hits which were the price he unconsciously paid ultimately to be possessed by his mother.

The psychoanalytic therapy *aimed first at obtaining the transference of the mother*, which was indispensable, so that I preferred to take the risk of never seeing either of them again, rather than not being honest during the first conversation which I had exclusively with the mother, despite the fact that the child was present. Luckily, on thinking it over, she could recognise an aspect of herself in her son and brought him back to us. *Armed with the transference of the mother, we sought to obtain that of Marcel*, and thanks to this transference, we revalued his agricultural calling in his eyes, that is to say, permitted the symbolic fantasies of the anal stage. Next time, the child brought us a drawing of four fruit, one next to the other, colourful and appetising. (He was giving us a present of his oral eroticism.) The feelings of inferiority had diminished, thanks to the position we took up and also to his success at his schoolwork without the continual intervention of his mother.

Marcel is transformed and *laughs. That very day*, he brings me two cats, admiring another one (offering us his oral passivity); and he allows himself a little tentative aggression towards his brother in a playful, vocal way.

We then sought to encourage his general aggressiveness (to make an effort to please us) and encouraged the conflict with his brother at the risk of arguments, as a result of which we obtained the new, single bed that his mother then bought him.

From then onwards, improvements at school began to take shape. Independence from his mother was no longer feared, ambivalence towards the Oedipal object, the brother, dissipated into an affectionate and admiring attitude towards his schoolmaster and open hostility towards his brother when he provoked him.

As far as the libido is concerned, Marcel is not yet very advanced, and our therapeutic role is not finished; but in effect, at home, "his brother and his mother find him good to be with", and at school he no longer feels an idiot.

Let's add that he has abandoned the idea of agriculture and is thinking about a commercial school, because "he wants to earn money and become rich", and he added: "Maybe I will do what Daddy does, be an agent for car parts, it pays well."

His expressiveness is still poor, limited to his mouth, he does not gesture and is not very talkative. But calm and thoughtful, he says what he wants to say and his words are carefully chosen. He gives the impression of a solid boy, with common sense, observant, and a little bit "noncommittal". It is thanks to this rather impervious character that he manages to resist the tumultuous atmosphere with which his mother surrounds him.

Let us leave him his armour, because actually he is happy; he told me so spontaneously. He would like to pass his exams and is thinking about his future. We are far from the boy who a year ago did not understand "the use of studying, when all he wanted was to become a farmer, there was no point, *it wasn't worth it*". He is now at the same level as many children of his age who become very adaptable adults, that is to say "normal", while never reaching the genital stage from an object relation point of view, which means that their sexual activity can be adult, but with an infantile affectivity and a love object chosen according to an Oedipus which is unconsciously homosexual: the phallic woman, authoritarian and frigid.

Note about Marcel

In 1967, Marcel, on a visit to France, managed to find me. At Bretonneau, I was unknown; the Medical Council informed him that Dr Pichon had died and gave him my married name and my address. He had never forgotten—about thirty years ago—that we got him out of a terrible morass. After that came the war. They remained in the provinces. He succeeded in his advanced commercial studies and decided to go far away to new countries. He got married at 29, they are a happy couple, with three children, a son, Jean, with whom he came today and two younger daughters. He has a commercial situation connected to agriculture in Africa. He is successful. His father has retired. His mother is still the same and an active, good grandmother when they see each other during the holidays. His wife gets on well with her. His brother has fragile health and got married after him; his wife and children have health problems; he has a good position and has remained near his parents.

As for himself, Marcel came with Jean so that I could tell him if everything is okay with his son who is now the same age as he was when he almost became an idiot instead of developing normally. He does not want his son to face the same risk. Marcel has become a tall, strong man, he has never had any other bouts of alopecia. He is calm, comfortable with himself, does not drink; this is a danger in Africa. He and his wife, and children are doing well and cope with the climate.

He thinks that his brother and his family's weak health comes mainly from the mind, and he would like to be sure that the mind of his son is healthy. Jean does quite well at school, he has friends, he prefers the outside to the inside, where he often fights with his sisters. He is also sometimes nasty to them as if he were jealous. This aside, he does not have major shortcomings, but there are days where one does not know what to make of him.

In reply to my asking him what he thinks about what his father is saying, Jean says: "Mummy and Daddy are always siding with them, it's always me who has to give in, I am fed up! I would prefer to stay with Grandmother, at least I would have some peace! I am not saying that I want to leave them … but it is always my fault." He had taken on a victim's tone.

– Wouldn't it bother you to leave Africa, your friends?
– Of course it would, but bah! I would make some more. My sisters, I am not saying … on their own, they are nice to me, but together they gang up and annoy me, and it is always me who is in the wrong!

Jean is sharp and intelligent. Only boy, eldest by five years of his two young sisters who are closer in age, he misses the time when he was an only child. The two little tigresses give him a hard time. Daddy and Mummy don't realise. He prefers his friends and even to spend time as an only child at his grandmother's, who has said that it would be better for his studies if he lived with her, he could be taken care of medically ("He is nervous … it is his age"). We speak, his father, the boy, and myself, of them and of him; his father has never had sisters, his mother did not have brothers; we speak of his place in the family, not easy faced with the intruders. "However", he said, "I was happy when I got my sisters. But after that, I would have liked a little brother."

Jean is towards the end of the latency phase. He wishes to maintain the life of a child and rediscover an imaginary tranquillity far from the conflicts of sexual difference with the sisters, and far from the parents who "do not understand him". At his grandmother's, he would be the big shot—no more Oedipal difficulties.

Jean feels less loved than his sisters. But he understands from this visit, and from all he has heard, that his father is interested in him and that his father wants to help him.

Father and son leave very happy about this visit to the lady doctor who had helped the father at a similar age. The three of us spoke together of the past, the present, and the future, of genital sexuality, and of puberty being close for Jean. As he was leaving, the father asks me "And what do we do about the beginning of term?"; I turn towards Jean: "What do you think about it?". He looks at his father and says: "Now I would prefer to stay with you, I'll tell grandmother that I changed my mind." I say to him: "Yes but what about your sisters?". He looks at me laughingly and says: "Oh, they are little and I will just have to stop bothering them ..."

Marcel's transference onto the clinic at Bretonneau had supported him, he needed confirmation from me of his success as a man, of the valour of his son, and of his ability to be a father and not to delegate his son's education to the mother at a time when Jean's puberty is making its presence felt. Marcel had never felt himself to be the son of his own father.

Marcel is the only case in Bretonneau, reported in this work, whose subsequent development I heard about.

Tote (aged four years and three months)

Fragments of the life of a child said to be normal.

I am treating her eleven-year-old brother who is seriously behind at school. He is inhibited having total inhibition towards everything except drawing, in which he is really gifted; their mother is good at drawing.

Tote feels unhappy because her brother does not give in to her any more. When he bothers her, she tells him that she is going to tell Mummy; and now he says: "Well, then go on and tell her", instead of immediately giving in as he used to. She feels sad, cries about nothing. She falls ill: heavy cold. But then she becomes like a baby, Mummy must not leave her, she makes guns out of paper and kills "the others" (Daddy and her brother).

Once recovered, she kept her revolver with her and when Daddy rustles his paper, she says "Bang", and if he stops moving she triumphs: "That's it, I have killed him." During her illness, she started sucking her thumb again more than ever. The habit started last year, at three and a half years old, during an ear infection from which she suffered a lot.

One evening, Mummy puts Tote to bed and sees her going back to her clothes; Tote says to her mother: "But somebody has taken it! Where is it?"

— "What?" asks the mother.

Tote does not reply, rummages in her drawers, in her knickers, looks on the floor around her, imitating a person who is looking for something.

— "What is it?" says Mummy.

Tote does not reply and carries on looking, then she replies:

— "But my willy! It was in my knickers, I had it and I can't find it again. You took it, eh, didn't you?" (said in a wheedling tone).

Her mother at first not understanding, but then amused, explains to her: but no, of course, I have not taken anything away from you. You didn't have one.

— "Yes, I did" and she starts crying.
  Her mother tries to explain the difference between the sexes.
— "That's just the way it is", and, she added, because she had herself suffered from a still not entirely resolved masculinity complex, "Well, my poor girl, what do you expect, that's the way it is, one has to get used to it, when one is a girl, even if it is not pleasant."

At four and a half years old, after her illness, Tote sucks her thumb when she is bored. One day after she had helped her mother to peel something which gave her thumb a bad taste, she shouted desperately: "Mummy my thumb is not good any longer", as if the world was only filled with distress. Her mother said to her "Use the other one".

— "No the other one has never been good, there's only one which is any good."

A few days after that, Tote said: "I would like to have a little willy like Michel (her brother). I want to pee standing up." Her mother tells her that girls are not made like boys and Mummies do not have a willy any more than she does. But she has a little pocket in her tummy that the boys do not have, it is to have children.

The same week, she says to her mother: "I don't want Daddy to kiss you or even touch you when he kisses you. I would like him to send you a kiss like that" (and she makes the gesture of sending a kiss with one finger on her lips). "Why?" says the mother.—"I want you to belong to me, not to him". (Was this response sincere?)

Later that week, she asks her mother for a big doll which she had been given as a present six months previously, but had found too big. She says this time: "My little ones are too small to play with". And she really begins "to play with" the big doll, speaks to her, undresses her, dresses her, sits her down and makes her eat.

The next week, Tote whilst opening the window, all of a sudden notices green leaves on the neighbouring chestnut tree. She gives a shout and comes to tell her mother: "Mummy our tree is full of lettuce!" Her mother explains to her that the buds are opening and the leaves are coming out. Tote says: "It's like chicks then".

The same day, she asks her mother: "Will I have big tummies (breasts) like you? Will these grow, these?" Her mother reassures her and says that yes.

A few days after that, Michel comes back from the seaside and recounts what he has seen: a lighthouse, and he explains what it is: it sees all over the sea and when the sea is rough, it prevents sailors from getting lost or drowning. Tote listens without showing it and all of a sudden when Michel stops speaking she says: "What a great story you tell, brother dear" (!) (*sic*) ("brother dear" as a grown-up might say).

That week she had formally invited her father and mother to a doll's tea party. Daddy had dressed up to "come and visit at four p.m.". Tote is becoming keener and keener on delighting her father. The following week, Tote kills her mother with her paper revolver and says: "I don't love you any more".

She comes back one day and tells her mother:

– When I am grown-up, I am going to marry Daddy.

Her mother replies:

– And what about me, then?
– Oh you …. you don't matter.
– But no, says Mummy, you will have another husband, Daddy is my husband, and he belongs to me.
  Tote does not reply.

One day after she had played happily with Daddy during the evening, Mummy undresses her and puts her to bed. Later she says to her father when he comes to say goodnight: "No go away, I don't love you" and refuses to kiss him. She says to her mother in a cross tone of voice a few minutes later: "I don't love Daddy any more". Then, after a silence and with passion: "He is too nice! I want to marry him, I want to so much!"

The next week, she cries to stop Michel leaving her. It is real despair. "You must come back!" She becomes nicer and nicer to him and coquettish with Daddy. Some friends come to visit, a man and a woman. Tote says: "The man is nice, I like him, but Daddy is much better." "You know, Daddy, it's you that I love best."

At the same time, she *no longer knows* how to dress herself. If she was left to her own devices, it would take two hours. She remains on the spot, waiting for Mummy, she *cannot* do it herself.

A few days later, to the great surprise of her mother, because Tote was not very interested in her clothes, she tells her mother: "I don't want to wear the dress I wore yesterday, I want another dress; at school the little girls have new dresses; mine is not pretty any longer."

Tote is a healthy little girl, this fragment of observation proves it, but she is living through, at four and a half, what she should have lived through at three. Had her older brother not been in treatment, she would have become, like her brother, a neurotic child. The father is mentally absent from his son's upbringing, he is disappointed in him. The son had seemed normal to the mother until the birth of her daughter, he had been sweet and gentle. He had never asked any questions regarding his mother's pregnancy and sexual difference. He did not show any jealousy, but was rather indifferent and passive. He did not go to nursery school, as the mother did not work. Tote's birth was very much desired, the mother having had a spontaneous miscarriage when her son was four. She was afraid she had become sterile and had had treatment. Michel had started primary school during his mother's pregnancy. Tote was born when he was six and a half. With his difficulties at school, which had required staying down in the two preparatory classes, one had been very tolerant, an IQ test had shown that he had little ability. He was a quiet child and luckily had inherited a gift for drawing from his mother. He was considered "retarded": it was only when he was eleven years old that his growing inhibitedness and problems relating to his school mates, coupled with his obvious depressive state, that a schoolmaster advised his mother to bring him to Dr Pichon's clinic. Michel suffers from an obsessional neurosis, which had, up to then, gone unnoticed. His case, which is in progress, has not been related here. I thought that the impact of the treatment of an elder child on his little sister—still mentally healthy—would interest the reader.

Denise (aged six)

Brought for enuresis. She wets the bed at least three or four times a week and wets herself at school once a fortnight; sometimes she asks to be excused at the moment that she starts wetting her knickers.

Good general state, normal reflexes. External genital organs normal. No abnormality of the vertebral column.

The child sleeps in a separate room from her parents, in the same bed as her sister Janine, who is two years older and who never wets the bed. It is a big bed and Denise sleeps on the wall side.

From a personality point of view, Denise is sweet and cuddly, like a baby; furthermore, at home she is spoken to as if she were a "baby"; she plays with children younger than she is. Denise pronounces as "t" all the hard "c" (or the "*qu*"). She will say: "*te j'ui dis*", instead of "*que je lui dis*" (what I say to her). Despite all this, the schoolmistress is pleased with her, she can write and is beginning to read.

I do not see Denise on her own because she is so babyish and, above all, extremely shy. I advise that she should no longer sleep against the wall and that a potty be put for her close to the bed. I also advise that Mummy get her up once before going to bed herself and, most important of all, that she encourages progress: being a little girl rather than a baby. I advise a consultation about her eyes, which, I notice, are tired and redden at the least effort (drawing). The mother is extremely myopic (1 March).

8 March:

Denise has not been incontinent at all during the week, either in bed or at school. She has only needed to get up once during the night, and she did it on her own without completely waking up.

The little one told her mother several times that "Mademoiselle Marette" (Françoise Dolto's maiden name; she married Dr Boris Dolto in 1942) had said that she was no longer a baby. The parents are delighted. Denise has never been more charming. There have been no incidents this week. The doctor says her vision is good.

Alone with me, she draws a pipe, an apple, a bird, and an aeroplane while writing under each drawing what it represents. Her eyes are no longer red.

22 March:

The mother brings her back to thank me. There has not been the least incontinence for the last three weeks and Denise is becoming "lively", although she is a little shy. Alone with me, she tells the story of Snow White and talks about songs. She would like to be a schoolteacher because one can write on the blackboard, and one can have babies (there is a nursery at her school) and one has pupils *"ti font ce t'on dit"*—"who do as they are told"—same desire as Zazie, from *Zazie in the Underground* (Zazie in the story also has fantasies of telling people what to do![1]).

29 March:

There was an accident in bed this week! Denise is very sorry, she has a shame-faced expression with me. Still good-natured. Good behaviour at home and at school.

Her eight-year-old sister, on the other hand, is becoming jealous and reacts by mendaciously accusing a little girl at school of sexual games and rude language. She later admits to lying because the other girl defends herself, but she also lies about nothing at home. The mother and the father believe that Denise is now cured despite the incident this week. They do not get her up at night, even once, as they were doing at the beginning of the treatment.

19 April:

The mother comes back. Everything had been perfect until the week after Easter, but in the last eight days, Denise has wet the bed three times.

---

[1] R. Queneau (1959). *Zazie dans le métro* (Paris: Gallimard). (Subsequently made into a film by Louis Malle in 1960.)

The only noticeable new thing in her life is that during the holidays she played with a little boy of her own age, Bernard. The parents think Denise should be sent to the country because she is a little pale.

Alone with me, Denise draws a little boy. She writes above "mimi". Now, Mimi is a boy with whom she has not played but whom she saw and "I found him beautiful because his hair was all curly and my hair doesn't make curls". (Denise is very proud of the bow on her head.) She goes on to tell me that she is afraid of the screen at the hospital which almost fell on her head earlier on, how afraid she had been! ... then continuing her circular appraisal of the room, she looks at the sink for a long time, then says: "At school, it's not the same (*c'est pas tomme ça*), the boys have "taps" (willies) but not like yours, smaller and not as high (she means the urinals with low pans) and the girls have closets so they can sit down, if not one does it (*sic*) in one's shoes; there is a door with a little hole, very small." (—in the girls' toilets, of course.)

She then goes on to say that she would very much like to have been a boy, "so as to have a "tap" (willy) like that. Daddy also ... (implied has got one too), but Mummy does not want us to go because we would have to go downstairs. And also we (us girls) would not have a bottom like that, so it would not be possible. And then Daddy says that the boys are not as good. He prefers girls, oh yes I am sure of that!"

What is interesting and amusing is the language used with its double meanings, real and figurative. Tap (willy) = boy's urinal (and Daddy's too), and the girls' closet is the word also used to symbolise the sex, because the door of the girls' closet is described as if the child wanted to illustrate the interest of the girls' closet through this little hole in the middle of the door as a compensation for the captivating "taps (willies) of the boys" and, by association, one understands that what Daddy prefers is the sex of the girls to that of the boys.

Despite Daddy's preference for girls, Denise is afraid that Janine, the eldest, will be preferred to her at home, and that now that she is becoming a big girl, she will not be loved as much.

Indeed, Denise continues to chatter while I am writing notes on her card and tells me that Janine wants to win all the time. "She is jealous 'cos I'm growing up", but there is nothing to be done about it, Denise says defending herself, "of course not!".

I tell the mother that it would be totally counterproductive to send her away to the country at this time.

I encourage Denise in her right to grow up without feeling guilty towards Janine. It is evident that she projects her own feelings onto Janine, although Janine has said nothing and does not admit her jealousy, Denise is probably right.

I say that straight hair is as pretty as curly hair, especially when one is pretty with such a lovely bow.

Denise asks me if I had kept the pipe (a drawing), which she had given me the other day: I say yes and show it to her.

29 April:

Denise has only wet the bed once. She tried to get up, but it was too late; that night Daddy had once more insisted that she slept against the wall on the side of the bed, on the grounds that she kicks her sister with her heels and pulls the cover over more to the outside and herself. Denise is better, is not pale any longer and is full of life.

She tells me dreams in which she sees her father eating and then he leaves her without saying goodnight.

– It's during the night and it is as if I really saw it.

I reply:

– But you know that Daddy loves you and would not do that sort of thing.
– Yes, I know.

Since then, everything is going well. The enuresis has stopped and Denise is developing normally.

Conclusion

Excellent prognosis. The clinical cure is probably sustainable.

Of interest in Denise's case is the relapse after a month of recovery. The symptom started again after a new surge of castration anxiety (the absence of a penis). (Having less beautiful hair, compared with a boy, such is the rationalisation of the unconscious that the wish for curls symbolises the envy "of another ornament" characteristic of Mimi and Bernard.) The symptom is linked to anxiety about growing up (because it means rivalry with the older sister who would be jealous, displaced Oedipal position), and coincides with the parents' wish to send her away for the holidays under the pretext that she was no longer bedwetting (an important and classic obstacle to sending children to camp).

The words of Denise deliberately reproduced here, word for word, are interesting, because one can see how the child reasons with her global thinking. The detail designates the whole and the object designates the part of the body it is destined to be used by. In this case, the understanding of the psychoanalyst, who listens and responds in the same natural tone: "of course, oh yes,—you think so,—how,—without any doubt" to the non-rational discourse of the child, and listens and responds in the same tone has a therapeutic effect. These conversations with double meanings were rich in underlying guilt feelings, because of the forbidden subjects at which they hinted and because of the penis envy they betray. The frank "conversation" with the adult opens the way to the anxiety hidden under the feeling of inferiority due to the girls' phallic castration; and once the anxiety is assuaged, the child can see the advantages of being a girl more objectively, especially with a mother who owns that she has no penis.

The symptom (enuresis), which reappeared, was due to the anxiety caused by the Oedipus complex. The affective inferiority towards the Oedipal object, shown in the anxiety dream (she is the only one Daddy does not say goodnight to) after having been talked about with the doctor, also disappears: "Daddy would never do that". The symptom is no longer underpinned by an emotional libidinal charge. It disappears. As far as the libido is concerned, it finds its direction again linked to Oedipal fantasies, with no danger to the superego, which is already on the way to a harmonious repression. Furthermore, we see that Denise has real possibilities of sublimation—that her tenderness for Daddy is encouraged even by her mother. The rivalry with Janine, instead of making her guilty, finds merit in the eyes of the parents and Denise, despite the natural jealousy of her older sister, is no longer compelled by unconscious feelings of guilt to self-punishing inhibition.

At the end of the treatment, Denise asked me if I had kept "the pipe" which she had drawn for me five weeks earlier. We would add that this question showed clearly the role of the positive transference towards the doctor, in the letting go of the symptom of her enuresis (masculine urethral protest); the question was symbolically hiding this one: "Do you realise the value of what I have given you: my recovery, renouncing being a boy? If you realise it, then it is because you are a Mummy who loves me as much as if I was a boy, whilst allowing that I love Daddy more than you."

Claudine (aged six years and nine months)

The child is brought to the hospital for her nervousness and daytime enuresis.

She is skinny and presents with polymicro-adenopathy. Reflexes are normal. The external genital organs are normal—skin test for tuberculosis positive. The X-rays show a slight shadow on the right hilum. Old calcifications also appear around the left hilum.

Parents are in good health. Two uncles, one on the paternal side and one on the maternal side, died of pulmonary tuberculosis before the child's birth.

For the personal history, the mother has nothing special to report except heavy colds and vague symptomatic events, dominated by sleep problems, anorexia, and nervousness. Claudine has a twelve-year-old brother, in good health.

Until last year, Claudine wet the bed every night and her knickers during the day. Most of the urinary incontinence during the day occurs at school, happening less frequently at home, and if it does, it is mainly in response to being scolded.

Last summer, the child was sent to camp where she wet the bed every night. On return to her family, and since October, the child only wets the bed occasionally because her mother gets her up twice a night.

But every day, she wets her knickers several times. The discharge is powerful and happens in the classroom, during breaks, at home, even though the child has only urinated a few minutes before. The schoolmistress is complaining. She won't let the child go to the toilet now because she would have to accompany her and it disturbs the class; furthermore, even these accompanied trips, tolerated before, do not exclude impromptu urination. At home, as soon as Claudine is scolded, she starts to scream "wee wee" very anxiously and, incapable of moving, stands rooted to the spot. If her mother does not come to her rescue, to take her to the toilet without delay, she does it in her knickers.

What is Claudine's behaviour at home and at school?

At home, it is necessary to distinguish between meal times and other times. *During meal times*, Claudine has very little appetite. She makes *scenes* according to the time-honoured expression used by her parents. Claudine pushes back her plate, cries, wants to leave the table, says she feels sick, needs to wee right away. Daddy gets cross, Mummy takes her then brings her back, her meal is reheated, they beg her, she has two spoons of soup and it all starts again. Parents are worried. She is skinny, she will become ill, they speak about the country, how the Paris air does not suit her. "It's like her uncles ", syrups, drugs, medicine everything is in question, it could be anything. Family meals are spoiled, mother is worried, Daddy is irritable. Daniel teases her, makes fun of her, and things are aggravated. In short, the mother begs us to give Claudine her appetite back (let us note that Claudine almost never eats between meals).

Outside mealtimes: At home, Claudine is a model child, but only when Daniel is not there. She is docile, happy, nice, affectionate with her parents, more so with her father, who returns her affection. But if her brother is there, nothing works. The mother says that he is a terrible tease with his sister and that she does not put up with it. There are shouts, arguments, fallings out, and demands from each of the children for the parents to get involved. As soon as Daniel has gone, Claudine becomes sweet and good again.

She started school in October. If it were not for the enuresis, the schoolmistress would be quite pleased with her. Fidgety, she doesn't concentrate, always needing attention to follow the work. Despite this, she can already read and write a little. She gets on well with her little friends.

In front of the child, we advise:

At night: that a potty is put next to Claudine's bed and that mother does not concern herself any more with getting her up. She is old enough to not need to have Mummy all the time. Never mind if she does not manage straight away. She is not to be scolded, and Daddy will be pleased with her when she shows him that she is becoming a big girl.

At mealtime: Claudine should not be forced, she should eat what she wants and leave the rest. I convince the mother to show no interest for at least three days. There are cases in which children a lot skinnier than her are put on a diet. Claudine is healthy, she can cope with missing a whole meal occasionally, which—I warn the mother—could be unconscious blackmail; she must promise me not to be upset by it. And I am convinced, I tell the mother, that it is in great part because of an unconscious desire to play at being a baby and to have everyone looking after her, that she has grown into these ritual daily family wrangles. She has to be helped to grow up. One eats when one is hungry. One stops when one is full. This is nobody's business but her own. The mother, a little worried, promises to follow my advice. Besides, I prescribe drops of a tonic, to be given to her at the beginning of the meal, this is to prop up the child emotionally but mainly to help the mother not to feel guilty about neglecting Claudine's health. I ask that Mummy insists at school that during the next few weeks the teacher allows Claudine to leave the class as often as she wants.

Alone with Claudine I ask her to draw whatever she likes for me. She draws a picture of herself and one of Daniel (see drawings p. 143), on two separate sheets of paper. We talk about her dolls, she has two favourites, Maurice and Snow White; so named because of the story she loves and Maurice because it is a beautiful name. But she doesn't know anyone called Maurice. I ask her if Maurice and Snow White get on well. She laughs and says, "not always, they quarrel". I say "well, Snow White who is so skilful and gracious in the dwarves' house has no reason to be jealous of Maurice, even if he is older than her".

– But she is not jealous; *they (masculine)* tease each other, and then I scold them. But *they (feminine)* are nice nevertheless. I love them both.
– Oh, you know, I tell her with a serious air, when dolls do not get on, it's like people, it's like you and Daniel.
– "You will explain to Snow-White that the handsome prince is not coming for Maurice, but for her with his beautiful white horse and that he will take her to his beautiful castle. Then it is Maurice who should be jealous. So you will have to tell Snow White to console Maurice instead of getting cross. And then you can explain to Maurice that he does not need to be nasty to Snow White because you love them both equally".

We agree to meet next week. And if the dolls have not understood, Claudine will just have to bring them to me. I would be pleased to see them and we would explain to them together.

We part good friends (22 February).

1 March:

Claudine has made huge progress. Mummy is over the moon. Claudine has not once wet the bed, or wet her knickers. Mummy gets her up only once in the evening before she goes to bed herself. Claudine has got up on her own some nights and on other nights did not need to at all.

During the day, she often runs to the toilets, but on her own.

At mealtime: after having eaten little the first day and almost nothing at breakfast the next day, she caught up at dinner and since then she has been eating normally.

At school, the schoolmistress is surprised by the compulsive, frequent need to wee, but no longer opposes it.

But there is still this *"nervousness, which worries me"* says the mother; "the states she gets into sometimes, especially when Daniel is scolded or punished. Claudine pulls her hair, scratches herself, stamps her feet, cries, screams, begs, she goes quite mad, it is impossible to calm her down; after that she is wrecked, exhausted for the rest of the day." There had been precisely such an event this week.

On her own with me, Claudine is a lot calmer; she has not brought her dolls (I do not mention this to her). She draws a house for me. "This is Daddy's house." She tells me that "there are some taps" in the house "like yours" pointing to the washbasin in the room. "Does that one work?" I reply: "Go and see." She does not and tells me "Sometimes they are broken, and then they are repaired." I agree.

I compliment her on her progress, she is becoming a big girl. I speak to her of her huge rage during the week, "she cannot remember a thing afterwards", she tells me.

I explain to her that, if she is in such a state when she sees Daniel being punished, maybe it is because inside herself, without telling anybody, she wants bad things to happen to him. He is stronger than her, this is annoying, maybe sometimes he also wants to show off to make Claudine feel that she is stupid, but she isn't. When Claudine is twelve, she will be as clever as he is. She replies that Daniel teases her much less now.

– "Maybe it is because you are also teasing him less", and I continue.
– "It is possible sometimes to be jealous and to think that it is lucky to be a boy. I know some little girls who are very nice who would have

liked to be able to pee like boys and they could not. It annoyed them, they thought that they were not made like anyone else. It is because they believed that ladies, Mummy, the lady doctor had a tap like Daniel. Boys have one, Daddies do too. But Mummies don't, nor do girls if they had one they would not be able to become pretty ladies or Mummies and the Daddies would not love them. It would not be pretty if Mummy and Mlle Marette had a moustache, a beard or a deep voice."

(Claudine laughs.)

– Oh no, of course not, I wouldn't want to be like that. I'd like to be pretty like Mummy.
– So you will be when you are grown up and Daniel will be like Daddy.

8 March:

Claudine urinates much less during the day. But that night, for the first time in a month, she wet the bed. The mother is not too cross about this accident, because she had not got her up before going to bed herself, and on the other hand, because Claudine had had a big boil on her buttocks for the last few days which burst yesterday but which had resulted in her staying in bed.

This week, there were no fits of anger. Claudine and Daniel are fighting much less, they still have little squabbles, but they manage on their own without telling on each other or asking Daddy or Mummy for help.

On the other hand, for the last few days (since she had the boil), Claudine is forever asking for something, mainly a drink for just one gulp or some sugar or a sweet.

On her own with me, Claudine makes me a drawing (p. 144) with phallic symbolism. She explains to me that it is a warship on the sea, that there are "thingies", flags and a man "who is looking through a big thingy".

I ask her who those two people are?

– "It's those who are left behind". I say: "Maybe it's you and Daniel." She laughs and says yes. (She is the person on the left, "the one who does not have anything for seeing far away".)

I explain to Claudine that she is sad at becoming a big girl. "It is difficult, one is afraid that Mummy will no longer look after you, but Mummy is not cross, on the contrary." I advise stopping the tonic, which had been suspended since the boil appeared and the eating difficulties do not reappear.

I suggest letting two weeks elapse before she is brought back to me. But before leaving me, Claudine takes her drawing back and taking a pencil she puts a big cross on it. I ask her why? She laughs and replies: "Because", then she hands it back to me.

22 March:

Claudine is very well. She no longer has a compulsive need to urinate. She now spends whole lessons without asking to leave the class. She is better behaved, has not had any fits of rage since the one we were told about on 1 March.

There is even some news on this point: a few days ago Daddy was threatening her brother with the strap, which he held in his right hand, while with the other he was preventing Daniel from getting away and Claudine found it entertaining to watch them "because they were funny going round and round" and she laughed "because Daddy is always grumpy, but he never really beats him".

Claudine makes a drawing (p. 144): all the family is holding each other by the hand, she places herself deliberately on Daddy's side who is separated from Mummy by Daniel. She does not have a big head as she used to have at the beginning, quite the contrary; she draws herself in compensation as tall as Daniel, but away from Mummy (renouncing her). Furthermore, when explaining her finished drawing to me and after having shown me Mummy's bag, she adds one for herself; she is no longer as in the preceding drawing "the one who has nothing" whereas the man and Daniel had "thingies", she opts for her femininity and gives herself "a bag like Mummy, but smaller".

29 March:

The mother brings Claudine back all pink with pride, to thank me because she is truly no longer the same. She is very well. No longer anxious or having fits of anger. She sleeps well and eats well. There are no longer problems with urination, Daddy and Mummy and the schoolmistress are all very pleased.

Coming back from the last consultation, the mother told me with laughter, Claudine went to fetch the strap from the closet and threw it in the rubbish bin. "So that Daniel will no longer be beaten."

Today, Claudine tells me, shyly and proudly, that she will be seven at one in the afternoon. I compliment her sincerely: "You really are a big girl."

Conclusion

In reading this case study, one cannot avoid being struck, as I was, by the progress between sessions and the minimal therapeutic intervention required. Each time the analyst got the maximum of what could be hoped for. One has to say that Claudine's mother is a feminine woman and that she has never offered any resistance to us, which is rare, and that the father takes up his place as head of the family perfectly, strict without really being harsh. He is looked up to and shows affection.

Claudine's symptoms conveyed the *refusal to admit the absence of a penis*. She remained babyish thus blackmailing everybody. The compulsive need to urinate disarmed Mummy and was used at school as vengeance against the phallic mother. But this aggressive symptom necessitated its infantile corollary, the need to be fed by Mummy, to have her pity her.

The acceptance of her aggression towards her father, and the mother letting go of control over her eating, gave her back the possibility of growing up. Notice that in Claudine's home, neither she nor the mother (whom I had asked) ever alluded to masturbation, and naturally I did not either. The desire for a penis was translated by a desire to inform herself about the lady doctor's willy (tap) (at the hospital). The next time, she had given up the big "thingies ", whilst remaining near the boat, then in crossing out the drawing, she renounced this type of fantasy.

Finally, with the bag, Claudine shows how the girl has an intuitive notion of the vagina, and she puts her bag between herself and Daddy.

Emotionally, she has arrived at the Oedipus complex, showing normal behaviour and no symptoms. The episode of the strap could probably be interpreted as a normal if masochistic manifestation of feminine sexuality and as a symbolic attempt to castrate the nasty father, so that he does not pay attention to Daniel (the only beneficiary of the strap). Thus she will be able to love him dearly and entrust her bag safely to him.

Fabienne (aged thirteen and a half)

The child is brought by her mother, a relatively older woman, indulgent with the child and worried about her health, about her very poor condition generally, but principally because of episodes which had started recently, were getting more and more frequent and which had a quasi-epileptic aspect.

There is no history of epilepsy in the family, which comprises:

- Mother, healthy, older-looking;
- Father, younger than the mother, "very anxious", invalided out of military service; stopped working a long time ago;
- André, thirty-one, in good health, married;
- Simone, twenty, in good health, married;
- Raymond, twenty, in good health, doing his military service;
- René, eighteen, in good health, workman;
- Odette, sixteen, in good health, seamstress;
- And Fabienne, thirteen and a half, the youngest.

In Fabienne's history, there is nothing particular to note. The developmental period seems to have been normal. There have not been any marked illnesses. She has not yet started her period.

The first episode happened at home for no apparent reason. Since then, these "occurrences" only happen at school.

The child faints and shakes for the entire duration of the episode which can last for up to half an hour. This is not true shaking, but a kind of shivering. The attack happens suddenly, it starts with the child feeling dizzy.

There is no initial cry, no biting of the tongue, no involuntary emission of urine and the fall is never hard. There is no "aura" nor hemicranial migraine after the crisis.

On the other hand, headaches occur daily, are short lived or tenacious depending on the day. The child is skinny, lacks appetite, has a waxy pallor, she has a glassy stare, generally her expression is sad and dispirited.

The examination and observations of our medical colleagues show no abnormality so the family has been referred to us.

The Binet-Simon test gives the child a mental age of eight years and six months, but, says Miss Achard, the test results fluctuate, and the child certainly has a true level above that provided by the test (26 June).

6 July:

I see her for the first time. Her shyness is extreme. If one speaks to her, her lips tremble before answering and she stutters a few monosyllables.

She is considerably behind at school. Her schoolwork has never been good, but until the age of nine, she "kept up". At present, whatever class she is put in she is unable to keep up.

She learns her lessons very conscientiously and repeats them to her mother quite well, but by the next morning she cannot even remember having known anything about them, or even what lesson it was.

Spelling can be very poor, or good by chance, for a few lines. Fabienne sometimes makes a mistake in a word which she had previously spelt correctly a few lines above.

Her arithmetic is appalling. In our presence, she manages to do very simple addition and subtraction, but even for that it is necessary that before writing down the answer which she announces timidly (without believing it) she looks at the adult all the time for confirmation. For multiplication and division, the difficulty is insurmountable. Fabienne knows her times tables if one asks her to recite them in their entirety, but she is incapable of using them for a calculation. "How many sixes are in thirty?" she repeats this question in a toneless voice and starts to cry whilst trembling. If one asks her how much is six times five, she says thirty, but she cannot establish any relation between this solution and the question which she asked herself shortly before.

In short, Fabienne has remained in the same class for the last three years with ten-year-old children, a class which she cannot keep up with and during break times plays with children younger than herself (between six and eight years old).

At home, she behaves like a little baby, loves to sit on her mother's knee and to curl up in her arms. She went through a phase where she was argumentative, impertinent and negative with her mother who was obliged to deal strictly with her. *This hostile attitude stopped at the time of the appearance of the attacks.*

At home, she is also treated like a baby. She never takes part in conversations. She sometimes wants something that her brother has in his hand, then she shouts, complains to her mother, who makes the older one give in "because she is little" and also because her father, always at home, does not want any noise.

The father is a nervous man, anxious, always ill since the war, where it is said that he was gassed. He was invalided out and the health of his lungs is in question. But he never has a fever or a real illness. In this family with numerous children, no one is invited to the house and the father forbids any association even with the neighbours. He only tolerates, at the request of the landlord, that their daughter plays with Fabienne in the courtyard. These landlords, rich, well dressed, and who have a car, impress the father. He is embittered and makes jealous remarks about them each time Fabienne mentions them. Nevertheless he considers it as politically useful to let the children play together. In fact, he is charming when these people speak to him, and without admitting it, profoundly flattered.

Besides this, the father does not take any notice of Fabienne, no more than of the other children. In a word, his behaviour is characteristic of neurosis.

There is another man in the house, René, who is eighteen years old and who, as we have seen, only has a puerile teasing interaction with Fabienne, and he always gives in. Anyway, he is not often at home outside meal times.

As far as the sister who is a seamstress is concerned, Fabienne speaks of her as a being whom she loves and admires, but without comparing herself to her. She belongs to the "grown-ups".

Such is the overall situation, indicating emotional retardation. The problems appear to have a hysterical origin, as a consequence of the episodes the child is excused from school for several days, and sometimes for weeks on end on the advice of the headmistress because Fabienne's attacks upset the children and have provoked the intervention of some parents.

I take Fabienne aside, because in front of her mother she is unable to answer and looks at her as if she were drowning and shouting to be rescued. At first, she always keeps her head lowered and answers in a whisper, politely like a well-brought-up but indifferent child: "Yes Madame, no Madame", with clipped tones.

Then when I comfort her, a bundle of nerves, eyes full of tears, her hands and her lips tremble, she remains pale and incapable of looking at me.

When I ask her if she has been as sad as this for a long time, she looks at me with a touched expression, cries, and contact is established.

From that moment onwards, she answers nicely, and little by little, a positive transference establishes itself.

I write summaries on her card, progressively, as I learn from her.

Her "sick feelings" happen at school when she has done something "wrong". For example: arriving late for school, not knowing her lessons. "Then she gets dizzy, she says, she feels uncomfortable", and she only wakes up when she sees people around her. Or then again, the attacks come in the school playground "when we play at bad games", for example: "playing at robbers, playing at catching each other", even though it's the others who are playing and she is watching them. She must, she explains, "not watch them".

The "sick feelings" are *a fear which is beyond her* and which *"hits hard"*, *"it crushes me"*. *Anxiety cannot be better described.*

Fabienne told me that, since her attacks, there has been less conflict with her mother, who now coddles her. There has been some conflict between her two brothers, six and four years older than her, ever since they were little—less in the last year, "because they are grown up".

Her depression and sadness come from her alarming preoccupation with "accidents in life, which could happen to her brothers". Last year, René had scarlet fever (it was before her attacks started), it was serious and we were worried. Now, "Mummy hides away to cry because of Raymond who is bored since he's become a soldier". (The mother herself is bored about everything now.) But "mainly because he is on the coast of Spain on a boat. And it is war and he will be killed." It is when she learned that he was going to Spain that she had her first episode. Besides, she does not know what the war in Spain is about or who is waging it.

Huge aggression—which she only acknowledges retrospectively— towards her two brothers. Continual scenes, reciprocal jealousy, blows, Fabienne cries which obliges the mother to intervene to make the boys give in under the pretext that she is "the little one".

But she did not love the mother any the more for that because, until the first attack, Fabienne systematically opposed to her mother in an impertinent way for the least thing, which provoked reprimands and slaps.

During this conversation, especially at the beginning, Fabienne makes repeated slips of the tongue. In two sentences, she says: "torpetlume" instead of *porte-plume* (pen with a nib) (she can't hold it any longer when her episodes start), "next year" instead of last year, her first "*quise—crisis—crommence—began*" her brothers "*quatinaient/*

taquinaient/teased her" all the time …, and so on. In short, she reverses the order of the consonants of the second syllables, which are put in the place of the first ones.

I somewhat alleviate her anxious guilt about "her past aggression" towards Raymond: maybe she felt sad as she was the last child, instead of being in his place. I tell her that nasty thoughts have no effect on reality.

I tell Fabienne's mother that she can go to school, there is no need to keep her at home, but that this is not very important because there is only one week left before the summer holidays.

She should try to help Fabienne to grow up, to look after the house, and to speak to her as if she were a woman.

13 July:

There have been no episodes though Fabienne has been going to school.

This is the last consultation for the school year.

I speak to the mother and help her understand the necessity of psychotherapeutic treatment; she is going to bring the child back every eight days from the beginning of October for a few months.

On her own with me, Fabienne speaks up and looks me in the face, she is much less emotional than the last time.

Referring to a conversation that I had had with two doctors from the clinic in front of her about another case, she says to me (after I had asked her "what do you think about all that?"), that she had not listened, because those things were not for her. I take advantage of this to explain that the precepts of politeness, which demand discretion, are there to make life easier for everyone, including those who submit to it. One abstains from hurting others by not saying unpleasant things, for example, but this does not prevent one having one's own opinion in one's own mind. When someone says things in front of you, which are not meant for you, this does not mean that you cannot listen, even if you cannot repeat them.

She then owns up to having listened a little, but she believed that it was bad. "The things which are not for me, I thought it was bad to listen to them, even if they were said in front of me".

Fabienne smiles (!) At my question: "how is it going", she replies: "I feel happier to be alive, it feels strange. I was always sad before!"

Her language is still full of childish things. Example: on holiday, she goes and plays with her *"petit'-amies"*—little friends and several other similar infantile expressions. The inversion of syllables has stopped.

12 October:

On the whole, the summer went well. Not a single episode. Fabienne did not go to the country but spent all her days in the company of a little girl of eleven who she likes a lot (the daughter of the landlord). She had a few dizzy spells, some on waking up, others after meals, but nothing major. She sat down and they passed.

She is much less emotional, smiles often, still shy, but no longer trembling, she flushes a little, but looks me squarely in the face.

She was still very saddened by the events at the end of September (the invasion of Czechoslovakia. Munich), she cried in bed at night, looked at the newspapers (when previously she had told me that it was bad to look at newspapers, that they were not for children) and on the whole she understood what was happening. Therefore, a very different attitude to that concerning Raymond on the Spanish coast.

She returns in eight days.

She had sent me a postcard this summer, but without writing her address, and I had not been able to respond. That had hurt her. She was afraid that I had forgotten her. We speak about her omission, maybe she says to herself that it is not true that I like her. (I tell her this because of her projections.)

19 October:

The mother finds her "rather better, anyway there is nothing to report".

Good start at school.

She tells me that she has discovered something: there are different types of schools, she had never noticed it before, but she now knows that there is the ordinary school and the public school, where there are nuns.

– What is your religion?
– I am a Christian, she says (but she does not know what it means. She did her "communion", but does not understand what that means

either: "One gets dressed in white, there is a candle and there is a celebration".)

In every conversation, one feels that she is trying to find a response according to the "book", and that she feels inadequate for not having studied it and remembered. That she could be able to reason with what she perceives with her senses seems to be beyond her understanding.

Using numerous examples, I try to stimulate her confidence in her own judgement. For example: "How are the objects that she sees made?"—"From wood"—"Where does it come from?"—"A cellar"—"How does it get into that cellar?"—"Somebody put it there"—"Where was it taken from?"—Attentive and humiliated, Fabienne replies: "I don't know, I haven't learnt it"—"Well, then, I say to her, a tree trunk, what is it?"—"They are trees"—"But it is wood"—"Oh, so this is why one can see trees being cut down?"—"Yes, and one takes them to be sawn to make planks and it is the planks which are put into a warehouse and are sold to workshops which employ workers." I lead her towards thinking in such a way about what most objects are made of, glass, straw, metal, fabric, and so on.

Fabienne then tells me about her sixteen-year-old cousin who learns "all the things about life in her book which tells you about all this" (*sic*), "how to bring up children and to tie up babies hands so that they don't rub themselves" (?).

I reply "Oh yes, it must be very interesting. If there are things that you would like to know and which are not in this beautiful book, you'll just have to ask about them. I will explain them to you."

Then we move onto arithmetic, and, in an attempt to move the issue from schoolwork onto that of adaptation to life, I speak of the change which is given back in a shop. Fabienne does not know the value of coins. "I never have coins. Oh no, I never run errands, I am too little. Yes I fetch the bread, but the shopkeeper puts it on account." I teach her the value of the coins while showing them to her and I tell her, "This is what you need to give to the baker for one kilogram of bread, this is how much a litre of milk costs, and so on ..."

We end up with playing at buying, addition, subtraction of sous, and handing back change. At the beginning, the answers are riddled with mistakes. Patiently, I start again.

A typical Fabienne answer goes like this (to my question "one franc minus thirteen sous?"): "six sous, no?"

All her replies are instant, without thinking and accompanied with: *no?*

2 November:

Fabienne says that she feels well.

At school, she talks to everybody; last year, she did not speak or play with anyone, and if somebody spoke to her she started crying, as she was so shy.

She is considerably behind, but now during playtime she goes and plays with those of her age from the older classes. She is still very infantile, likes to cuddle up to Mummy and to sit on her knee.

We start the play shopping again. We spend a quarter of an hour on half of five francs, the five francs being represented by four coins of one franc and two coins of fifty centimes. She gives me every possible answer except two francs, fifty centimes, and this despite having divided the six coins into two equal piles.

Finally, at the end of this quarter of an hour (during which I patiently encourage her), and after having been on the edge of tears, she suddenly manages it, completely bewildered that she had not understood it earlier. I explain to her that everything I am asking of her is just as easy and that she can do it.

I ask her if she has any idea about what she wants to do later on. She has ideas, she would like to be a shop assistant, because she likes playing at being a shopkeeper. I say: "why not" and show her the practical way to get there, first really knowing how to give back the right change, then knowing how to wrap parcels properly, and then knowing a shop where they would take an apprentice. "It will come soon, it's next year, you will be fourteen soon! In four years, you will be able to get married." All this is completely new to her. She wanted to be a shop assistant like a little boy might want to drive a train or become a general. The thought that it could happen appears to her extraordinary.

On the whole, good progress in behaviour. There is a certain amount of mental retardation, however seeing the progress made since July, one can hope that Fabienne will adapt to a reasonably satisfying social life.

9 November:

Fabienne had a fainting episode. She has not been to school since. I deliberately see her very quickly, just enough to tell her in front of her mother that I am not worried at all, that she is afraid of growing up and without doing it on purpose wants to play at being a little girl. I forbid mother to take her on her knee like a baby. We will speak together next week, I will only see her if she has no episodes.

She must go back to school right away this afternoon. All this is said in a firm voice, but taking Fabienne affectionately by the shoulder.

16 November:

Being unwell, I am not there and in my absence, Mrs Codet sees her and notes: "She is well, no episodes this week. Appears much better than when I had a glimpse of her six months ago."

23 November:

Fabienne looks much better than she did a fortnight ago. No further episodes.

She tells me her fears when she is falling asleep.

She *"sees big heads"*. These big heads are neither ugly, nor grimacing, nor terrifying, but nevertheless "I hide my face in my arms and I am very frightened".

I say nothing and Fabienne continues: "Also at night, I recite my lessons to myself and in the morning I have forgotten them. They call me *tête de linotte* (linnet head; "featherbrain"). I ask her:

– What does it mean?
– I don't know, she says, it's bad, it's something bad.
– Do you think so? What is a linnet?
– A little bird.
– Yes, then what about the head of a linnet.
– Ah yes, it means the head of a little bird.
– Of course, and when you are afraid of the big heads, it is because they are reproaching you for not remembering your lessons as if "it was bad", as if you did it on purpose. A linnet is very nice and she knows enough things to make her nest, sit on her eggs, look after her babies which are not old enough to leave the nest, she has a heart which can love just as much as the big sillies who have big know-all heads.

She tells me that she is often tired before meals because she is very hungry and that she cannot eat enough to last until the next meal without being tired. She has not taken any medication since June.

14 December:

She is well, has more colour, and says that she feels stronger. There hasn't been the least incident, either in health, or behaviour since 23 November. *The night terrors have stopped.*

Fabienne tells me about little incidents at school, with the volubility that boarding school children's stories have. This is new. "… I tell her … she says … that she is going to tell the teacher … that they say … that we do, etc." Altogether, she demonstrates her well-being.

We start the attempt at calculating money again. Better results than at the beginning, and good later on. Up to now, it was only a question of francs and sous. I risk patiently explaining the respective value of centimes and sous? (one sou equals five centimes). She understands, but does not yet manage to calculate the centimes.

After which, Fabienne asks me if she can tell me something that she would like to know. I reply:

– Of course.
– How are babies made?

First, I ask her what she thinks. She tells me that she thinks that the man gets involved, but she does not know how, maybe "by wounding", and the children are born from the side of the tummy, "it tears or else the man or the doctors give it a big stab with a knife to open the tummy. It's called labour, it is terrible and one often dies."

My unembarrassed explanation causes her to become very attentive, seems to reassure her a lot, and even to please her. I also explain to her the meaning of the word "pre-pubertal" that her mother often used about Fabienne. She told me that she believed that it was "something bad" and that "it was not for children" to hear.

Fabienne owns up to the fact that she wanted to ask me the truth, because it was her cousin, so up to date on things about life, who had told her all this. Today she understands that with all her air of knowing, in fact she knew nothing. She thanks me and is very happy about it.

Taking her back to her mother, I tell her that her daughter has become a big girl and that I think she no longer fears growing up.

The mother is happy and tells me that Fabienne has changed, that she is interested in housekeeping and listens to the radio.

25 January:

Fabienne has progressed even further since last time, it is a psychological as well as a physical transformation, she had her first period normally and without tiredness nor pains, she was very proud about it.

On her own with me, she looks contented and calm, she smiles. She will leave school. She still wants to be a shop assistant and there is a haberdasher where her mother shops who could perhaps take her, she takes young girls who begin as apprentices. She will go and ask her.

There is considerable progress with sums. She gives change very well and even does simple mental sums. She says to me that she has often asked her mother to pretend to give her change, and "once I knew how, I told Mummy that I would go and do the shopping, and her mother agreed".

At home, her attitude is therefore much better. As far as René is concerned, she is annoyed that he is not nice to her. She wrote to Raymond again so that he is less bored. She does not think about war anymore. "We will see, nobody knows."

In class, she is not brilliant, except for sewing. She does not sew as well as Odette, who is a seamstress, but Odette says that it's good. Fabienne likes knitting and sewing. I urge her to make something (a scarf, for example, or a sweater) for René for his name day. That way, he will know that she has become a young woman, and may become nicer to her.

I also advise her to go to a church club on Sunday. She tells me that there is one in particular where her school friends go. "And when the weather is nice, they go into the woods for a picnic." I tell her mother, who is all for it. "It will be against Daddy's wishes, but never mind", says the mother.

Since 25 January:

I was only meant to see Fabienne again if something was not going well. I did not see her again. In any case, the last session presaged well-adapted behaviour despite the deficient mental level.

Conclusion

One can see in this case, on the one hand the feelings of inferiority, and on the other, of anxiety; the envy of power (big head) and the wish for domination over the brothers being nothing but penis envy.

The feelings of inferiority, already legitimate, were re-enforced by a self-punishing inhibition, due to the return for the child of the death wishes primitively directed onto her brothers. Dangerous scarlet fever for René and the war in Spain for Raymond seemed to confirm the all-powerful magic.

Castration anxiety went as far as inhibiting the entire development of the child, forbidding her "to look at", "to listen", "to think", because of an obsessional contagion which like an oil stain provoked the phobia of everything that, through an association of ideas, could be qualified as being "a bad thing".

The child was then obliged to regress all the way back to the passive oral stage to satisfy the pleasure principal at the easiest and more rudimentary level (to be cuddled on Mummy's knees).

The Oedipal aggression towards the mother, which had been expressed through impertinence, had to be repressed secondarily under the threat of the superego and had made room for the infantile and masochistic attitude of the hysterical episodes which disarmed and worried the schoolmistress and the mother. The episodes then occurred each time "a bad thing" (aggressive games or awareness of her academic inferiority) provoked a resonance with the castration complex.

Monique (aged fourteen and a half)

She is not a child whose immediate family would think that she was ill and herself even less so.

They come for a consultation so that after examining her I can tell them whether or not she is capable of continuing with her studies as far as the Brevet (GCSE), because her teacher is trying to dissuade her and predicts failure if she attempts them. They thought of bringing her to us at Bretonneau because we are treating one of her cousins, who has nervous tics, at the Wednesday clinic and he is much improved. Her parents present Monique as normal. We will see how deeply neurotic she is.

Monique's mother is a nurse; intelligent, neat and tidy-looking, with a feminine face and flirtatious, despite the fact that she is very soberly dressed in a slightly masculine fashion. Outwardly, she is calm and friendly, her language is composed, and she seems to dearly wish for success for her daughter, to whom she speaks very kindly.

Monique is a young girl who already has periods, with a body starting to take shape, unkempt, with black nails and dirty hands, which while speaking she brings up to her face in an embarrassed gesture.

Her hair is greasy, uncombed, pulled back, and held by a dirty ribbon. Her eyes are not unbeautiful, but her look wavers, her smile is grimacing and embarrassed, and she laughs unnaturally, turning her head from side to side and showing dirty teeth; there are buttons missing on her dress; her collar is dirty and half-unstitched.

She tells me about the situation at school and her difficulties with memory, not for her lessons but in everyday life (she cannot perform two tasks without forgetting one). I notice that she cannot say a word without looking at her mother, as if to check for tacit approval.

She passed her Certificate last June at thirteen and a half, although she was in the class below the Certificate. There were five of them who did the same thing. One took the initiative to put herself in for the Certificate and the four others followed, all five passed. But at school, they were judged very harshly, apparently, and in the class they were "taken a dislike to".

The schoolmistress claims that Monique is incapable of moving to the second year of the class.

But Monique would like to become a gymnastics teacher, which requires "GCSE" levels. She brings me her schoolbooks. Unlike herself, they are well kept.

The Binet-Simon test shows a normal mental level, but difficulty in letting go of one task and adapting rapidly to the next, which Miss Achard translates into "lack of mental agility, a child with muddled responses, often in bad French; unsure how to measure the relative importance of the answers." All the tests together give a total mental age of fourteen years, four months, with a real age of fourteen years and six months. But detailed observation of the test questions and results is particularly interesting, emphasising what we have been thinking about the difference between Monique's mental level and intelligence, on the one hand, and her neurotic intelligence, on the other.

Having answered all the questions at the nine-year-old level correctly, Monique fails two out of five "age ten" questions, passes all "age twelve", four out of five "age fifteen", and two out of five "adult".

Looking at the overall test results, one can see that Monique *fails in the tests that demand significant engagement of the senses, practical memory, and judgement, in which objectivity and a sense of initiative come into play, that is to say, common sense.*

This is where she failed:

- Arrange in order five weights (ten years);
- Reproduce two drawings from memory (ten years);
- Interpret an engraving (fifteen years); she described it as a ten-year-old would;
- Pattern cutting (adults);
- Reconstruction of a triangle (adults);
- Difference between abstract words (adults).

On the other hand, she passed all the questions where book knowledge is indispensable (three rhymes; king and president), or where verbal memory comes in (repetition of numbers, sentences). Intellectual astuteness and philosophical reflection about life are also accessible to her (difficult issues, Hervieu's thought).

In Monique's behaviour, the same lacunae are found on another level. In the same way as she remains stuck in incomplete reasoning for a long time, she remains in a libidinal position of late infancy from which she is having great difficulty emerging.

In a conversation which I have on my own with the young girl, she tells me that she has been going camping for a long time, but before it was not "as it is now". She tells me that the boys tease (the girls) "when they are together"—"They are after them", and when coming out of school "they give them a hard time and say things to them". "One cannot be left in peace." "So it is not their fault" (the girls). Her companions laugh and run off, do not talk about it and sometimes grumble a bit, but it's driving *her* mad! She is "afraid that people think that she is happy about it, that the concierge sees her and tells the neighbours or her mother". In brief, she is at war with the boys, she retorts with offensive remarks, she is furious, she hits them, then she takes shelter, is hunted down in doorways, and takes refuge in unfamiliar staircases, and, above all, she dare not dress as a teenage girl and she is dirty and looks boyish.

She is beginning to "find out about life" from what other people are saying, she admits blushing, but she is terribly afraid of her mother. When I tell her that her mother would give her the explanation she wants, she answers that she could never ask her anything

From the conversation I had with the mother, I did not get the impression that she tried to curb her daughter in any way, quite the contrary. So after a lot of hard work with Monique, she allows me to call her mother in and to speak in front of her. Monique shakes, begs me not to, then gives in with huge apprehension. As I expected, the mother demonstrates complete understanding and speaks to Monique exactly in the same way as I would have about the stories with the boys. The mother tells me that the boyish and unkempt looks of her daughter annoy her and that she pushes her to go to mixed camps so that she can get acquainted with boys and become a little bit coquettish. She laughs about Monique's fears and tells her that she should be proud that the young men tease her and be amused by it.

But turning towards me, she adds: "I have always told her father that he was wrong; he wants his daughter to be sporty, to be brave, tough, also he always wants me not to look smart or wear makeup, and he likes his daughter to be the same."

Sometimes I tell him: "But she is too old for you to treat her like a boy, soon she will be a woman, she does not even know how to sew and nothing to do with housework seems to interest her." He replies: "She knows plenty, and I hope that she will not be so stupid as to become like all those little geese who dress like film stars." In brief, her father loves her in his own way, he does a lot with her, encouraging her to become a gymnastics teacher, but only wants to see boys' qualities in her, and, adds the mother: "He is anxious and demanding with her, he's never satisfied."

Such is the psychological picture of this case. Monique's behaviour is typical of neurosis.

It is obvious that Monique has the intellectual capacity to pass the Brevet and other exams in which "pure learning" forms the greater part. It is more than likely that the unfavourable opinion of the schoolmistress is dictated by a certain bias with its own motivation. But to pass exams, especially competitive entrance exams, there are not only the written tests or what is said during the orals. There is also all the individual marks concerning the matter of how one presents oneself, speaks, behaves, the team spirit and so on, and all this goes against Monique, and will be a serious handicap for her in her social life. It is certain that Monique's behaviour is neurotic, which is to say badly adapted to reality—note that "reality" is not a synonym for "real".

From a diagnostic point of view, we are dealing with a non-negotiable Oedipus complex because of the unconscious hostile attitude of the father towards women; and all the reactions of the "ego" have led to a masculinity syndrome.—see p. 85.

Monique was obliged to regress to a pregenital stage; for her, the most satisfactory is the anal sadistic stage. She is then in an infantile situation of raging refusal faced with the muscular and phallic superiority of the boys, to which she reacts by overvaluing her studies and with aggressive behaviour. But this is irrational and the unconscious protest does not modify reality and the result is anxiety, the terrifying panic that forces her to tragi-comic retreats in unknown buildings. The boys' pursuit is unconsciously *triggered* by this ridiculous, exhibitionistic attitude of rebellious frailty and this awakens guilt towards the super-ego. "People are going to believe that she is doing this on purpose" and "tell the neighbours and her mother". Castration anxiety begins to resonate, an absolutely irrational anguish when one knows the mother! It is not she, nor the neighbours that the child is afraid of, it is of her own superego whose voice is that of an all powerful and magic phallic mother. This superego is a representation of the mother that all little girls have at the anal sadistic pre-Oedipal stage; it is further endowed with jealousy by the child at the beginning of the Oedipal stage which is nothing more than the child's own jealousy projected onto her mother.

The Oedipal stage remaining unresolved, Monique has a harshly subjective attitude towards the external world arising from the archaic attitude of the anal stage—which is, we know, ambivalence.

All feminine beings are homologous with the mother. In the ambivalent position, "the mother" cannot, very simply, be, she must be "good" and "bad" all at once in varying proportions of negative and positive.

Towards the schoolmistresses, substitutes for the bad mother, Monique behaves critically, with impertinence and rebelliousness, from a feeling of inferiority, which unsurprisingly provokes reprimands. The child is then only too pleased to justify her grudges by rationalising them, she says "the schoolmistress took a dislike to me" and goes and complains about her to the "good mother" (her mother). But, even towards the mother, the attitude is not totally positive, the child fears her because unconsciously she (the child) is hostile to her. This is demonstrated by her masochistic attitude: infantile submissiveness and the need for her constant approval, of her words and slightest efforts. This necessary attitude arises because of unconscious ambivalence, it balances the other, the sadistic aggressive attitude towards the schoolmistresses and the school directors.

At the same time, the objects of Monique's affection are of the unconscious latent homosexual type, which binds her friendship with girls "similar to herself", that is to say, driven by the same conflicts (the four rebels taken a dislike to).

Vis-à-vis other young girls, childhood friendships fall apart because they react to the boys' attacks in a different way and abandon the bizarre and unkempt Monique to her sad position of emotional retardation. A gap appears between Monique and the other girls of her generation, increasing still further her inferiority feelings towards women.

Monique is therefore not equipped for life. However intelligent she is, she lacks common sense and can only succeed on the margins of what is the norm. She is animated by huge feelings of inferiority. She will not know how to compete in daily social life and triumph over other women. Furthermore, the unconscious restriction to the free play of her aggression—even when it is not at the service of a taboo femininity—renders her incapable of succeeding in the fight for her sexual life without sabotaging herself.

We will see later on the prognosis of such a case without psychoanalysis. Psychoanalysis cannot be advised for Monique at the moment, as neither the parents nor the child can understand the seriousness of the situation, especially with a father who would offer insuperable resistance. As long as his daughter is legally under his authority, it is impossible to treat her without placing her in a situation, which would be, in all humanity, too painful to bear.

We therefore said nothing about psychoanalysis, we tried the only weapon left to us: which is to answer the question for which we were consulted in the first place, while taking advantage of that occasion to have direct action on the superego in confronting it with the reality: the non phallic, non jealous, non castrating mother. I reassured her completely about her mental level and intellectual capacity, I, a "woman-doctor" ("who commands" the nurses), therefore who should be a "masculine phallic woman" and "dangerous in the extreme", spoke with simplicity and common-sense words about the fights with the boys. I stimulated her coquetry by pointing out her natural qualities, which she could enhance, without even having recourse to lipstick or powder, we added. "Because there are some charming and feminine women who do not use makeup."

I *congratulated* her on her rebellious initiative with the Certificate and tested the hypothesis that perhaps she may have some responsibility for the fact that she has become "disliked" by the schoolmistresses. Did she not celebrate her triumph ineptly to "annoy", as if the really strong position to have taken might not rather have been, once success was assured, to play the modesty card! This argument made her laugh, because it found a fertile echo in the defence mechanism of "cunning" allowed by her sadistic anal superego. Furthermore, my objective manner of speaking gently about her father and his obvious envy of women did not shock Monique. Despite her fear, which had revealed itself to be without foundation, the cooperation that I solicited at the end of the conversation, will perhaps have a healthy corrective effect on the superego of the young lady.

However, in my heart of hearts, I am doubtful. The prognosis in Monique's case appears to us very bad. Psychotherapy could only achieve superficial and momentary results. It is too late. She would need real psychoanalysis, but this will only be possible when Monique's father has *died*.

Without psychoanalysis, such young women cannot become women who are sound in body and mind. If they manage to behave like everybody else, or for any other reason linked to social mores or liberation from the family, manage to "take" a lover or to get married, they are frigid in normal sexual relations (vaginal insensitivity), may even be totally frigid, and they are contemptuous of "sexual matters", which they call (according to the expression relating to excrement) "shitty". This will vary according to the degree of their unconscious guilt feelings at usurping another woman's place.

Their unresolved aggression towards the masculine sex renders them unbearable and *castrating* towards men, amongst whom, in preference they will choose those who are inferior to themselves (milieu, wealth, intelligence). If they are with potent men or men who are obviously superior to them, they will attempt to "castrate" them in every way, to render them impotent (vaginismus), or to publicly ridicule them (public fights, *faux pas*, over-spending, overt extramarital affairs). If they do not manage to lessen their vitality, they will project all their sadism into them and play the victim, be ill, crushed, betrayed, played with, and sadistically ruined through themselves provoking or unconsciously privileging the conditions that satisfy their masochism.

If these women have children, these will not be invested with maternal love of the oblative genital stage but with an ambivalent "love", possessive and authoritarian, bearing the mark of sadomasochistic object relations of the anal stage. These women may behave with refined cruelty towards their children, depending on the social class to which they belong—teaching them to despise or misjudge their father, posing as the "self-sacrificing woman" to whom everything is owed, and whom it would be criminal to abandon in order to lead their own emotional and sexual lives as healthy males and females.

Here is once again an eloquent example of what we call family neurosis. In Monique's case, we can see the heavy responsibility of a neurotic father—himself an enemy of women and a homosexual who does not know it. Nevertheless, let us not accuse him too fast. He himself may be passing onto his daughter the suffering which was imposed on him in his youth by a frigid mother, or by castrating sisters against whom he was unable to react, and who unconsciously he will never forgive. Anyway, we know that he suffers, because, despite the submissive neurosis of his daughter, he is never satisfied with the child.

Conclusion

- The Oedipus complex is unavoidable in the course of individual human development.
- It erects obstacles on the life path for many of us.
- In all cases in which the Oedipus complex has not been resolved, one witnesses anomalies (restrictions or exaggerations) of aggressive and passive libidinal tendencies, the free play of which is indispensable to social adaptation.
- In fact, castration anxiety imposes three positions.
- One, submission is the only happy and appropriate solution to resolve the Oedipus complex which leads to what is considered normal social adaptation.
- The other two are, on the one hand, flight from castration anxiety, and on the other, rebellion and open fight against it.
- When there is flight, the subject expresses this either by a total inhibition of activity, or by instability, mental flight, and sometimes through actual escape. (We did not give any examples of these, because these children are taken directly to psychiatrists.)
- When there is a vehement protest of the unconscious faced with the cruel dilemma, which is imposed on it, the subject expresses it through personality problems accompanied by regression to archaic, structuring stages of sexuality. These are manifested in a more or less marked way by anti-social behaviour and perversion. Because of the incestuous effects, which they aim at defending against, these satisfactions,

even though regressive, bring about unconscious guilt. This has to be appeased, for fear of anxiety. If there is no punishment, the anxiety becomes intolerable, self-punishment through failure becomes necessary. But if punishment does occur, it further reinforces the feelings of inferiority and of revolt, which, in their turn, trigger new forms of aggression. One sees therefore what a "race to death" a subject can be led towards, the case of Jean being an eloquent example. They can also lead the subject to delinquency.

Behind the symptoms, which are superficially similar in girls and boys, there exists a real difference in the castration complex of the girl and that of the boy.

Castration anxiety in a boy is an anxiety about phallic castration. It is linked to the Oedipus complex.

Castration anxiety in a girl has two stages: the first, phallic castration anxiety happens in the pre-Oedipal environment; the second, utero-ovarian vaginal castration anxiety is the only one linked to the Oedipus complex, it is the punitive anxiety of the evisceration of female genital desire.

This work did not allow me to broach the very numerous questions which can be asked about the castration complex. Its aim is to introduce our non-psychoanalytic colleagues to the fundamental moment that is the Oedipus complex in the story of the individual's development and its role in the aetiology of symptoms in physical functioning and behavioural problems.

May it show the therapeutic benefit of psychoanalysis in its application to the problems of physiological, mental, and character development in children.

INDEX

repression 7, 10, 25, 32, 35, 43, 64, 67,
    72, 78, 82, 106, 120, 173, 202
    cultural 43
    mechanisms 10
    of sexuality 78
    reinforcing 9
    sexual genitality and
        pregenitality 64
    witness 126
romantic fantasies 83, 91

sadistic
    aggressive attitude 225
    and masochistic components 21
    fantasies 29
    possession 31, 139
    pre-Oedipal stage 225
sadomasochistic ambivalence 24
secondary anxiety 7
secondary infantile masturbation 25
secondary masturbation 24, 98
sedatives xxii–xxiii
    fantasies 49
self-punishing mechanisms 97
sexual
sexual curiosity 25, 32, 71
    spontaneous 45
sexual intercourse 156
    child witnesses 31
sexuality 4, 13, 33, 36, 56–57, 82, 89,
    106, 228
    activity of child 52
    archaic components 33
    boy's 76
    consequences for 56
    desire 32, 59
    external manifestations 48
    fantasies 53
    female 89, 209
    genital 35, 66, 81, 85–86, 194
    genital life 14, 67
    genitality and pregenitality 64

genital-oblative mode 69
health 38
in individual development 38–43
infantile xx, 45
inferiority 104
interest 32, 35, 44–45, 56
normal 52
normal components 18
of girl 73–75
phallic 70, 78
refusal of 17
relations 72, 86, 227
role of 38
satisfactions 57
sensuality 70
sexual mutilation 71, 150, 171
    fear of 154
    magical suppression of 150
silence and immobility 29
social adaptation 62, 121, 228
social prognosis 182
solitary sexual activity 69
sonorous resonance 27
sphincteral erogenous zone 97
sucking pleasure 15
superego 4–5, 7–8, 25, 40–41, 62, 66,
    80, 82, 159, 182, 225–227
    acts 7
    archaic 48
    boundless civilisation 91
    boy's 64
    collective 125
    dynamic element of 9
    formation of 115
    full of grace 91
    governance of 10
    homosexual anal superego 22
    masturbation 86
    of sexual partner 92
    resistances of 122
    rigid 7–8
    severity of 167